MULTICULTURAL E[

James A. Banks, ~~Series Editor~~

"To Remain an Indian"

Lessons in Democracy
From a Century of
Native American Education

K. Tsianina Lomawaima

Teresa L. McCarty

Teachers College
Columbia University
New York and London

Published by Teachers College Press, 1234 Amsterdam Avenue, New York, NY 10027

Library of Congress Cataloging-in-Publication Data

Lomawaima, K. Tsianina, 1955–
    To remain an Indian : lessons in democracy from a century of Native American education / K. Tsianina Lomawaima, Teresa L. McCarty.
      p. cm. — (Multicultural education series)
    Includes bibliographical references and index.
    ISBN-13: 978-0-8077-4716-2 (paper : alk. paper); ISBN-10: 0-8077-4716-5 (paper : alk. paper); ISBN-13: 978-0-8077-4717-9 (cloth : alk. paper); ISBN-10: 0-8077-4717-3 (cloth : alk. paper);
    1. Indians of North America—Education.   2. Off-reservation boarding schools—United States—History.   3. Indian students—United States—History.   4. United States—Race relations.   5. United States—Social policy.   I. McCarty, T. L.   II. Title.   III. Multicultural education series (New York, N.Y.)
    E97.L66 2006
    371.829'97—dc22
                                           2006043864

ISBN-13:   ISBN-10:
978-0-8077-4716-2 (paper)   0-8077-4716-5 (paper)
978-0-8077-4717-9 (cloth)   0-8077-4717-3 (cloth)

Printed on acid-free paper

Manufactured in the United States of America

13   8 7 6 5

Dedicated

to the memory of

Elsa N. Setima Adams, the

first Hopi woman to earn a teaching degree at

Arizona State Teacher's College

And to

Agnes Dodge Holm,

Bilingual educator, clear-eyed leader, friend,

first university teacher of Navajo, and cofounder of the Rock

Point Bilingual Education Program,

who invented a way to teach Navajo with high academic

expectations and genuine care for her students

The position taken, therefore, is that the work with and for the Indians must give consideration to the desires of the individual Indians. He who wishes to merge into the social and economic life of the prevailing civilization of this country should be given all practicable aid and advice in making the necessary adjustments. He who wants *to remain an Indian* and live according to his old culture should be aided in doing so.

—Lewis Meriam et al. (1928, p. 86, emphasis added)

Contents

Series Foreword

The nation's deepening ethnic texture, interracial tension and conflict, and the increasing percentage of students who speak a first language other than English make multicultural education imperative in the 21st century. The U.S. Census Bureau (2000) estimates that people of color made up 28% of the nation's population in 2000 and predicts that they will make up 38% in 2025 and 50% in 2050 (El Nasser, 2004).

American classrooms are experiencing the largest influx of immigrant students since the beginning of the 20th century. About a million immigrants are making the United States their home each year (Martin & Midgley, 1999). More than seven and one-half million legal immigrants settled in the United States between 1991 and 1998, most of whom came from nations in Latin America and Asia (Riche, 2000). A significant number also come from the West Indies and Africa. A large but undetermined number of undocumented immigrants also enter the United States each year. The influence of an increasingly ethnically diverse population on the nation's schools, colleges, and universities is and will continue to be enormous.

Forty percent of the students enrolled in the nation's schools in 2001 were students of color. This percentage is increasing each year, primarily because of the growth in the percentage of Latino students (Martinez & Curry, 1999). In some of the nation's largest cities and metropolitan areas, such as Chicago, Los Angeles, Washington, D. C., New York, Seattle, and San Francisco, half or more of the public school students are students of color. During the 1998–1999 school year, students of color made up 63.1% of the student population in the public schools of California, the nation's most populous state (California State Department of Education, 2000).

Language and religious diversity is also increasing among the nation's student population. In 2000, about 20% of the school-age population spoke a language at home other than English (U. S. Census Bureau, 2000). Harvard professor Diana L. Eck (2001) calls the United States the "most religiously diverse nation on earth" (p. 4). Islam is now the fastest-growing religion in the United States. Most teachers now in the classroom and in teacher education programs are likely to have students from diverse ethnic, racial, language, and religious groups in their classrooms during their careers. This is true for both inner-city and suburban teachers.

An important goal of multicultural education is to improve race relations and to help all students acquire the knowledge, attitudes, and skills needed to participate in cross-cultural interactions and in personal, social, and civic action that will help make our nation more democratic and just. Multicultural education is consequently as important for middle-class White suburban students as it is for students of color who live in the inner-city. Multicultural education fosters the public good and the overarching goals of the commonwealth.

The major purpose of the *Multicultural Education Series* is to provide preservice educators, practicing educators, graduate students, scholars, and policy makers with an interrelated and comprehensive set of books that summarizes and analyzes important research, theory, and practice related to the education of ethnic, racial, cultural, and language groups in the United States and the education of mainstream students about diversity. The books in the *Series* provide research, theoretical, and practical knowledge about the behaviors and learning characteristics of students of color, language minority students, and low-income students. They also provide knowledge about ways to improve academic achievement and race relations in educational settings.

The definition of multicultural education in the *Handbook of Research on Multicultural Education* (Banks & Banks, 2004) is used in the *Series*: Multicultural education is "*a field of study designed to increase educational equity for all students that incorporates, for this purpose, content, concepts, principles, theories, and paradigms from history, the social and behavioral sciences, and particularly from ethnic studies and women's studies*" (p. xii). In the *Series*, as in the *Handbook*, multicultural education is considered a "metadiscipline."

The dimensions of multicultural education, developed by Banks (2004b) and described in the *Handbook of Research on Multicultural Education*, provide the conceptual framework for the development of the publications in the *Series*. They are *content integration, the knowledge construction process, prejudice reduction, an equity pedagogy,* and *an empowering school culture and social structure.* To implement multicultural education effectively, teachers and administrators must attend to each of the five dimensions of multicultural education. They should use content from diverse groups when teaching concepts and skills, help students to understand how knowledge in the various disciplines is constructed, help students to develop positive intergroup attitudes and behaviors, and modify their teaching strategies so that students from different racial, cultural, language, and social-class groups will experience equal educational opportunities. The total environment and culture of the school must also be transformed so that students from diverse groups will experience equal status in the culture and life of the school.

Although the five dimensions of multicultural education are highly interrelated, each requires deliberate attention and focus. Each publication in the series focuses on one or more of the dimensions, although each book deals with all of them to some extent because of the highly interrelated characteristics of the dimensions.

The struggles, disappointments, hopes, and dreams of Indians in the United States reveal the values and possibilities of U.S. society because of the unique and integral role and presence that Native Americans have in American history and culture. The Declaration of Independence states "that all men are created equal, that they are endowed by their Creator with certain unalienable Rights, that among these are Life, Liberty, and the pursuit of Happiness." As the Founding Fathers crafted these lofty words in 1776, the experiences of Native Americans as well as the enslaved experiences of African Americans (Painter, 2005) strongly contradicted these ideals and revealed that "men" referred to White males with property and that White women, Native Americans, and African Americans were excluded from the Founding Fathers' concept of citizens who "are created equal."

Throughout the history of the United States, the treatment of Native Americans has been the canary in the coal mine that revealed the extent to which the United States was realizing or contradicting the ideals stated in its founding documents, such as the Declaration of Independence, the Constitution, and the Bill of Rights. As Myrdal stated in his classic study of African Americans in 1944, the gap between American democratic ideals and practices such as institutionalized discrimination and racism creates an "American dilemma" that has been a powerful force in America's response to and construction of the images of its marginalized groups of color, such as Native Americans and African Americans.

In "*To Remain an Indian*," an incisive, well-researched, and informative history, Lomawaima and McCarty describe how the American dilemma has been manifested in the U.S. response to American Indians and their quests for self-determination, empowerment, human rights, and democracy. They argue convincingly and with compelling evidence that Native American cultural differences have historically been conceptualized and responded to as either safe or dangerous. The levels of tolerance of cultural difference have been cyclic. However, the quest for a "narrow zone of tolerable cultural difference" and the eradication of cultural differences perceived as dangerous has been the dominant theme in the U.S. response to Native Americans as they struggled for social justice, democracy, and an education that would allow them to retain their languages, cultures, and religions.

Lomawaima and McCarty use their cogent and insightful conceptualization of a safety zone of allowable cultural differences to describe how this idea has been used to justify the denial of self-determination to Native American groups, operate boarding schools that eradicated Native languages and cultures, and to prevent Native people from "remaining Indian." A safety zone of allowable cultural differences is a trenchant idea that helps us to understand the experiences of groups such as African Americans and Mexican Americans, as well as the experiences of ethnic, cultural, and language minorities in nations outside the United States (Banks, 2004a). The laws in states such as California and Arizona that prohibit bilingual instruction and the contentious debate over Black English that occurred in the Oakland Public Schools in 1996 when the district proposed using Black English as a vehicle to teach African American students standard English are examples of actions taken by the dominant U.S. society to eradicate cultural differences that are beyond its idea of tolerable cultural differences.

This gracefully written and insightful book teaches important lessons about democracy in the United States and how Native Americans have struggled against great odds and overwhelming forces to gain social, civil, political, and cultural rights, a struggle which is continuing because their dreams and possibilities remain unfulfilled. The hard lessons that this book conveys poignantly and explicitly are that democracy can never be taken for granted, that it is always an incomplete project for which nations that aspire to be democracies must pursue with diligence and determination, and that when a nation denies rights to a group such as Native Americans, the rights of all groups—including mainstream powerful groups—are seriously jeopardized. As Martin Luther King (1963) stated, "Injustice anywhere is a threat to justice everywhere."

This book is significant and timely not only because it documents the long and unfinished struggle by Native Americans for the realization of democracy and social justice in the United States, but also because it reveals the extent to which democracy is imperiled for all Americans. I hope this book will be widely read and will inspire its readers to act to make democracy in the United States less fragile and more consistent with the nation's founding ideals. The Civil Rights Movement of the 1960s and 1970s brought the nation closer to its democratic ideals. However, memories of the Civil Rights Movement are fading (West, 2004) and are not part of the life experience of a new generation of educators. New initiatives and actions are needed to revitalize the nation's commitment to democracy and human freedom. A serious and committed reading of this heartfelt and erudite book is a promising and enriching place to begin to renew our commitment to human justice, freedom, and democracy.

James A. Banks
Series Editor

REFERENCES

Banks, J. A. (Ed.). (2004a). *Diversity and citizenship education: Global perspectives.* San Francisco: Jossey-Bass.
Banks, J. A. (2004b). Multicultural education: Historical development, dimensions, and practice. In J. A. Banks & C. A. M. Banks (Eds.), *Handbook of research on multicultural education* (2nd ed., pp. 3–29). San Francisco: Jossey-Bass.
Banks, J. A., & Banks, C. A. M. (Eds.). (2004). *Handbook of research on multicultural* education (2nd ed.). San Francisco: Jossey-Bass.
California State Department of Education. (2000). Online, http://data1.cde.ca.gov/dataquest
Eck, D. L. (2001). *A new religious America: How a "Christian country" has become the world's most religiously diverse nation.* New York: HarperSanFrancisco.
El Nasser, H. (2004, March 18). Census projects growing diversity: By 2050: Population burst, societal shifts. *USA Today,* p. 1A.
King, M. L. (1963, April 16). *Letter from a Birmingham jail.* Retrieved February 24, 2006, from http://www.nobelprizes.com/nobel/peace/MLK-jail.html
Martin, P., & Midgley, E. (1999). Immigration to the United States. *Population Bulletin, 54*(2), pp. 1–44. Washington, DC: Population Reference Bureau.
Martinez, G. M., & Curry A. E. (1999, September). *Current population reports: School enrollment, social and economic characteristics of students* (update). Washington, DC: U.S. Census Bureau.
Myrdal, G. (with R. Sternal & A. Rose). (1944). *An American dilemma: The Negro problem in modern democracy.* New York: Harper.
Painter, N. I. (2005). *Creating Black Americans: African American history and its meanings, 1619 to the present.* New York: Oxford University Press.
Riche, M. F. (2000). America's diversity and growth: Signposts for the 21st century. *Population Bulletin, 55*(2), pp. 1–43. Washington, DC: Population Reference Bureau.
United States Census Bureau. (2000). *Statistical abstract of the United States* (120th edition). Washington, DC: U.S. Government Printing Office.
West, C. (2004). *Democracy matters: Winning the fight against imperialism.* New York: Penguin Group.

Acknowledgments

This book has been a long time in the making. The thoughts and analyses expressed here have been developing since our work in American Indian education began more than two decades ago. The authorial debts accumulated over such a long period are immense, but we begin by expressing our sincere gratitude to Professor James Banks, who provided the invitation and the opportunity to bring our work together on these pages. He believed in the worth of the project and throughout its duration was a source of both freedom and direction, patience and helpful structure. We also thank Brian Ellerbeck, Wendy Schwartz, Aureliano Vázquez Jr., and the staff of Teachers College Press for the editorial expertise that clarified and improved the manuscript.

In Chapter 5, our analysis has been inestimably aided by the recent publication of Rebecca C. Benes's *Native American Picture Books of Change: The Art of Historic Children's Editions* (2004). Benes focuses on the Native artists, such as Fred Kabotie and Alan Houser, who made the first editions of the Indian *Life Readers* exquisite works of art. The Museum of New Mexico Press reproduced many of the original illustrations; no fan of children's literature should miss the clarity of design and charm of Fred Kabotie's illustrations for *The Five Little Katchinas*. In our analysis we approach the Indian *Life Readers* from different perspectives than did Benes, but her research into the history of the Bureau's production of the *Readers* has greatly enriched our understanding, and we are indebted to her work.

The textual analysis of Navajo language publications in Chapter 5 is the work of Professor Mary Willie, Department of Linguistics/American Indian Studies, University of Arizona. Professor Willie is bilingual and biliterate in Navajo (her first language) and English. We are deeply indebted to her generosity as a friend and colleague as well as her willingness to contribute to our deeper understanding of the Navajo *Life Readers*. Her insights give us precious glimpses into the constraints and opportunities faced by the original translators of these stories. The textual analysis of the Hopi–English reader *Field Mouse Goes to War* was generously provided by Hartman H. Lomawaima, Director, Arizona State Museum and American Indian Studies faculty, University of Arizona.

We thank Dr. Wayne Holm for his sharp insights into the development of American Indian bilingual education and for sharing details on the life and accomplishments of his late wife and education partner for more than 50 years, bilingual educator Agnes Dodge Holm, to whom we co-dedicate this book. We are further indebted to Agnes and Wayne Holm for allowing Teresa McCarty to interview them in January 1996; excerpts from those interviews appear in Chapter 6. To Teresa McCarty's longtime colleague, friend, and co-researcher, the late Galena Sells Dick, we owe a special debt of gratitude for the material on the Rough Rock Navajo bilingual education program. As Galena knew so well, Indigenous bilingual/bicultural education was a primary tool for rupturing the federal "safety zone," thereby helping to realize sovereign tribal goals.

As this book was going to press, the field of American Indian education lost one of its legendary leaders, Dr. Robert A. Roessel Jr. Known to all as Bob, his leadership changed the contours of Indian education policy in the latter part of the 20th century. In 1959, Bob Roessel established the Center for Indian Education at Arizona State University—still the only center of its type—and shortly thereafter, the *Journal of American Indian Education*, still the preeminent scholarly journal in the field. In 1966, with Navajo tribal and community leaders, he cofounded the first American Indian community-controlled school at Rough Rock, Arizona (discussed in Chapters 6 and 7). He went on to cofound the first American Indian community college, now called Diné College and located at Tsaile, Arizona. His work was instrumental to the passage of the 20th century's landmark legislation: the Indian Education Act of 1972, the Indian Self-Determination Act of 1975, and the Native American Tribally-Controlled Colleges Act of 1978, all of which are described on these pages. Robert Roessel's name appears periodically here, but his contributions weave between every line of the account from mid-century onward. He and his wife, Ruth Wheeler Roessel, have been special friends to Teresa McCarty; without their mentorship and support, much of this story could not be told. We also thank Bob and Ruth's son, Monty Roessel, who currently heads the school his father cofounded, for his ongoing support of the work reported here on Rough Rock, and for his friendship.

Others to whom we have looked in documenting the vision of Native American education presented here include Mary Eunice Romero, Lucille Watahomigie, Akira Y. Yamamoto, and Ofelia Zepeda, whose work in American Indian bilingual education also is described in Chapter 6. We thank Drs. Romero and Zepeda for their additional contributions as co-principal investigators, with Teresa McCarty, on the Native Language Shift and Retention Project discussed in Chapter 7.

For their contributions to the Rough Rock English–Navajo Language Arts Project (RRENLAP) discussed in Chapter 6, in addition to the late Galena

Dick and her husband, Ernest W. Dick, we thank Sally Begay, Dan Estell, Juanita Estell, Lorinda Gray, Emma Lewis, Afton Sells, Evelyn Sells, Gloria Sells, Lynda Teller, Lorena Tohe van Pelt, and the late Rita Wagner and her family. For their assistance with the Navajo youth interviews discussed in Chapter 7, we thank Community Research Collaborators Sally Begay, Mary Benally, Leroy Morgan, Twylah Morris, Darlene Redhair, Delrey Redhair, Treva Yazzie, and Marvin Yellowhair. We are especially grateful to the youth who candidly—and powerfully—shared their thoughts and hopes for their language and culture. We also thank Fred Bia for photographs from Rough Rock School.

Our sincere thanks to the many colleagues whose work and collegiality have served as inspiration: Ray Barnhardt, Thomas Biolsi, Bryan Brayboy, Thomas Buckley, Courtney Cazden, Brenda Child, Philip Deloria, Donna Deyhle, Joshua and Gella Fishman, Perry Gilmore, Rayna Green, Shirley Brice Heath, Nancy Hornberger, Valerie Lambert, Julian Lang, Jerry Lipka, Stephen May, N. Scott Momaday, Nancy Parezo, Lorna Rhodes, Maureen Schwarz, Tove Skutnabb-Kangas, Bernard Spolsky, Jay Stauss, Julie K. Stein, Karen Swisher, John Tippeconnic III, John Troutman, Gerald Vizenor, Terrence Wiley, and Harry Wolcott.

The historical chapters depended on the professional assistance of the talented and dedicated staff at numerous libraries and archives; thanks to all and special thanks to the staff at Special Collections, University of Arizona main library; Ann Cummings, Richard Fusick, Ken Hawkins, Mary Frances Morrow, and staff at the National Archives and Records Administration, Washington D.C., and the National Archives, Still Pictures Branch, in College Park, Maryland; Paul Wormser, Director of Archival Operations at the National Archives and Records Administration, Pacific Region, at Laguna Niguel, California; archivists at the National Archives and Records Administration, Southwest Region, in Forth Worth, Texas, and Pacific Alaska Region in Seattle, Washington; staff at the National Anthropological Archives, National Museum of Natural History, Smithsonian Institution; the Museum of Native American Arts and Culture, Spokane, Washington, whose collections are now housed at the Northwest Museum of Arts and Culture, and whose archival staff, including Larry Schoonover, Rose Kraus, and student interns offered generous assistance tracking down photographs; the Toppenish Public Library, Toppenish, Washington; and Kathy Hubenschmidt, Jeannette Garcia, and Karen Luebbermann of the Arizona State Museum photographic archives.

Many other colleagues, as well as our students, provided advice and feedback as we worked on the manuscript. Deep thanks to David E. Wilkins for feedback on Chapters 1 through 5 and for incomparable, intellectually enriching friendship. For their comments on Chapter 8, we thank Sylvia

Hendricks, Alex Mendez, Delbert Ortiz, Andrea Ramon, Alison Reeves, and Naomi Takuda, whose corrections to information on Native charter schools were invaluable. For listening and sharing substantive suggestions with Teresa McCarty on a seemingly endless flight from Siberia to the United States, thanks are due to Professor Perry Gilmore of the University of Arizona Department of Language, Reading and Culture. We thank all of the students enrolled in AIS 677, The History of Indian Education, at the University of Arizona during the spring 2005 semester for their careful reading and invaluable comments on an early draft of the manuscript; and thanks to Karen Capuder for her editorial assistance with references.

Financial support for Teresa McCarty's work on this book was provided, in part, by the Alice Wiley Snell Endowment in Education Policy Studies at Arizona State University and the U.S. Department of Education Institute of Education Sciences. We especially thank Alice (Dinky) Snell for her faith in this work.

Finally, we thank those who have listened, advised, and stood by us as friends and family members throughout the long days (and nights) of researching and writing: our parents, Curtis T. and F. Marilyn Carr; Virginia Doulin, Mildred McCarty, and the late James L. McCarty; our siblings, Jan Blackman, Valerie Mussi, Julie Pitchford, and their families; and friends Caren Creutzberger, Karyn Gitlis, Jan Kegelman, Diana Pardue, and Diane Zipley. We reserve our final expression of gratitude for our husbands, Hartman H. Lomawaima and John F. Martin, who have greatly enriched our writing partnership by their own mutual friendship, and without whose intellectual, moral, and emotional support this work would not be possible.

Preface

Each and every [Lakota] parent was a teacher and . . . all elders were instructors of those younger than themselves. . . . We learned by watching and imitating examples placed before us. Slowly and naturally the faculties of observation and memory became highly trained. . . . The training was largely of character . . . and continued through life. True Indian education was based on the development of individual qualities and recognition of rights.

—Luther Standing Bear (Lakota) (1933/1978)

America can be revived, rejuvenated, by recognizing a native school of thought. The Indian can save America.

—Luther Standing Bear (Lakota) (1933/1978)

Imagine America's response to Standing Bear's offer in 1933. Imagine it today. It is a daunting task, to focus the attention of a powerful, self-assured nation on the peoples whose very existence today might appear as a rebuke, a reminder that this place called home was not always yours. And then propose that Indian people have something valuable to teach, that a "Native school of thought" might rejuvenate the nation. What a thought.

We are fascinated that Standing Bear chose the term *school of thought*. Schools have for so long been at the center of debates over national purpose, identity, and vitality. And schools have been at the center of the onslaught to "civilize"—to eradicate Native thought, language, culture, and education. What might the nation-state learn about itself from the lessons drawn from a century of Native experiences with schools?

 We might learn about choice.
 We might learn about self-determination.
 We might learn about the potential for national strength embedded in cultural and linguistic diversity and the dangers propagated by homogenization and standardization.
 We might learn enough to forge, together, a new vision of democracy.

Federal and mission schools set out to "civilize," assimilate, and "Americanize" Native peoples. Whatever the label, education policies and practices have been designed to erase and replace. Erase Native languages; replace with English. Erase Native religions; replace with Christianity. And so on. But paradoxes immediately complicate the picture. If the government was committed to obliterating Indigenous cultures and languages, how do we explain early 20th-century classes in federal schools teaching Native arts and technologies? How do we explain the federal production of bilingual primers, for use in bilingual classrooms, in the 1940s? How do we reconcile late-20th-century federal policies of Indian self-determination with regulations that thwarted self-determination at every turn?

By comparing and analyzing federal policies, educational practices, and individual experiences, we discern patterns in the apparent anomalies that pepper the last century of education imposed on Native peoples. U.S. society and government were not, we propose, simply vacillating through "swings of a pendulum" between tolerance and intolerance. Each generation was working out, in a systematic way, its notion of a safety zone, an area where dangerously different cultural expressions might be safely domesticated and thus neutralized.

In this book we lay bare the social-structural and historical forces underlying the safe/dangerous paradigm. In so doing, we reveal the falseness of fears attached to notions of dangerous cultural difference and the promise of diversity as a source of national strength. We explicate how Indigenous America's fight to protect and assert educational self-determination enriches national and international education debates.

The title phrase *to remain an Indian* derives from a section of the 1928 Meriam Report, an investigation into the federal administration of "Indian affairs" that more than 70 years ago advocated for the right of choice:

> He [*sic*] who wishes to merge into the social and economic life of the prevailing civilization of this country should be given all practicable aid and advice in making the necessary adjustments. He who wants to remain an Indian and live according to his old culture should be aided in doing so. (Meriam et al., 1928, p. 86)

Even though the authors of the Meriam Report erred in inferring a static or backward "old culture," they rightly grasped the principle of choice—the ability "to remain an Indian"—as an essential human right.

The words *diversity, democracy,* and *self-determination* are not simple abstractions. They represent whole domains of human experience. Insofar as these words constitute a shared vocabulary—a shared, although contested, field of reference—they are built on the backs of human lives, human stories, and individual reality. What has been the reality for Native peoples in U.S. schools and in the American democracy? In the chapters that follow,

we endeavor to excavate, recover, and place at the center those Native individuals, voices, and experiences that official historical master-narratives have
overlooked or pushed aside.

OVERVIEW OF THE BOOK

We trace the journey of Indian education from instruction in Native homes
and languages; through federal incarnations of colonial education; through
transfer of educational powers and responsibilities from federal schools to
state-supervised public schools; to shared powers with Indian tribes and
communities; to the possibilities once again of Indian education being envisioned and implemented both *by* and *for* Native people. In our journey we
never lose sight of choice and tribal self-determination, the key lessons that
American Indian education offers all citizens, as they embody the promises
at the core of a critically conscious democracy.

We begin by proposing a theoretical framework, which we label the
safety zone, to explain shifts in federal educational policies and practices over
the past century. Forging beyond the metaphor of policy shifts as the "swings
of a pendulum," we view federal Indian policy as a sociocultural (and therefore ideological) process in which federal authorities *appropriate* policy to
serve particular interests and goals.

Chapter 2 overturns dangerously delimiting stereotypes of American
Indians as one-dimensional learners. We let the voices of Native people demonstrate the complexity of Indigenous education as language-rich, consciously
designed systems based on Indigenous theories of intellect and emotion.
Chapter 3 maps the terrain of safe and dangerous cultural difference in early-
20th-century schools. Complex Native cultural life could present daunting
threats to federal control but could also be imagined as "primitive," thus
innocuous, "arts and crafts" or "harmless" children's lullabies.

The publication of the Meriam Report in 1928 marked a shift in federal
constructions of safe/dangerous difference. The Meriam Report proposed a
remarkable possibility: that the federal government should support Native
people who *choose* to "remain an Indian." As Chapter 4 illustrates, putting
that remarkable proposal for choice into action proved to be a complicated,
contentious task. Native and non-Native players struggled with the boundaries between safe and dangerous difference, revealing the deeply contested
power relations at the heart of federal policy.

In Chapter 5, a close reading of the bilingual readers produced by the
Bureau of Indian Affairs in the 1940s and 1950s reveals a fascinating inter-
play among non-Native educators and Native translators. The Bureau's Hopi,
Lakota, Navajo, and Pueblo *Life Readers* offer glimpses of the tug-of-war

between Bureau control and Native implementation in this pioneering development of bilingual education.

Perhaps the most revelatory self-determinant initiatives involved the birth of Indigenous bilingual/bicultural programs in community-controlled schools, a movement we detail in Chapter 6. During the late 1960s and 1970s—when, in the words of one of the architects of Indigenous bilingual/bicultural education programs, "the government wasn't down on us so hard" (Wayne Holm, personal communication, 1996)—Native communities began transforming Indian education from the inside out, "growing their own" bilingual/bicultural teaching staff, curricula, and pedagogies.

Yet Indigenous bilingual/bicultural education has not been sufficient to reverse the language dispossession resulting from genocide, the boarding schools' English-only policies, and, more recently, the forces of globalization. In Chapter 7, we analyze what we call (following Svensson, 1981) the "new American revolution": the struggle by Indigenous communities to reclaim and retain their languages as fundamental expressions of choice and self-determination.

In Chapter 8, we take up the standards movement, the most recent challenge to Indigenous educational self-determination. Emphasizing reductionist literacy programs and high-stakes tests, this movement can be seen as a regulatory response to "dangerously" increasing numbers of students of color, English-language learners, and poor and working-class students. Among other initiatives, Native communities are resisting these standardizing pressures by developing Indigenous counterstandards, such as those for culturally responsive schools.

Can linguistic and cultural diversity be promoted and maintained without concomitant economic, political, and social marginalization of historically oppressed groups? Can the truly dangerous forces of standardization be resisted and transformed? Can Native and non-Native parents and communities be trusted with the powers of choice and self-determination in educating their children? Our answer to these questions is a resounding "yes!" —but as we suggest in the Coda, these goals require significant, even revolutionary, social change.

WHERE DO WE STAND?

History is a social construction. We do not claim to be neutral observers, but no historical account is disinterested or politically neutral. As scholars of American Indian education trained in social-cultural anthropology, we bring a strong interdisciplinary orientation to our work and a stance as both "insiders" and "outsiders."

Our individual and shared experiences weave in and out of the chapters in this book. Although much of the writing has been completed shoulder-to-shoulder, we have each had a "heavier" hand in certain parts of the book. Chapters 2 through 5 derive from Lomawaima's teaching and research. Chapters 6 through 8 are grounded in McCarty's ethnographic and oral historical research. Working together, we have sought to create a coherent portrait of American Indian education over the past century. As we critically reevaluate taken-for-granted education policies and practices, we ask our readers to carefully consider their meaning for social justice and democratic citizenship.

CHAPTER 1

Choice and Self-Determination: Central Lessons from American Indian Education

> Following the life patterns they knew . . . [the schoolgirls] would set up camps in the several corners of the playground, complete with tepees made of unbleached muslin, about two feet high for the families of Indian dolls made from sticks, covered with brown cloth, with beads for eyes and real hair clipped from their own braids. . . . One could see as many as fifty tepees at one time. . . . Frequently, there could be seen a dozen or more braves squatting on the high ground looking down upon these miniature camps with nostalgic interest.
> —T. H. Morgan (1958, p. 29)

So Thisba Huston Morgan described the Ogalalla Boarding School as she reminisced, years later, about her experiences as a teacher in the spring of 1890. The scene seems to contradict everything we know, or think we know, about federal and mission schools for American Indian children. After all, "Indian schools" were created to "civilize" Native children, to eradicate Native identities, languages, and cultures. Why would the children at Ogalalla be allowed to act out the "uncivilized" camp life their teachers were certain was destined to perish? And in full view of only recently "pacified" Lakota (Sioux) adults? Historian David W. Adams (1995), whose attention also was caught by this remarkable description, called it student "resistance" and said simply, "The teachers chose not to interfere" (p. 234). But *why* not interfere? Interfering with Native lives was, quite literally, their job. Perhaps these teachers were sympathetic to their young charges? Perhaps this school was an exception to the rule of late-19th-century federal policy that forbade every expression of Indian-ness? As it turns out, Morgan was not the only Indian Service teacher who "chose not to interfere," and Ogalalla was not the only school home to such a scene.

Two historic photographs match Morgan's description of the transformed playground at Pine Ridge, and neither comes from Lakota country. The papers of Estelle Reel, Superintendent of Indian Schools from 1898 to 1910, are housed in the Northwest Museum of Arts and Culture in Spokane, Washington. The Reel collection includes hundreds of photographs of Indian

1

schools and schoolchildren, including "Little Girls' Play Ground, Crow Agency, Montana" (see Figure 1.1). The National Anthropological Archives, Smithsonian Institution, in Washington, D.C., contain a similar photo, "Cantonment Indian boarding school, with girls' play tipis in front yard 1900," taken or collected by Jesse Hastings Bratley while teaching at the school for Cheyenne children in Oklahoma (see Figure 1.2).

The playground at Ogalalla Boarding School was not an aberration; it fit into a pattern. Historic photographs and Thisba Morgan's memoirs reveal how federal powers were focused to "domesticate" the most dangerous Indians of their day, the recently hostile northern and southern Plains tribes whose war-bonneted warriors stood—and stand—as iconic American images of the "last free Indians." Photographs such as these showed Americans how dangerous cultural difference was being contained, made safe within the Indian boarding schools, arguably the most minutely surveilled and controlled federal institutions created to transform the lives of any group of Americans. The schools controlled a physical *safety zone* in their classrooms and playgrounds that could symbolically neutralize the Native languages, religions,

[handwritten margin note: purpose of NA schools continued]

Figure 1.1. "Little Girls' Play Ground, Crow Agency, Montana, Early 1900s." Photo in the collection of Estelle Reel Papers, Northwest Museum of Arts and Culture/Eastern Washington State Historical Society, Spokane, Washington.

Figure 1.2. "Cantonment Indian Boarding School, with Girls' Play Tipis in Front Yard, 1900." National Anthropological Archives, Smithsonian Institution/(Neg. #53312).

economies, polities, family structures, emotions, and lives that seemed to threaten American uniformity and national identity. The sites and tribes involved in these scenes were not accidental, as Thisba Morgan's continued commentary on the Ogalalla playground makes clear:

> Frequently, there could be seen a dozen or more braves squatting on the high ground looking down upon these miniature camps with nostalgic interest. They said it reminded them of their camps in the hills and they would recall their exploits on the Little Big Horn. . . . Their brave spirits were broken. The buffalo was gone. They were utterly bereft of such perfect freedom as no other race of free men had ever known in our free land. Should a shower come, the tepees, the tepee poles, wagons and dolls would be hurried inside the schoolhouse and stowed away to reappear on another sunny day. The camp must be forgotten. The children must learn to live in the white man's world. (Morgan, 1958, p. 29)

Colonial supremacy forged this nostalgia as the victors pacified the conquered, the last perfectly free men [*sic*] "in our"—not their—"free land."[1] The United States created its national self-image as an exceptional, divinely

American

ordained democracy by juxtaposing its "civilization" against its assumptions of an Indigenous "primitive." The United States asserted its rights as a sovereign nation, the land of the free, as the natural heir to Indian freedom and the heir to Native lands as well (see Adams, 1988).

SCHOOLS AS "CIVILIZING" AND HOMOGENIZING INSTITUTIONS

The "civilized" nation assumed that its right to dispossess Native nations went hand in hand with a responsibility to "uplift" them, and mission and federal "Indian schools" were established as laboratories for a grand experiment in cultural cleansing, Christian conversion, and assimilation of laborers and domestic workers into the workforce (Littlefield, 1989, 1993). The so-called civilization of American Indians, at times simply termed "Americanization," mandated the transformation of nations and individuals: Replace heritage languages with English; replace "paganism" with Christianity; replace economic, political, social, legal, and aesthetic institutions. Given the American infatuation with the notion that social change can best be effected through education, schools have logically been vested with the responsibility for Americanizing Indigenous peoples as well as immigrants. Educational historian David Tyack (1967) clearly identified the schools' difficult role balancing safe uniformity versus dangerous diversity in educating immigrants:

> From the time of the Revolution forward, substantial numbers of Americans supposed that the free citizen was the uniform man, that diversity somehow endangered the promise of American life since it threatened cohesiveness. Others saw a free society as a place where it was safe to be unpopular, comfortable to be different. The common school in successive decades expressed both points of view in differing degrees, seeking to strike the precarious balance of ordered liberty. The task of Americanizing the immigrant posed in all its complexity the problem of unity within diversity. (p. 234)

Reservations were also envisioned as laboratories to implement the scientifically phrased project of "elevating a race." Just as reformers and Reconstructionists a few decades earlier had viewed slavery, criminal as it was, as the "civilizing engine" of uplift for Blacks, so the extraordinary federal policing powers of reservation life were seen as necessary instruments to "civilize" American Indians (Hoxie, 1984/1989; Lindsey, 1995; Pommersheim, 1995). Even the reservations' repressive power regimes, however, could not match the totally controlled environments aspired to by school administrators. Within these totalizing institutions, selected elements of Native cultures might be made safe as they were encapsulated, domesticated, and aired out on a sunny day.

Federal Indian schools were largely superseded by public schools in the late 20th century, but forces to transform Native students and control a safety zone of allowable cultural expression continued largely unabated. Public education in the United States was founded on the principle of local control, but that right, like citizenship, was not immediately offered to all Americans. For American Indians, African Americans, immigrants, and others, schooling has been an engine of standardization, not of parental choice and control, as powerful interests within the dominant society endeavored to fit diverse Americans for their assigned places within established economic and social hierarchies.

The interests at work in shaping schooling have not held a unified vision of a single ideal "American," but rather a vision of multiple roles and varying opportunities depending on a complex intersection of citizenship status, "race," color, gender, national origin, and religion. This multifaceted vision has nonetheless had homogenizing or standardizing goals. Often masquerading as a tool for equal educational opportunity, standardization has segregated and marginalized Native peoples and others as it has circumscribed a narrow zone of tolerable cultural difference.

Drawing the boundaries between safe and dangerous cultural difference and illuminating the safety zone of American national culture lie at the heart of our history of American Indian education. The dilemma of the safety zone has endured to the present day. Which Native beliefs and practices might be judged safe, innocuous, and tolerable? Which beliefs and practices are too dangerous, different, and subversive of mainstream values? How best to manage or eradicate dangerous cultural expression? Federal Indian education policies and practices reveal how our nation defines itself and how it acts, to varying degrees, in liberating or repressive ways toward groups defined as different. Native experiences and perspectives—both resistance to imposed education and the creation of alternative models—reveal the liberating power of choice and the importance of self-determination for communities who make up a nation unified by critical democratic ideals, rather than by linguistic or cultural homogeneity. The history of Native education well illustrates the costs of repressive, standardizing schooling that abrogates the rights of local choice and control.

The education of American Indian children has been at the very center of the battleground between federal and tribal powers; the war has been waged through and about children, and the costs of colonial education have largely been borne by Indian people. Economic and social indicators that quantify status and quality of life in the United States are notoriously grim for Native Americans: lowest per capita incomes, highest rates of infant mortality, extraordinarily high rates of depression and teen suicide (Snipp, 1989). Educational statistics are no better. Of the more than 500,000 American

Indian students in U.S. schools in the early 1990s, 60% left school before graduating (National Center for Education Statistics, 1995). These statistics are the legacies of decades of repressive administration, when Native parents and communities were denied the right to local control over education, when they were denied the privilege of choice.

SAFETY ZONE THEORY: EXPLAINING POLICY DEVELOPMENT OVER TIME[2]

According to Felix S. Cohen (1953), Assistant Solicitor in the Department of the Interior in Franklin D. Roosevelt's administration,

> Like the miner's canary, the Indian marks the shift from fresh air to poison gas in our political atmosphere; and our treatment of Indians, even more than our treatment of other minorities, reflects the rise and fall of our democratic faith. (p. 390)

Cohen, scholar of international and American Indian law and legal ethics, understood the strategic use of American Indians as exemplars of how U.S. justice has been applied and misapplied. He pointed to shifts in Indian policy as indicators of the "rise and fall" of democratic ideals. The periodicity of the pendulum is regularly evoked in summaries of Indian policy: The pendulum swings from allotment to reform, from New Deal tolerance to Cold War xenophobia, from tribal termination to Indigenous self-determination (see, e.g., Deloria & Lytle, 1983; Washburn, 1988). As Arthur Schlesinger Jr. pointed out in *The Cycles of American History* (1986), the pendulum metaphor has been used extensively in American political science. Like Schlesinger, Native historian Don Fixico (2002) has criticized the "oscillating pendulum" model; it describes, but does not explain, change over time.

As an explanatory alternative to the pendulum, we propose a theoretical model of the safety zone that traces the "swings" of Indian policy—including educational policy—to an ongoing struggle over cultural difference and its perceived threat, or benefit, to a sense of shared American identity. The federal government has not simply vacillated between encouraging or suppressing Native languages and cultures but has in a coherent way—using salient criteria such as gender, childhood, "aesthetic" versus "economic" life—attempted to distinguish safe from dangerous Indigenous beliefs and practices (Lomawaima, 1996, 2002; Lomawaima & McCarty, 2002b).

American Indian education offers powerfully revealing evidence of how each generation, Native and non-Native, has competed and cooperated to determine where and when Indigenous cultural practices might be considered benign enough to be allowed, even welcomed, within American life.

More often than not, however, the outcome has been not to welcome but to marginalize, repress, or even criminalize Native life. As the focal institutions charged with remaking Native people, schools have proved the most sensitive barometers of America's safety zone. As the Board of Indian Commissioners wrote in their 1902 annual report, "Schools alone cannot make over a race, but no one instrument is so powerful in producing desirable changes in a race as are schools for the young" (Annual Report of the Commissioner of Indian Affairs [ARCIA], 1901, p. 781).

As ideas of American identity and democracy have shifted over the past century, influenced by social movements, economic developments, and world events, the boundary line distinguishing safe from dangerous cultural difference has shifted as well. From the rigidly racialized hierarchies endorsed by early-20th-century science; through the progressive reform movements of the 1920s; the New Deal social programs of the 1930s and 1940s; the Cold War retrenchment of the 1950s; the civil rights movements of the 1960s and early 1970s; the move toward self-determination in Indian country over the 1970s, 1980s, and 1990s; to the current turn-of-the-century promise to "leave no child behind," the U.S. government and many of its citizens have struggled with "the Indian problem." The problem is that Native communities have persistently and courageously fought for their continued existence as *peoples*, defined politically by their government-to-government relationship with the United States and culturally by their diverse governments, languages, land bases, religions, economies, education systems, and family organizations.

The "problem" posed by the survival of Native peoples and languages is a profoundly political one because of the inherent sovereignty of Native nations and their historical and contemporary relations with other sovereigns such as England, France, Spain, and, more recently, the United States. We cannot understand the creation and defense of the safety zone as a purely "cultural" question. Culture, language, politics, and legal status are inextricably bound together in the fabric of U.S./Indian relations. This requires an explication of terms and concepts before we can proceed to the theoretical and methodological approaches that guide our history of Indian education.

KEY TERMS AND CONCEPTS

Terms for Peoples

We use the terms *American Indian*, *Native*, *Native American*, and *Indigenous* interchangeably to refer to peoples indigenous to what is now the United States. Personal identity among Native peoples is often layered: rooted in a particular tribe; encompassing a sense of shared American Indian identity; and expressed in intersecting layers of tribal, state, and national citizenship. We use the term *American* in a national sense, referring to the United States of America and its citizens, recognizing that there is a larger understanding of the term referring to Latin American nations and peoples.

Educational Terms

We often use the term *American Indian education* to refer to the colonial education of American Indian people within school systems dedicated to "civilizing" and standardizing goals. A similar term, *Indian schools*, has referred to the on- and off-reservation mission and federal schools. In recent decades, the term *Indian education* has broadened to include public school education of American Indian, Native Alaskan, and Native Hawaiian children. A more ancient but still vital meaning of *Indian education* refers to the culturally based education of Native children by their parents, relatives, and communities (traditionally and sometimes today in a Native language). This book is devoted to the effort to bridge the immense but not insurmountable gap between these disparate and often conflicting systems of "Indian education."

Political and Legal Terminology

Critical Democracy. We do not define democracy as simple rule by the majority. We view democracy as a value, a policy, and a practice that respects, protects, and promotes diversity and human rights. A democratic citizenship requires civic courage (Freire, 1998) and a multicultural consciousness that acknowledges and confronts the historical and institutional roots of oppression. Our concepts of democracy and diversity are premised on a critical construct of the democratic ideal (see, e.g., Aronowitz & Giroux, 1985; Darder, 1991; Freire, 1978, 1998; Giroux, 2001). We purposefully frame critical democracy as an ideal, recognizing the "contradictions between an espoused theory of democracy and a lived experience of inequality" (Darder, 1991, p. 63). We argue that this ideal can and should stand as a vision of what our democracy aspires to and might become.

Critical democracy demands that the United States be a nation of educational opportunity for all, not merely a homogenizing and standardizing machine. We conceive of more than a benignly neutral diversity that "celebrates" cultural differences while muting the ideological forces that privilege certain differences and marginalize others. Rather, diversity embodies the heart and soul of promise, of opportunities, of what might be, for a socially just and fully democratic nation. A fully democratic society cannot systematically deny privileges or choices to certain citizens, or selectively deny full citizenship to its members, or systematically privilege elites. To flourish, individual human beings as well as social groups need room, opportunity, and resources to develop and implement their values, philosophies, and beliefs. They need opportunities to exercise educational choice. They need places where difference is not perceived as a threat, even as the pressures for standardization gather momentum across the United States and across the globe.

Choice. Our use of the word *choice* should not be misunderstood as an endorsement of current political arguments that tout educational "choice" while stripping away all historical and social context and, most importantly, while they mask the operations of race, social class, language, and power that determine who has "choice" and who does not. Especially in Native America, choice operates in linked domains of individual choice and community self-determination that are rooted in the inherent sovereignty of Native nations. Perceptions of and real opportunities for choice are deeply conditioned by generations of poverty, discrimination, federal control, oppressive schooling practices, and economic and infrastructural underdevelopment. In this context, parental choice operates at the level of the family but is embedded within systems of shared values. Enabling choice does not mean an abrogation of public responsibility to build and adequately support vibrant, challenging, high-quality educational institutions.

The Centrality of Sovereignty. Native peoples in the United States are distinguished from other "ethnic" minorities by their status as members of sovereign nations. Sovereignty is the inherent right of a people to self-government, self-determination, and self-education. Sovereignty includes the right to linguistic and cultural expression according to local languages and norms, the right to "write, speak, and act from a position of agency" (Giroux, 2001, p. xv). As a political reality, sovereignty does not require complete independence. What nation today is completely unfettered? The United States, for example, contracts treaties and agreements with other sovereigns, and the federalist system balances federal sovereignty against sovereignty of the states. The fact that tribes are not completely independent polities does not contradict their status as sovereign polities (Wilkins & Lomawaima, 2001).

Constitutional Basis of Tribal Sovereignty. The singular legal status of tribes both predates and is recognized by the Constitution (see Castile, 1998; Castile & Bee, 1992; Deloria & Lytle, 1983, 1984; Deloria & Wilkins, 1999; Philp, 1986; Pommersheim, 1995; Prucha, 1984; Wilkins, 1997; Wilkinson, 1987; Williams, 1990). The commerce clause delegates to Congress the power "to regulate Commerce with foreign nations, and among the several States, and with the Indian tribes." The Constitution empowers the president to negotiate treaties with foreign nations (ratification requires a two-thirds vote by the Senate), and the formative United States used the treaty process, as did earlier colonial powers, to conduct diplomatic relations with Indian nations. The Constitution, federal legislation, bureaucratic rules of the federal agencies supervising Indian affairs, and judicial decisions are all tributary to what we call federal Indian policy (Wilkins & Lomawaima, 2001).

Tribal Powers. Examples of tribes' sovereign powers include the right to determine their membership, administer justice through tribal courts, govern their citizens, and regulate use of their land base. A direct government-to-government relationship articulates tribal relations with the federal government (and increasingly with state governments as well), and is critical to understanding how rights—such as the right to operate tribal departments of education or casinos—are negotiated and implemented.

METHODOLOGICAL AND THEORETICAL APPROACHES

We cannot understand the present divorced from the past. Current ideologies, policies, practices, and experiences do not simply appear out of the ether but are firmly rooted in the lives of earlier generations. Our vantage point, scanning more than a full century, enables us to track the contours of the safety zone through changing circumstances.

Analytical Perspectives

Analyzing the moving target we call the safety zone requires us to integrate three perspectives: those of federal policy, institutional practices, and Native and non-Native individual experiences (Lomawaima, 1993, 1995, 2002; see also Adams, 1995). Scholars of American Indian education and education policy in general have often assumed that policies involve government action (or inaction). This assumption tends to overstate the reality or force of formal state policies and documents. Representing policies as objective "texts" obscures how complex, contested, and deeply ideological they are. Instead, we view policy as a sociocultural process—as modes of human interaction, negotiation, and production mediated by relations of power (McCarty, 2004). Within this framework, policy is the "practice of power" and of normative decision making (Levinson & Sutton, 2001, p. 1).

In the case of American Indian education, federal authorities, school superintendents, teachers, and others have normalized certain cultural and educational practices while defining others as threatening to federal authority and therefore impermissible. We intentionally focus on these dynamics, examining episodes of Indian education policy-in-practice. How has federal Indian policy been appropriated by different actors to promote particular interests at particular moments in time? How have Native people experienced and responded to federal policy-in-practice?

The views from the vantage points of policy, practice, and experience are distinctive. Sometimes they seem to be focused on different planets, and thus their juxtaposition teaches us more than any one view can provide. The statements of federal policymakers framed in rhetorical flourishes reveal ideologies and dearly held beliefs about the United States and about Native Americans. A significant corpus of policy has emanated from Washington, D.C., far removed from much of Indian country. Policy tends to be national in scope, homogeneous and coherent within specific political administrations or eras, and marked by transition and reformulation as administrations change. It is richly documented by evidence housed within the National Archives. The key players include well-known, highly placed political appointees within the Office of Indian Affairs, elected officeholders, and politically and economically powerful citizens active in reform groups. The players have written profusely and been profusely written about.

Quality and Character of Archival Records

The Indian Office quest to Americanize American Indians, in the tradition of all great bureaucratic endeavors, was (and is) continually in process. Surveillance, data collection, record keeping, and the production of reports have been the lifeblood of the bureaucracy. In 1926, Superintendent of Education Peairs directed all Indian Service teachers to prepare for curriculum revision by surveying their community, to "actually go into the homes of the Indians" to determine the "present stage of the Indians' advancement physically, morally, mentally, socially, and economically"; to collect, tabulate, and assess data (NARA, Entry 135, 1926). Our indebtedness to the federal mania to collect and store information about Native Americans is profound and perverse; this book would be impossible without it, but it stings to be so deeply indebted to those who set out to document Indian deficiencies.

In an ideal world, official "authorizing" policies generate practices in rational, predictable, and understandable ways; that has sometimes even been the case in Indian education. Practices are local: the daily activities of administrators, teachers, and staff. Practices also tend to be richly documented in collections held in church archives and Federal Regional Records Centers, where papers from individual schools and agencies are deposited.

We do see variability in the character of these documentary records over time. In the first half of the 20th century, records tend to be voluminous, detailed, revelatory of the character and opinions of the recorders, and often revealing about individual Native students or employees as well. After the 1940s, these records tend to become more quantitative than qualitative; they present aggregate statistics, for example, such as daily or quarterly attendance records, rather than the detailed descriptive records or commentaries on individual students that were more common in earlier years. Similarly, later records contain less correspondence and commentary by individual superintendents, reservation agents, or similar record-makers. These differences in records over time may reflect different record-generating or record-keeping strategies, or both.

Native "Archives" in Memories and Documents

The perspective offered by individual experiences is as central to the chronicle of Indian education as those of authorizing policy and practice. The most important perspective for the story told within these pages can be heartbreakingly ephemeral. Gaps and fissures fragment our knowledge of Native experiences over the last century, reminding us of the many "stories that fall just beyond our grasp," in N. Scott Momaday's words (personal communication, 2002). We call these the "black holes" of American Indian Studies, and some days they seem to carry most of the weight of our universe of knowledge. Despite the black holes, many Native experiences have been documented in written and photographic forms. Perhaps surprisingly, federal documents in the National Archives contain abundant evidence of Native lives, although many accounts were not recorded *by* Native authors. Like all records, they demand careful and discriminating use. Some were authored by Native people, though, as Brenda Child's (1998) scholarship on the letters exchanged by parents and students of boarding schools attests.

Life Histories Are Gifts. American Indian Studies is blessed with a rich autobiographical and biographical literature that is critical to our intellectual development (Brumble, 1981). As scholars we are bound in an ethical relationship with our sources. Native life histories speak to us with the voices of our relatives, our grandparents and parents, our aunts and uncles, our clan, our kin, and our people, who offer us their stories as gifts. What the stories can teach depends on us, on our motivation and the energy we are willing to invest. Gifts imply generosity; generosity inspires respect, attention, analysis, responsibility, and affection for the giver.

Responsibilities of Indigenous Scholarship. Affection may strike some as an inappropriate responsibility of scholarship, a dangerous finger— or fist—on the scale of allegedly objective analysis. The emotional ties—and responsibilities—that knit scholars to the communities we "study" and serve also apply to the personalities behind life histories and archival documents (Lomawaima, 2000). The analytic strategies of comparison, cross-checking, and verification are not vitiated by affection (Lomawaima & McCarty, 2002a). Offering our sources the affection they deserve implies our respect for *their* emotions, a relationship required for effective education. Anthropologist Thomas Buckley offers a pertinent lesson from his Yurok mentor, Harry Roberts (the adoptive nephew of Robert Spott, known as anthropologist Alfred Kroeber's "last and perhaps most influential informant"). Spott told Roberts, "At first," the old Yuroks "told the anthropologist [Kroeber] personal things, but when they saw that they were not understood, they stopped. Never give someone something that they can't understand" (Buckley, 1997, p. 4).

Finally, we draw on our own firsthand ethnographic research. Ethnographic inquiry is relevant to our account of recent developments in American Indian education: of the struggle to realize the "unthinkable" through the first Indian-controlled bilingual/bicultural education programs, to reclaim endangered mother tongues, and to resist the new standardizing regimes that operate under the pretense of "leaving no child behind." In our ethnographic reporting, too, we have sought to be attentive to and respectful of the voices and perspectives of cultural insiders, allowing them to teach us through lived experience.

"Footprints" of Native Peoples in Education

We search for the footprints of Native presence in a century of American Indian education, looking for the unexpected, the overlooked, the seemingly paradoxical results of and responses to domineering policies and institutions. Our use of the term *footprint* is deeply influenced by our understanding of the Hopi concept of "footprint" or "track," which metaphorically refers to the physical markers left on a sacred landscape (Hopi Dictionary Project, 1998). When ancestral Hopis emerged into this world, they made a covenant with Màasaw, its spiritual steward. Màasaw directed them to live according to a harsh but rewarding way of life. The "establishment of ritual springs, sacred trails, trail markers, shrines and petroglyphs . . . and other physical evidence [manifested] that they had invested the area with their spiritual stewardship and fulfilled their pact with Ma'saw [*sic*]" (Dongoske, Jenkins, & Ferguson, 1993, p. 27). Footprints not only trace physical presence but stand for an enduring emotional, moral, and spiritual commitment to a way of life.

Within the history of American Indian education we are searching out the conditions under which Native people have created or fought for a sense of self and community, often under tremendous duress. We specify a sense of self as well as community because the concept of the individual is not absent from Indian communities. A sense of the individual is critical to many Native communities' sense of empowerment and choice, as it is up to each individual to muster the drive, knowledge, and dedication necessary to nurture a healthy, productive community. Our goal is to begin an "inquiry whose aim is to rediscover on what basis knowledge and theory became possible" (Foucault, 1970/1994, p. xxi). Our abiding interest in understanding the roles played by Native people throughout the past century leads us to the following questions:

- How have Native students, parents, teachers, and others found or built niches of educational opportunity or achievement over the last century, even as federal policies and practices were designed to fuel the assimilationist engine?
- How have Native people helped shape or shift, or responded to, widespread notions of safe or dangerous cultural difference?

Robert Dumont (Dumont & Wax, 1969) referred to the creative responses of Indian children—the production of new identities within boarding schools and manipulations of silence to subtly enforce their values in standardizing classrooms—as "autonomous developments" in Indian education. Perhaps *autonomous* is not the best word to describe Native people chipping out spaces to express Indian-ness within institutions controlled by others; they may not have been completely autonomous but they were motivated by deep commitments to culture and community. They each made choices—often difficult or unpopular choices that countered official policy, institutional practice, even the opinions of kin and neighbors—to change the ways people thought about and enacted learning, teaching, schooling, and education. They inserted Native voices into the narrative of Indian education, and they put Native perspectives and values into action in the daily life of Indian schools. Their leadership may have been the exception, not the rule; the programs and practices they developed may have been ephemeral; but they were not alone and we believe the incremental legacy of their efforts made a difference over time.

As chroniclers of Indian education, we bear the responsibility to seek out footprints of Native presence and understand them—not as singular exceptions but as moments in the historical narrative that help us link past to present, that help us traverse the territory between 1900 and the present. In this journey we can begin to appreciate, for example, how Native people took advantage of the window of opportunity for Native-language instruction and freedom of religious expression under Commissioner John Collier in the 1930s. We can better understand the enormous strides made by Native people in the 1960s and 1970s because we have glimpses of the legacies, however tenuous and suppressed, they built upon.

How can we hope to produce a story about Indian education that marries the dominant narrative—buttressed by powerful storytellers, well-rehearsed storylines, and a virtual landfill of supporting documentation—with the traces of Dumont's "autonomous developments"? Writing a "balanced" history that equitably apportions page space and narrative punch to a vast federal bureaucracy and local Native realities is difficult. Point and counterpoint are not evenly matched. We hope for a historical account whose quality is not measured solely by the cubic volume of archival boxes or linear feet of library shelves devoted to its sources. Finding the overlooked, recovering what has been suppressed, and recognizing the unexpected requires excavation, rehabilitation, and imagination. All history does.

†

CHAPTER 2

The Strengths of Indigenous Education: Overturning Myths About Indian Learners

One day some white people came among us and called a meeting of the parents. . . . They had come after some boys and girls and wanted to take them a long way off to a place about which we knew nothing. I consented at once, though I could think of nothing else but that these white people wanted to take us far away and kill us. . . . To me it meant death, but bravery was part of my blood, so I did not hesitate.

—Luther Standing Bear (1931/1988, p. 157)

The place "a long way off" was Carlisle Indian Industrial School, in the Pennsylvania countryside. Luther's father honored his bravery with a give-away; Luther remembered "I was going with the white people, and perhaps might never return; so he was sacrificing all his worldly possessions" (Standing Bear, 1928/1975, p. 125). Standing Bear faced his fate with the fortitude developed by his Lakota education, unaware of the ways his actions, demeanor, and language might be (mis)interpreted by school staff. What circumstances shaped the coming collision between Luther's Lakota upbringing and the educational culture of Carlisle? Figure 2.1 shows the young Standing Bear at Carlisle, in a photograph taken by John Choate when the elder Standing Bear traveled east to visit his son.

INDIGENOUS EDUCATION VERSUS AMERICAN SCHOOLING

"Primitive" Native societies were assumed to entirely lack or possess only rudimentary forms of the building blocks of a civilized society, such as governing bodies, codes of law, or organized religion. U.S. educators assumed that Native societies also lacked educational systems. Just as communities were assumed to be deficient in pedagogical theories and methods, Native individuals were assumed to lack the verbal, cognitive, even motor skills necessary to succeed in schools.

16

Figure 2.1. Luther Standing Bear and his father during his father's visit to Carlisle Indian School, Carlisle, Pennsylvania. Photo by John Choate. National Anthropological Archives, Smithsonian Institution/(I.D. #06842400).

The ideology that juxtaposed "civilized" against "primitive" justified land dispossession, political subjugation, and forced assimilationist schooling. Stereotypes about Native learners—as "silent," "stoic," or "visual"— have strategically reinforced the necessary difference and distance between "civilized" and "primitive" students. We propose that any "theory" that posits human beings as one-dimensional learners does great damage to the truth of human complexity.

HOW—AND WHY—DO STEREOTYPES ENDURE?

Before we begin our analysis of the last century of Indian education, we must address how and *why* Native educational systems and learners have been

characterized as deficient. Alleging Native deficiencies has invested schools
with the institutional "right" to "civilize" American Indian students. These
allegations persist to the present day. If Native parents and communities hope
to exercise the human rights of educational self-determination and choice,
then we need a broader understanding of the strengths of Indigenous educational systems designed and refined over the centuries.

In late-19th-century schools, teachers expected stoicism of their Indian
students. The stoicism—in public at least—should come as no surprise. Children were in enemy territory; everything about them was under attack. Who
would willingly admit to weakness before the enemy? Even if the cause were
"only" homesickness, emotions were better kept to oneself, and Native reminiscences of boarding school life are full of tears shed in private (Archuleta,
Child, & Lomawaima, 2000; Johnston, 1989; LaFlesche, 1900/1978;
Lomawaima, 1994). Federal employees used stereotypes of Indian "deficiencies" to "explain" student stoicism and justify the reshaping of Indian emotional life. In a newspaper interview published in 1900, Superintendent of Indian
Schools Estelle Reel (see Figure 2.2) "explained" Indian children:

> [The Indian child's] face is without that complete development of nerve and
> muscle which gives character to expressive features; his face seems stolid be-
> cause it is without free expression, and at the same time his mind remains
> measurably stolid because of the very absence of mechanism for its own ex-
> pression. (quoted in Lomawaima, 1996, p. 14)

Reel's ungenerous rationalization of Indian "stolidity" conveniently masked
the English-only discipline of the schools. Children were not allowed to speak
their language, and that meant that many children had no language—no
"mechanism of expression"—at all.

> The new-comer [to the Presbyterian Mission School among the Omahas in the
> 1860s], however socially inclined, was obliged to go about like a little dummy
> until he had learned to express himself in English. (LaFlesche [Omaha] 1900/
> 1978, p. xvii)

Silence has been an essential part of the discipline and regimentation
imposed on Indian children by colonial educators for five centuries. As early
as the 1530s, Franciscan teachers in Mexico City subjected boys to a "discipline of silence" while girls were "uplifted" through "silence and prayer"
(Barth, 1945, pp. 82, 102). In a memoir recounted to her friend Louise Udall,
Helen Sekaquaptewa recalled the Keams Canyon School on the Hopi reservation in the early 1900s: "We didn't understand a word of English and didn't
know what to say or do" (Udall, 1969, p. 43). Half a century later Galena
Sells Dick experienced similar silencing at Chinle Boarding School on the

Figure 2.2. "Estelle Reel, Superintendent of Indian Schools, 1898–1910." Photo in the collection of Estelle Reel Papers, Northwest Museum of Arts and Culture/ Eastern Washington State Historical Society, Spokane, Washington.

Navajo reservation: "It was confusing and difficult. . . . If we were caught speaking Navajo, the matrons gave us chores . . . or they slapped our hands with rulers. Some students had their mouths 'washed' with yellow bar soap" (Dick & McCarty, 1996, pp. 72–73). The stereotypic image of Indians as stoic and silent has endured for centuries because colonial educators have created and sustained it.

Scholars including Bryde (1970), Dumont (1972), and Philips (1972, 1983) have documented Indian children talking *less* over time as they progress through school. Their research provides chilling evidence that the myth of the "silent Indian learner" has served colonial education well, by focusing blame on students, not schools, as the source of a "problem." We must remember that every learner is sometimes silent and sometimes verbal; that learners choose among visual, aural, and kinesthetic modes. We must unmask and overturn any and all myths that tell us all Indian students are somehow one-dimensional learners, whether stoic, silent, visual, cooperative, or non-analytical. We do not intend to deny the reality of diverse learning modes, but rather to deny the dominating essentialism of myths that reduce Native learners to single dimensions.

We tackle these myths with evidence from the rich archive of knowledge about Indigenous educational systems. Native voices articulate the diverse, complex character of Indigenous education. The domains addressed here (many more remain to be explored) include Indigenous theories of intellect; the consciously designed structure of educational systems; the language-rich character of education; learning through watching, doing, and making; and instruction through relationships with others—with corn, for example, or animals placed in our care. Before we turn to Indigenous education, however, we need to reflect on definitions and concepts of education that surround us in the contemporary world. These terms and ideas help explain why myths—such as the silent, stoic Indian—are so powerful and enduring. They last because they are useful, not because they are true.

WHAT IS EDUCATION?

Ask ten Americans to *define* education and you will likely hear lofty aspirations —education develops life and job skills and hones critical thinking. Ask ten Americans to *describe* education, and nine times out of the ten you will hear about schooling: teachers and students in age-graded classrooms, testing, grades, homework, reading and writing and arithmetic. Our everyday ideas about *education* are constrained by a narrow vision of *schooling*, a thin slice out of the panoply of educational theories, strategies, and experiences developed over human history.

The ubiquity of the education = schooling paradigm partly explains why so much ink has been spilled over the "problems" of students from "different" backgrounds. The schooling paradigm has often targeted "difference" as uncivilized, disadvantaged, or worse; it has defined difference as a problem. The alleged attributes of Native students' difference constitute a lexicon of marvelous abundance (see Lomawaima, 1995, 2003): Nez Percé kindergarten students who possess "less developed" visual perception (Lowry, 1970, p. 303) and "severe linguistic inadequacy" (Ramstad & Potter, 1974, p. 493) are among the fundamentally "disadvantaged" children from "cultures of poverty" (Crow, Murray, & Smythe, 1966; Salisbury, 1974; Webster, 1966).

Less loaded language classifies Indians as silent learners (Dumont, 1972; Guilmet, 1978, 1981; More, 1989; Rhodes, 1988; Ross, 1989; Wauters, Bruce, Black & Hocker, et al., 1989); observational or "private" learners (Appleton, 1983; Brewer, 1977; John, 1972; Longstreet, 1978; Swisher & Deyhle, 1989; Wolcott, 1967); cooperative versus competitive learners (Brown, 1980; Miller & Thomas, 1972); visual learners (Kleinfeld & Nelson, 1991); field-dependent or field-independent learners (Dinges & Hollenbeck, 1978; Ross, 1989); "right-brained" or "whole-brained" learners (McShane & Plas, 1984; Rhodes, 1990; Ross, 1989; see Chrisjohn & Peters, 1989, and McCarty, Wallace, Lynch, & Benally, 1991, for rebuttals to ideas of racially or culturally programmed hemispheric dominance); and "ecological," "holistic," or "spiritual" learners (Cajete, 1994; Locust, 1988; Van Hamme, 1996).

We do not want to dismiss out of hand the literature cited above. Much of it is instructive, well-crafted research. Just as importantly, we absolutely know that culturally rooted practices produce distinct orientations toward teaching and learning (see, e.g., McCarty et al., 1991). We must recognize the serious error, however, of reducing our ideas of any learners to one-dimensional proportions. Unfortunately, many teachers and scholars—even Native parents and students—reproduce the myths of Indian students as one-dimensional learners, despite commonsense knowledge and scholarship that tells us otherwise.

The task at hand is to explode the narrow schooling paradigm, and to accomplish that we must answer the questions *why* and *what*. Why does the ideology of schooling sometimes generate a profusion of one-dimensional stereotypes of students? What can we do about it?

An array of scholarship compellingly illustrates the complexity of Indigenous educational and knowledge systems (Barnhardt & Kawagley, 2005; deMarrais, Nelson, & Baker, 1992; Johnston, 1976; Kawagley, 1995, 1999; Lipka & Ilustik, 1997; Lipka, Mohatt, & The Ciulistet Group, 1998; Okakok, 1989). Films, museum exhibits, and books display the rich diversity of Native experiences within mission, federal, and public schools (Archuleta et al., 2000; Ellis, 1996; Hyer, 1990; Johnston, 1989; LaFlesche, 1900/1978; Lomawaima, 1994, 1999; Riney, 1999). Scholars detail the achievements of Indian-controlled classrooms, programs, and schools over the last few decades (Dalton & Youpa, 1998; Dupuis & Walker, 1989; Lipka, 1991, 2002; McCarty, 2002a).

But the myths persevere, despite what we know about the complexity of Indigenous languages, the nuances of intercultural communication, and the pitfalls of intercultural miscommunication (Au & Jordan, 1981; Cazden & Leggett, 1981; Greenbaum & Greenbaum, 1983; Philips, 1972, 1983; Scollon & Scollon, 1981; Van Ness, 1981). The myths persevere despite evidence that oversimplified notions of teaching/learning styles do not capture the complexities of human interaction (Swisher & Deyhle, 1987, 1989). Research by McCarty and her colleagues (1991) showed Navajo children blossoming from silent "concrete" learners into talkative, analytical students when an experimental social studies curriculum was organized around Navajo content and values. But the myths don't fade. How can that be?

Part of the answer lies in the corporate, standardized nature of schools. Myths of one-dimensional learners were created to serve schools-as-institutions. Imagine the seductive power of the myths for administrators struggling to make ends meet, for teachers in overcrowded classrooms striving to serve diverse students. Imagine the sigh of relief when a learned professional journal offers the "single best way" to teach Indian students or reveals their dominant "learning style." Simplifying students appears to make a teacher's life easier.

Some myths do not flatter Indian people or intellects; others cast a rosy glow on Indians as "natural" artists, athletes, or ecologists. Some myths justify practices used to diminish students: Indians are visual, just show films; or Indians are nonverbal, debate is not culturally sanctioned. Sorting "positive" from "negative" myths, however, is pointless. The job at hand is not to sort myths but to expose them as dangerous and overturn their power to seduce.

Narrow, standardizing institutions demand myths that simplify the world. Expansive, liberating places of education demand realities that complicate it. Human beings are not one-dimensional learners or teachers. We select from a repertoire of preferences appropriate to our age and skill, consciously deciding how best to approach a new situation. Are we learning how to cook or committing a ceremonial song cycle to memory? Are we teaching teenagers to drive or grandparents to use a computer? Are we trying to master a heritage language or a mountain bike? We deploy aural, verbal, visual, kinesthetic, emotional, and cognitive skills and strategies that intersect in anticipated and unimagined ways. On less conscious levels, we are shaped by our upbringing, environment, language(s), ties of love and friendship, age and gender, health or illness. To enrich, not simplify our understanding of Native educational systems, we turn to Native lives and voices.

NATIVE VOICES TEACH LESSONS OF SHARED HUMANITY

Native autobiography requires and rewards close reading, which discloses the language-rich character of Native education. Francis LaFlesche (Omaha) (1900/1978) wrote in the preface to *The Middle Five*, his memoir of attending a Presbyterian mission school in the late 1800s: "Like the grown folk, we youngsters were fond of companionship and of talking. . . . We chattered incessantly of the things that occupied our minds, and we thought it a hardship when we were obliged to speak in low tones when the older people were engaged in conversation" (p. xvii). On the other hand, Charles Eastman (Dakota) (1902/1971), whose life was roughly contemporaneous with LaFlesche's, recalled, "As a little child, it was instilled into me to be silent and reticent" (p. 9). The contrast between the two descriptions reminds us of the complexities of human lives and the ways ends shape means. Both men wrote to educate primarily White audiences at the turn of the 20th century, when anti-Indian sentiments were rampant.

Eastman's (1902/1971) comment about reticence falls in a passage where he impresses upon the reader the "gravity and decorum" necessary to train a warrior and hunter; in his view, this training provided "the foundations of patience and self-control" (p. 9). LaFlesche (1900/1978) described "incessantly chattering" youngsters in his preface, where he stated the express "object of this book . . . [is] to reveal the true nature and character of the Indian boy" to the average American, whose "misconception of Indian life and character . . . [is] largely due to an ignorance of the Indian's language, of his mode of thought, his beliefs, his ideals, and his native institutions" (pp. xv, xviii).

We share LaFlesche's and Eastman's goal—to overturn misconceptions about Native people. They aimed to impress their audiences with the basic, civil humanity of Indian tribes: chatty children and old folks, moments of humor and solemnity, attention to correct diction, the beauty of language. They were not trying to reduce the complexity of Native life to one-dimensional myths— Indian children are chatterboxes, or Indian children are reticent—they were describing the human complexity of Native lives.

INDIGENOUS KNOWLEDGE GUIDES HUMAN SOCIETIES

To understand Native peoples over time, we strive to understand their theories of the origins of life, their ethics to maintain life, and their methods of constructing the past and envisioning the future. Native theories and histories are expressed in accounts of creation, which we study as we would study any philosophy or science; they share a status as systems of thought, explanatory theories guiding human decision making over the centuries. Explanatory theories provide moral and intellectual frameworks for understanding the world; they guide human beings as we do the following:

- *Observe* our surroundings, including environment, climate, celestial bodies, other living beings, and other human beings
- *Organize* our knowledge of the past
- *Explain* what we see and who we are
- *Cope* with circumstances through adaptive strategies, both "tried and true" or new and innovative
- *Plan* for the future

As we approach Indigenous knowledge systems, we need to remember
our limitations. Each system requires a lifetime of study to master its deep-
est levels. We are also handicapped by our reliance on English, given the
pitfalls of translation. Published accounts, including those composed in English, have been abbreviated or rearranged for many reasons—to achieve a
Western chronology, to suit editorial tastes, or to protect private information. Given all these limitations on our understanding, one might ask: Why
bother? Our reward is a glimpse of something profound.

The Native people who have published life histories have invited us into
their lives—into their homes, in a sense. Many of us understand the boundaries between public and private spaces when invited into a home. The kitchen
is a welcoming space, but a guest should not explore bedrooms, closets, or
medicine cabinets. Native epistemologies also have public and private spaces.
Not all knowledge is open to all learners, even within Native societies. Clans
possess proprietary rights to knowledge or skills—as historians, storytellers,
potters, administrators, or guardians. In Pueblo cultures, for example, each
kiva (religious society) possesses proprietary knowledge not shared with other
kivas. Within each kiva, initiates progress through levels of education according to their age, gender, intellectual capacity, and interest—no one assumes that all will reach the highest levels of understanding pursued by a
dedicated few.

Multiple Levels of Understanding

> The legends I have told were told by the old Pimas many, many years ago to
> entertain and instruct their children. . . . They show what life was like in those
> old days and what bothered people. . . . They show us what our ancestors
> thought was important. They help us to understand what is important today.
> (Webb, 1959, p. 116)

George Webb hints here at the multiple levels of understanding folded into
Native oral traditions. At one level simple "fairy tales" enthrall children, but
at other levels social charters direct behavior and stories encode the past as
well as the present. Indigenous epistemologies are complex philosophical
instruments subject to analysis, interpretation, and metaphoric unpacking.
In 1993, Harry Walters, director of Diné (Navajo) Studies at Diné Community College, and Maureen Schwarz, a non-Native anthropology graduate
student (now on the faculty at Syracuse University) discussed Diné explana-
tions for the "mystery illness"—hantavirus—stalking the southwestern states.
They focused on the origin story that described a time when human women
gave birth to monsters.

HW: OK, that is level one, right there. Level one.

MS: Level one? OK.

HW: Yeah, level one, but there are twelve levels [of analysis of Diné stories]. When you get to it, it is very complicated, even for me, I know, I think I will just stay at the two levels.

(quoted in Schwarz, 1995, p. 385)

[handwritten margin note: Most people take some NA stories as fairytale, actually quite deep.]

Walters discussed the possibility of monsters standing as metaphors for disease or immoral behavior. His analysis moved from level one "on to the next level of abstraction," while acknowledging "the elementary level . . . that is just gonna read like a fairy tale" (quoted in Schwarz, 1995, p. 389). Outsiders who do not speak Native languages most frequently encounter Native philosophies at the "fairy tale" level but should not assume that is all there is to it.

Indigenous Intellectual Property: "It Is for Us to Solve"

Native epistemologies demand that we respect what is shared, the boundaries of proprietary knowledge, and the rights of Native intellectual property. In the early years of the 20th century, an Arikara storyteller known as Hand shared the story of Arikara origins with George Dorsey, ethnographer for Chicago's Field Museum. Hand concluded the story: "This will give an idea to all how the Arikara originated under the earth. Yet it seems a mystery to us, and it is for us to solve" (quoted in Dorsey, 1904, p. 25). Hand minces no words in his powerful statement of Arikara intellectual property. Clearly he anticipates a large, interested audience when he addresses his story "to all." He signals that their understanding will be partial, only "an idea," a glimpse of how the Arikara world came to be. Hand warns us: This story is hard to understand; it is a mystery. Mysteries demand intellectual engagement; they do not give up their lessons easily to the dilettante. Hence, "it is for us to solve." Hand's statement is not only one of ultimate ownership— "it is for us"—but also of ultimate learner responsibility. Hand is saying "it is *up to us* to solve"; it is our profound responsibility as Arikara, learning to be fully Arikara, to solve this mystery.

[handwritten margin note: Horal]

The Learner's Responsibility: "It Is Up to You"

The listener/learner's responsibility lies at the core of many, perhaps all, Indigenous theories of intellect. As we have labored over the past 25 years to learn how to act appropriately in societies different from those in which we were raised, Lomawaima as an in-law in Hopi society and McCarty as a long-resident guest and coworker in Navajo society, we have often asked for advice.

"What should I do?" The most common answer is "It's up to you." You must shoulder the responsibility of putting lessons learned into operation. You must work at solving the mystery.

Knowledge, Sovereignty, and the Individual

What connects discussions of tribal education as it once was, past and current Indigenous epistemologies, and contemporary life? Karuk writer Julian Lang reminds us that "this ancient knowledge, created by the genius of our ancestors, contains the very essence of our tribal sovereignty" (1989, p. 3). If we understand sovereignty as a bundle of society's inherent human rights to self-government, self-determination, and self-education (Wilkins & Loma-waima, 2001), then Lang's "ancient knowledge" is the bundle—philosophies, skills, ceremony, material culture, interaction with a living environment—that gives sovereignty life in the daily world. In order to live properly in the world, children must be educated in ancient knowledge—politics, law, moral order, and the social contract that binds together a society's citizens.

Lang's (1989) description of his revelation about the sacred California High Country is worth quoting at some length, as he beautifully illustrates the engaged learner "at work," tussling with his people's ancient knowledge:

> In 1980, I returned home to our Center of the World and the Klamath River [in northern California]. . . . The most important spiritual peaks for us and two neighboring tribes were in danger of being destroyed by the planned construction of a highway, the G-O Road. This area, locally known as the "High Country," has for ages until the present been the site where the strongest doctors have gained their power. In 1981, I was racking my brain, researching endlessly, to find the myth-evidence which proclaims its sanctity. I never found the evidence I was looking for. Then one day in late 1987 I was talking about the G-O Road with my great aunt Ramona Starritt. She emphasized the taboo about going to the High Country for "no reason." Those peaks up there, Doctor Rock, Chimney Rock, Peak Eight and others, after all, were special people. She asked me rhetorically, "You know why those peaks are so powerful, don't you?" "No." "Because they were left behind to guard the headwaters of all the creeks." BINGO! A creation myth I had long since stored away in memory shot into my brain, a very perplexing myth. It was obviously important, but I was simply unable to locate the geography where the creation occurred. The myth was speaking of the High Country! This comment by my relation was the key to putting it all together. (p. 3)

Lang literally walks us through his thought processes, wedded to a sacred landscape, as he reaches a deeper understanding of Karuk ancient knowledge.

Lang's (1989) title, "It's Hard to Be an Indian," can also be understood at several levels. On the one hand he refers to the "wall twenty feet thick of misconception" that confronts Native peoples everyday (p. 3). His title is also an everyday saying in Indian country, referring to the challenge of living right, of joyfully assuming the responsibilities and obligations of adult life as a Karuk, or Dakota, or Arikara. We can see an Indigenous theory of intellect—It's up to you! It's hard, but it's worth it!—working to put sovereignty and ancient knowledge into practice.

CAREFULLY DESIGNED EDUCATIONAL SYSTEMS

> It is commonly supposed that there is no systematic education of their children among the aborigines of this country. Nothing could be farther from the truth. All the customs of this primitive people were held to be divinely instituted, and those in connection with the training of children were scrupulously adhered to and transmitted from one generation to another. (Eastman, 1902/1971, p. 41)

In the American imagination of education, we often refer to everything within schools as formal education and everything outside school walls as informal. This popular but artificial dichotomy fails to describe the complexity of American education inside and outside of schools. Its failure regarding Native educational systems is even more profound because it communicates that they are "accidental" or "unplanned."

"Formal" Education Means More Than Schools

Because the school = formal education equation is so powerful, Native education has usually been equated with *informal*, since Indigenous education over the last five centuries has usually occurred "out of school" (although in recent decades community-based and school-based education for Native children have begun to overlap and merge).[1] The label "informal" is another one-dimensional strategy used to denigrate and marginalize Native education, but close examination reveals that all educational systems incorporate both formal and informal aspects.

What are the characteristics commonly used to describe formal education? The system is consciously designed; pedagogical theories—of how students learn, for example—are spelled out, as are "best practices" to achieve educational goals; content and method are calibrated to students' age or development—grades K–12 are a widespread example; "higher" education is more restrictive or specialized than "lower"; education takes place within specific sites such as schools or classrooms; instructors are authorized by a certification process; student "progress" is judged by testing that determines continued movement through the system. Specific pedagogical methods can also be termed more or less formal—lectures, for example, compared to "hands-on" experimentation (this measure often correlates with the degree of control exercised by the "teacher" versus the "student").

In a purposeful contrast, informal education makes up the rest of the universe. If formal education is institutionalized, informal education is not. It occurs in everyday, mundane contexts, not in specially marked sites and times. It occurs according to happenstance, not as part of a consciously designed "curriculum." Anyone can be a teacher; anyone can be a student; knowledge is not restricted to particular classes or categories. Informal education is so "unmarked" in contrast to the marked characteristics of formal education that it may be completely unconscious—"learning by osmosis." Informal education has no rules, no pressure, no tests, and might even be "fun."

The formal/informal contrast developed to suit the circumstances of Western, industrial societies as institutionalized schooling grew to dominate notions of education. As such, there is little reason to suppose it would adequately describe Native educational systems, but one by-product of the school = formal model is the expansion of "informal" to subsume *all* non-Western modes of education. Indigenous modes of education have thus been suppressed or silenced. Native testimony effectively destroys the pretense that "informal" accurately describes Indigenous education. As the following evidence demonstrates, Indigenous systems incorporate many attributes of "formal" education (just as much of what goes on inside of schools can be called informal).

Patterns Within Indigenous Education

Native educational systems are formalized, intentionally designed to achieve pedagogical goals, as Charles Eastman points out in the quote that began this discussion. Frances Manuel (Tohono O'odham) (Manuel & Neff, 2001) made the same point about the pattern within Indigenous education. "My grandmother must be a very wise woman—she taught me a lot. Up to this day, things she said fit into a pattern" (p. 6). The Tohono O'odham and Dakota patterns are not identical to one another or to other tribes' patterns. The details of how a specific society organizes its education will not hold true across all Native communities, but the tribally specific evidence presented here illustrates that a system of organization exists in each case.

Education for Strength. According to Eastman, Dakota education was systematic, divinely ordained, and scrupulously adhered to. Basil Johnston (1976) described Anishinabe education as systematically constructed to meet the basic needs of society and the individual, which included leadership, protection, sustenance, learning, and physical well-being. Florence

Edenshaw Davidson remembered how young Haida boys left their mother's home around age 10 or 11 to receive strict instruction from an uncle. "Under the tutelage of his mother's brother a boy received formal instruction in ceremonial roles and assisted his uncle in various economic activities. He was toughened by harsh discipline and rigorous physical activity" (Blackman, 1982, p. 27). Similarly, Navajo youngsters were taught to "make themselves strong" by running toward the dawn light or by rolling in the snow on early winter mornings. "Make yourself strong," Thomas James recalls being told by his mother, "Test yourself. This is how I was taught" (quoted in McCarty, 2002a, p. 33).

Education According to Gender. The conscious designs of educational systems reflected gendered social life. From their father's sisters, Haida girls "received formal instruction in womanly behavior: how to behave toward one's husband, how to rear children properly, standards of etiquette" (Blackman, 1982, p. 28). Navajo girls learned parallel lessons from their maternal aunts or "little mothers," *shimá yaazhí* or *hamá.* The *kinaaldá* ceremony, celebrating a girl's first menses, still teaches physical and mental endurance, inducting girls into their "tasks as a woman and mother" (Begay, Clinton-Tullie, & Yellowhair, 1983, p. 71).

Education According to Age. Basil Johnston (Anishinabe) recalled that three stages structure the Anishinabe education system (Johnston, 1976). From birth to approximately age 7, children learn from women and elders in the home; then they apprentice, by gender, to learn life skills such as hunting; in the third stage, adults seek wisdom from those recognized for their study and understanding. Medical training in particular required a long and rigorous apprenticeship (see Begay et al., 1983, and McCarty, 2002a, for related educational practices in Navajo society).

Education for Leadership. According to Johnston (1995), Anishinabeg had a model for choosing leadership—or instruction—appropriate to the task at hand.[2] Communities were best served by resourceful, independent individuals who felt strongly obligated to their kin and neighbors. The paramount goal of the educational system was to develop such exemplary individuals, called *ogimauh,* who would be chosen to lead a given project only through completion.

Education According to Clan or Rank. Clan affiliation provides another way to allocate and authorize intellectual property rights and educational responsibilities. Among the Anishinabeg, the Crane and Loon clans possess the knowledge to train potential chiefs in leadership, while the Bird clan provides spiritual guidance (Whaley & Bresette, 1994). Among the Hopi, Bear clan trains the village civil leadership in administrative skills, while Coyote clan is known for its storytellers, each contributing to the corporate whole known as *Hopituh*, "people who live according to the Hopi way of life" (H. Lomawaima, personal communication, 2004). Clan prerogatives include the pedagogical knowledge of how to best train people in assigned areas of life. One clan will not trespass on the prerogatives of another, and some clan knowledge is transmitted only to its members (it is "secret").

Indigenous societies also developed hierarchical levels of instruction. Among the Anishinabeg, the Midewiwin (or Grand Medicine society) recognizes four to eight levels of participation, each correlated with a level of knowledge (Gill & Sullivan, 1992; Johnston, 1976). Society members study music, Indigenous knowledge, and herbal medicines in order to extend and enrich human life (Vizenor, 1984). We mentioned earlier the fairy tale–like character of the first level (of 12) of analysis within Diné stories of creation; the highest levels are reached only by those few individuals who dedicate their lives to intellectual engagement with the system (Begishe, n.d.; Schwarz, 1995).

Survival as the Ultimate Test. What of the stress of testing in formal education and the allegedly more enjoyable contexts of informal education? Indigenous societies may not have had institutionalized SATs, bar exams, or qualifying boards, but their educational goals were profound—to produce competent, caring adults—and consequences for failure were equally profound. The ultimate test of each human educational system is a people's survival. When Alaska Native Poldine Carlo (1978) was 10 years old, she visited a 16-year-old girl who was ill with tuberculosis.

> I'd sit by her just watching her unraveling flour sacks. She'd undo it strand by strand and twist it into a long thread. She made a fish net out of it. She did such long and patient work because it was her way of contributing to a means of life. (p. 80)

Basil Johnston (1976) reminds us that children were encouraged to draw their own inferences rather than having conclusions imposed upon them, but tests were severe: dangers encountered on the battlefield, in the vision quest, in medical training, or in the struggle to keep one's family clothed, sheltered, and fed. Hunger and starvation are recurring themes in many Native oral literatures, for good reasons. Frank Mitchell, noted Navajo ritual specialist, remembered that his father-in-law "wanted me to know that he had been depending on me as a strong young man to look after the livestock and the farm when he was away. . . . Now the time had come for me to take charge of things because there would be nobody for me to depend on" (quoted in Frisbie & McAllester, 1978, p. 195).

LANGUAGE-RICH CONTEXTS FOR EDUCATION

The word in the Pima language for "Something Told" is *ha'ichu'a·ga*. In the winter evenings while Rainbow's Ends [my mother] was roasting corn over the fire, we would ask Keli·hi [my father] to tell us something. Sometimes he would tell us how to behave so that we would grow up to be good people, or he would tell us things that happened when his father . . . was a boy. All these things are *ha'ichu'a·ga*. (Webb, 1959, p. 91)

Certain realities underpin the myth of the silent Indian learner. Languages and the cultural systems they express differ in many ways: in sound and grammatical structures, nuances of vocabulary, and rules of social interaction. In her seminal research at Warm Springs, Susan Philips (1972, 1983) demonstrated significant differences between local and national norms of linguistic and social interaction, or "communicative competencies." These are the deeply internalized, even unconscious rules we all employ in everyday interactions. Competent individuals have learned the subtle verbal and nonverbal cues that signal a listener's rapt attention, whose turn it is to speak, and the length of appropriate silences (Basso, 1989).

Communicative competency includes both speaking and listening behaviors as we interact with others. Philips (1983) calls the system of rules that organize these interactions "participant structures" (p. 119). In her research, she observed different participant structures organizing Warm Springs Indian interaction and Anglo American, teacher-dominated classroom interaction.

Thus in regard to both the structuring of attention and the allocation of turns at talk, Warm Springs Indian children learn culturally distinctive systems for socially appropriate education.

At the age of six, the Indian children enter a classroom where the organization of interaction is Anglo in its hierarchical structure, and in the control of talk that one individual exercises. . . . The organization of classroom interaction at the first-grade level is designed to fit with or build on the interactional skills the Anglo children have acquired during their first six years of life. That organization does not, however, completely fit or build on the interactional skills acquired by the Warm Springs Indian children. (Philips, 1983, pp. 126–127)

These differences "result in miscommunication between student and teacher in the Indian classrooms" (1983, p. 127). Compared to Anglo students, first-grade Warm Springs students responded less often to their teachers, and by sixth grade, Indian students talked much less even than their first-grade counterparts (1983, p. 96).

Philips's research raises several important issues. Warm Springs Indian people use silence in different ways than the majority culture does. At the same time, patterns of hierarchy, control, and power acted out by Anglo American teachers and Indian students in classrooms discouraged students from talking, and they talked less and less as they progressed through the grades. These phenomena are related, but they are not identical. The cultural distinctiveness of Warm Springs rules governing speech and silence should not be interpreted to mean that Indian children lack the cognitive equipment to learn through verbal interaction. Warm Springs educational systems are just as language-rich as classroom systems, but they use language and silence differently. "Mainstream" teachers can wield very real powers over students to discourage community language patterns and privilege normative patterns, and as a consequence, students may simply stop talking. The moral here is that difference should not be equated with deficit, and the exercise of power in classrooms can never be underestimated.

Native education systems share the human goal of creating competent, caring adults who share core values. Achieving this goal requires language-rich activities and instruction to develop communicative competencies. All human learners are creatures of language, the human "tool of tools," and language lies at the center of all educational systems.

Indigenous Instruction Embedded in Names

"A child's name was given him as a kind of prayer" (Wilson, 1927/1981, p. 8). Naming is a central component in the development of individual human beings. Gerald Vizenor (1984) describes the names an Anishinabe person has in a lifetime: the nickname given by parents and, most important, the sacred or dream name presented to a child by a specially chosen person. The namer's gift includes the name and its associated power, derived from dream. The child's responsibility is to develop that power or potential (Vizenor, 1984). Once again, we can see the educational maxim "it is up to you" in operation in Native life.

Hopi names also clarify the position of the named as a "conscious individual agent" in a shared society. Whiteley (1992) shows how Hopi names are "poetically composed . . . oral texts"; they are "tiny imagist poems" (p. 209). A Hopi receives many names, at birth and levels of religious initiation, always being named by members of another clan. Names convey, in highly compacted form, information about the named, the name-giver, their social relation, the landscape, ceremonial activities, color, freshness, motion—the possibilities are endless (Whiteley, 1992). The name Lomawaima simply translated means "beautifully walking." As a name, it also contains a story about a unique person, time, and place: Hartman Lomawaima's great-grandfather striding out of the village early one morning, on his way to his fields. It had rained overnight, after an extended dry spell, and he rejoiced at the prospect of seeing his corn refreshed and rejuvenated. He was literally "walking on air."

Indigenous Instruction Embedded in Songs

Names are only one aspect of the individual that situate him or her in a language-rich environment packed with metaphor and allusion. Songs and stories enrich the tapestry.

> My father often sat and sang me to sleep by the firelight. . . . He had many songs. Some of them were for little boys. Others were for little girls. Of the girls' songs, there was one I liked very much; it was something like this:
>
> > My sister asks me to go out and stretch the smoke-flap.
> > My armlets and earrings shine!
> > I go through the woods where the elm trees grow.
> > Why do the berries not ripen?
> > What berries do you like best?—the red? The blue?
> >   (Wilson, 1927/1981, pp. 13–14)

Music, sometimes called the universal human language, has an emotional power few would deny. Combined with lyrics, music has the power to indelibly impress words into memory. Songs evoke inspiration and nostalgia. They reinforce emotional ties to ceremonies, memorial dates, and life celebrations. Societies that depend on accurate oral transmission of knowledge strategically use song to encode hours, days, even weeks of material into memorable form. Native societies continue to highly prize compositional skills in melody and lyric. Song is a powerful educational tool, from lullabies internalized by infants and young children to days-long song cycles painstakingly memorized by apprentice ceremonialists.

Indigenous Instruction Embedded in Stories

Anna Moore Shaw (Pima) was born in 1898 on the Gila River reservation south of Phoenix, Arizona. She learned well the lessons imparted through stories when, after a long day of chores, she would join the family on mats around the fire to hear stories and receive still more advice on becoming a wise and good woman (Shaw, 1974, pp. 29–30). Her father's "favorite advice was the kind that came through the old legends" (p. 31). Storytellers would make the moral clear when addressing young children: "Do not steal. It is very wrong" (p. 32), or "Do not be *s-chu tha'a* (selfish)" (p. 30). At other times the listener had to apply herself to understand a story's reference. Anna wondered why young babysitters were called *chukugshwad*, cricket: "We did not rub our legs together to chirp lullabies, but we did like to sing and hum to put the little ones to sleep, so maybe that was how we got our name" (p. 111).

Navajo sand painter Hasteen Klah told his biographer Franc Newcomb, "At night, after the family had gathered around the . . . fire, it was customary for [my] uncle to sit in the place of honor and, when all were seated, to relate a legend or describe a rite" (Newcomb, 1964, p. 101). Youth "listened carefully," Klah recalled, "for this was intended to be part of their education" (Newcomb, 1964, p. 101; see also Cruikshank, 1998). Abbreviated children's versions or "little stories" (Manuel & Neff, 2001, p. xv) might be told year-round, but the "real stories" mobilized power that demanded respect. Contemporary Crow writer Alma Hogan Snell was raised by her grandmother, Pretty Shield, who told her, "Words are holy. Treat them with respect. There's power there" (quoted in Snell, 2000, frontispiece).

One indication of the power of words was careful instruction in proper speech. Francis LaFlesche (Omaha) (1900/1978), wrote:

> From the earliest years the Omaha child was trained in the grammatical use of his native tongue. No slip was allowed to pass uncorrected, and as a result there was no child-talk such as obtains among English-speaking children. . . . A boy of ten or twelve was apt to speak as good Omaha as a man of mature years. (pp. xvi–xvii)

Tangibly powerful language educated by working directly on the listener's mind and emotions, and rhetorical skills were highly valued. Poldine Carlo (Athabaskan) (1978), who grew up on the Yukon River in the early 20th century, recalled the power of oratory:

> At the big potlatches when all the chiefs would get together in one village, each chief would stand up in the hall and make a speech. . . . These people were well educated in their Indian ways and the words they used were all very high words. (p. 56)

According to Basil Johnston (1976), stories are not necessarily—or even appropriately—devised for the listener to interpret literally, but rather "freely, yet rationally according to the Ojibway views of life" (p. 8). Anishinabe educational theory assumes responsible listeners, who develop conclusions according to their intellectual capacities: "There is no instantaneous understanding" (1976, p. 8). Johnston's teachers guided him while stressing his responsibility to develop his own understandings, but sometimes the guidance provided by Native teachers was much more direct.

Catechism as a Teaching Method

> cat·e·chize 1. To teach orally (the principles of a religious creed) by means of questions and answers 2. To question searchingly or persistently. (Morris, 1975, p. 212)

The definition of *catechize* in the *American Heritage Dictionary of the English Language* pithily sums up current pedagogical assumptions, deeply rooted in Western cultural traditions of schooling: language-rich instruction means question-and-answer interchange. If we look more closely, the dictionary traces *catechize* to the Greek *katēkhein*, to teach by word of mouth. We must turn to this earlier, broader meaning to capture a commonality of human pedagogical systems and to realize the specific cultural privilege that the question-and-answer format, idealized as the Socratic method, has been awarded in Western thought and educational practice.

[margin note: Teaching by word of mouth]

The question-and-answer exchange between teacher and student is not foreign to Native educational systems, although it seldom dominates to the degree seen in school classrooms. According to Francis LaFlesche's (1900/1978) memoir, an Omaha "father or mother would ask . . . 'Who was that you were playing with?'" as they "warned their boys and girls against a free association with the children of persons who did not bear a good character" (p. 10). Johnston (1976) describes evenings before story time, when Anishinabe "children were frequently asked questions, 'What did you see today that was beautiful? What did you hear, that was pleasing? What did you touch that was moving?'" (p. 122). Charles Eastman (1902/1971) describes the early training of Dakota youngsters in "legends"; they would hear a story one evening, and be required to repeat it the next, as "the household became his audience, by which he was alternately criticized and applauded" (p. 42). Eastman provides particularly rich detail about the process his uncle, "a strict disciplinarian and a good teacher" (1902/1971, pp. 43–44), used to instruct him:

> When I left the teepee in the morning, he would say "Hakadah, look closely to everything you see"; and at evening, on my return, he used often to catechize me for an hour.
>
> "On which side of the trees is the lighter-colored bark? On which side do they have most regular branches?"
>
> It was his custom to let me name all the new birds that I had seen during the day. I would name them according to . . . anything about the bird that impressed me as characteristic. I made many ridiculous errors, I must admit.

He then usually informed me of the correct name. Occasionally I made a hit and this he would warmly commend. (1902/1971, p. 44)

Eastman recognized this educational process of observation, analysis, and deduction as science, and labeled it accordingly. Navajo caretakers use similar pedagogical methods to teach children to herd sheep. Children first observe sheep, then identify what they have seen. Finally, their teachers help them organize their observations: "What you see is what sheep eat during the day. This is good for them, but if they eat [a poisonous plant], they can become sick and die" (McCarty et al., 1991, p. 50). Shirley Begay et al. (1983) describe a similar process for Navajo girls learning to weave. Mothers, aunts, and older sisters encourage young weavers to observe and test their hypotheses; they support and expect experimentation.

Lectures, Directions, and Plain Speaking

In addition to songs, stories, speeches, and catechism, Native caregivers marshaled language through lectures, directions, encouragement, and scolding to shape children's thoughts and behaviors. Buffalo Bird Woman recalled that her Hidatsa grandfather often talked to her and scolded her when she was naughty (Wilson, 1927/1981). Francis LaFlesche's (1900/1978) Omaha mother carefully explained why food was placed on the grave of deceased relatives, and Pima parents (Webb, 1959) "[e]very so often . . . lectured to their children regarding manhood and womanhood" (p. 36).

Anna Moore Shaw's (1974) Pima parents used "strong lectures" of oft-repeated words to "instill in me the important Indian values which they had learned from their parents" (p. 108), and Alma Hogan Snell (2000) related that "Crows believed that the best way to teach their children was to give them vivid examples of desired behavior and abundant encouragement" (p. 10). Hasbah Charley's Navajo parents and grandparents demonstrated, "We are teaching you here; this fire [home/hearth] that we've built for you, you will make that your school" (McCarty, 2002a, p. 34). Helen Sekaquaptewa (Hopi) articulated the advantages of plain speaking: "my mother told me about the sex side of life, although even when I was younger she had not neglected that subject. She didn't try to make it sound nice nor beat about the bush but told me in plain language so I would understand" (Udall, 1969, p. 117).

Centuries of plain language, perplexing myths, lyrical songs, demanding questions, scolds and lectures, words of comfort and love and more—all have contributed to the language-rich life surrounding and nurturing Native people. Language has been a key, but not exclusive, medium of instruction in Indigenous educational systems. Human beings draw on a wide range of media and modes of learning that overlap with and integrate with language use. In English we often use the term *learning by doing* to encompass a range of educational activities, including observation, imitation, repetitive practice, and the actual physical "doing" of skills we are trying to master, whether cooking, construction, gymnastics, or yoga.

LEARNING BY DOING

Some "doing" skills are developed as we harvest, acquire, and modify materials. Design and construction depend on material characteristics, such as tensile strength, flexibility, or rigidity. Other "doing" skills involve bodily preparation, such as muscle training for strength, flexibility, or endurance. Physical training is often intimately tied to mental, emotional, and social "discipline."

Indigenous educational systems are not unique in using diverse modes and media of instruction, but compared to contemporary schooling practices they may privilege hands-on learning by doing. In certain contexts, they might also place a higher value on instruction that is operationalized through interaction with other lifeforms (such as plants and animals) and interaction with the technologies of material culture.

Learning Through Observation

> [When the old ladies dug prairie turnips] I'd watch them, and I noticed that they *did* care. . . . They had a routine about it. They didn't just go carelessly around; they did these things patiently and correctly. . . . They would dig the roots with their sticks; then they would replace the soil and tamp it down just like nobody had bothered it. They always said *Aho* (thank you) to the Creator, and if there were any wild seeds, they would scatter them about for more turnips to grow in another year. (Snell, 2000, pp. 35–36)

Alma Hogan Snell (Crow) learned by watching her elders. Careful, patient, and correct observation of actions led her to deduce the pattern guiding actions. She learned lessons that were moral (always say "thank you") and ecological (scatter the seeds, tamp down the soil). The ineluctable relationship between the moral and the ecological is part of the very structure of this lesson. Native California basket weavers maintain similar caring relationships with the individual plants—sedge, junco, and others—that provide the materials necessary to construct this most sophisticated technology (Bibby, 1996). Pomo basket weavers in northern California teach their daughters, granddaughters, and nieces to walk quietly and respectfully among the sedge beds. Young children are taught not to carouse around the beds while older women are gathering. No woman will enter the beds or work on baskets while menstruating. They sit quietly among the plants, taking their time, talking to them, carefully harvesting the straight sedge roots as they weed, clean the soil of rocks and aerate it as well, transplant young plants, and look after the health of the beds (Sherrie Smith-Ferri, personal communication, 1990). Contemporary resource managers in California speculate that some plant species are currently endangered not because of human "interference" but because Native human care has been removed from the environment (Blackburn & Anderson, 1993).

Learning in the Home

"Everything is based here, everything is based here, here in the home. May nothing, may nothing disturb it" (Manuel & Neff, 2001, p. xxii). This English prayer translates the O'odham phrase that Frances Manuel's grandfather spoke whenever he delivered "wise words." Shirley Begay et al. (1983) note the importance that Navajo parents traditionally attach to home, livestock, and land: "Let all that has been given to you be your thought" (p. 37). All human societies, including Native ones, recognize the home as a central educational institution. Helen Sekaquaptewa described the game of bone dolls, where sheep bones are used as simple likenesses of family members. Young girls (and sometimes boys) arrange the dolls to play out their roles in life and the community (Ferrero, 1983). Buffalo Bird Woman remembered how little Hidatsa girls played at housekeeping through their games and with their dolls (Wilson, 1927/1981). "Playing house" is a ubiquitous childhood activity, not restricted to Native lives. However, in the last centuries imposed school education has purposefully pushed aside or eradicated home-based education for American Indian children. In order to imagine Native-based education again, we must remember how important the seemingly simple activities of "playing house" can be.

Taking children out of Native homes has disrupted much of the instruction in life cycles that is important to maintain physical and mental health. Many Native societies recognize the important changes at puberty for girls and for boys, and many sequestered young women for intensive instruction (Begay et al., 1983; Frisbie, 1964; Schwarz, 1997). Athabaskan Poldine Carlo (1978) tells us, "When a girl became a young woman, she was put away for a year. . . . While the young woman was behind the curtain, she was learning how to sew and to do other different things a woman is supposed to know when she gets married" (p. 15). Miles removed from the Yukon, in the southwestern desert, O'odham Frances Manuel (Manuel & Neff, 2001) explains her puberty confinement, "They said that the reason they did all this is because I was going to be tough and ready to meet up with whatever would come" (p. 27). Native educational systems were designed to draw strength from the cycles of life within the human body and in the larger world, in the fields and gardens and animal communities that provided models of instruction.

Plants and Animals as Teachers

> We cared for our corn in those days, as we would care for a child; for we . . . loved our fields as mothers love their children. We thought that the corn plants had souls, as children have souls, and that the growing corn liked to hear us sing, as children like to hear their mothers sing to them. (Buffalo Bird Woman, quoted in Wilson, 1927/1981, p. 94)

Even as women and their corn fields learned from and nourished each other, Buffalo Bird Woman learned by training her dog to pull a travois. "Owning a dog, and invited to go with my mothers to get wood, I felt that in spite of my girlish years I was almost a woman now" (quoted in Wilson, 1927/1981, p. 86). The successful training of her dog as helpmate marked a milestone in her development into a competent adult. Myriad Native voices speak of the fundamental ethical lessons embodied in relations among humans, animals, and plants. Basil Johnston (1976) notes that the Anishinabe story of life's origins embeds a lesson in the order of creation: first plants, then animals, then humans. Plants sustain all life as nourishment and medicine; animals help sustain human life as teachers, food sources, and companions (especially dogs). Humankind is the last and the least of creation, dependent on plants and animals for survival, distinguished by the ability to dream, and invested with the responsibility to learn from visions.

Diné elders give lambs to young children so the sheep can help teach youngsters the principles of correct living. At about age 6 to 8, "the Navajo child is charged with herding sheep . . . and performing other tasks independent of parental supervision. An earmark or brand is placed on the child's sheep, a symbol of increasing responsibility and independence" (Begay et al., 1983, p. 27). The sheep herd is known as *shimá*; the same word refers to the earth and one's biological mother. In the film *Seasons of a Navajo*, Chauncey Neboyia speaks of his lifelong relationships with his animals—his dogs, sheep, cattle, and horses—saying, "without animals, I don't know how I would feel" (Borden, 1988). "Without livestock," Hasbah Charley says, "there's no you. You're nothing" (quoted in McCarty, 1984, p. 21). For these and other Native people, emotional identity itself springs from the relationship with animals.

A RETURN TO CHOICE AND LOCAL CONTROL

Ya know,
I think it's kind of a SHAME
That we don't sit our kids down and tell stories about this
and that.
Maybe it's our own fault
but we don't have time to tell the story
on account of SCHOOL
on account of ACTIVITIES
on account of something else.
              (Manuel & Neff, 2001, pp. vv–xvi)[3]

Frances Manuel poignantly and pointedly sums up the challenges confronting families today. How do we balance the demands of a "busy modern life," the hours consumed by school and after-school activities, and the human need to connect our children to their legacy? Where and when do we tell the stories that transmit the hard-won, priceless knowledge of those who came before us? How do Native languages survive, embodying centuries of human theory, practice, and creative moral engagement with the world? How do we use ancient knowledge to guide vital, adaptive Native societies into the future? How do we build expansive, liberating places of education that teach our children how to thrive in a diverse, demanding, technological, fast-moving modern world? It's up to us.

Native people have rarely backed away from these responsibilities, but over the past century many forces have conspired to push them away. Despite seemingly unrelenting pressures to surrender their Indian-ness, Native peoples have courageously and stubbornly refused to give up. They have chosen "to remain an Indian." Native individuals have been deeply affected by their schooling, but Indigenous knowledge and education systems have proved resilient. Luther Standing Bear (1933/1978) recalled in his third book that his years studying at Carlisle Indian School (see Figure 2.3 for a picture of his lesson slate) and working for Wanamaker's department store in Philadelphia did not alter his essential identity:

> I returned from the East at about the age of sixteen, after five years' contact with the white people, to resume life upon the reservation. But I returned, to spend some thirty years before again leaving, just as I had gone—a Lakota. Outwardly I lived the life of the white man, yet all the while I kept in direct contact with tribal life. While I had learned all that I could of the white man's culture, I never forgot that of my people. I kept the language, tribal manners and usages, sang the songs and danced the dances. I still listened to and respected the advice of the older people of the tribe. (p. 235)

Figure 2.3. Lesson Slate by "Luther Otakte," Luther Standing Bear, at Carlisle Indian School. Photo by John Choate. National Anthropological Archives, Smithsonian Institution/(I.D. #06814000).

"Formal education [schooling] did change my behaviors and attitudes," Galena Sells Dick (1998) writes in her autobiographical narrative. "At the same time, I maintained a strong belief in my language and culture" (p. 24). These sentiments, widely shared among the generations who came of age in the 20th century, have formed the ideological reservoir from which new Indigenized forms of schooling have been constructed. In concluding our discussion of Indigenous educational systems, we cannot improve upon Luther Standing Bear's (1933/1978) unequivocal commitment to Lakota education, which concluded *Land of the Spotted Eagle*:

> So if today I had a young mind to direct, to start on the journey of life, and I was faced with the duty of choosing between the natural way of my forefathers

and that of the white man's present way of civilization, I would, for its welfare, unhesitatingly set that child's feet in the path of my forefathers. I would
raise him to be an Indian! (pp. 258–259)

In the coming chapters, we trace a century's journey as Native parents and
communities have fought for the right of choice, to raise their children in the
way of their forebears.

CHAPTER 3

Women's Arts and Children's Songs: Domesticating Indian Culture, 1900–1928

Now, are we a better people than we were years ago when we sang our own songs, when we spoke to the Great Spirit in our own language? We asked then for rain, good health, and long life; now, what more do we want? What is that thought so great and so sacred that can not be expressed in our own language, that we should seek to use the white man's word?

—John Lolorias, a Tohono O'odham (then called Papago) graduate of Hampton addressing the Board of Indian Commissioners meeting at Lake Mohonk. (quoted in ARCIA, 1901, pp. 824–825)

At the turn of the 20th century, Lolorias was not alone in his criticism of English-only and other repressive measures being enforced throughout Indian schools and homelands. Those fighting for the rights of Native expression, however, may have felt they were losing their battle. Over the first three decades of the 20th century, the Indian Office and its allies constructed an extraordinarily narrow safety zone where selected Native traits and expressions might be tolerated. Federal powers over Native societies arguably reached their peak in these decades, when Native men were jailed for wearing long hair, for not wearing "citizen dress," and for keeping their children out of school. Perceptions of Native peoples as simple-minded and childlike and of Native cultures as lacking religion, morality, or social order rationalized the extreme exercise of federal powers during this era.

The deeply paternalistic attitudes and oppressive practices of the early 20th century were rooted in the need to domesticate the most dangerous cultural differences—those defining Native peoples—that threatened American identity as a nation divinely ordained to "inherit the earth" from Indigenous nations. The moral authority of America's inheritance seemed to require the obliteration of American Indians, if not literally then linguistically and culturally.

Zero tolerance was the norm applied to most Native lifeways. Safe differences fell within a narrow range defined by the cultural norms of Western

43

society, including mythical tales told to children, lullabies, and the women's work that produced arts, crafts, and a few Native foods. The home and hearth inhabited by women and children, the Victorian wellspring of civilized living, helped define the safety zone. Even child life or women's work fell outside the safety zone, however, if it was connected to religion, involved competitive economies (such as buffalo hunting or gill netting of salmon), or required harvesting of foods (such as acorn) or materials (such as sedge for basketry) on White-owned lands.

The ways in which federal employees parsed safe and dangerous cultural differences along gender lines deserve more scholarly attention. All of the arts we consider in this chapter—Navajo rug-weaving, Pueblo pottery, beadwork and basketry across the western United States—fell squarely into the domestic sphere of women's work, a less threatening arena than the potential competition posed by male Indian loggers, fishermen, farmers, ranchers, printers, or tradesmen. We only begin the work necessary to adequately compare the relative safety of a Native domestic sphere—perceived as safe as long as it was being transformed by the social engineers of the federal school system—with the dangerous realms of male economic activity early in the century.

Cultures, economies, legal status, and social mores intersected and clashed as early-20th-century America struggled with Native difference. Using culturally loaded and legally significant notions of gender and childhood, federal policymakers defined Indian peoples as "insensible wards," sharing the diminished legal status of children. Replicating an ideology of familial power relations, federal agents assumed the powers of parents over Native wards and stripped Native parents of choice in schooling their own children. From about 1870 to approximately 1920, increasing federal powers evolved hand in hand with changing expectations of Native peoples. The optimism of the late 19th century, which envisioned "civilized" Native peoples assuming an equal place with other citizens, gave way to an impoverished, racially defined view of social hierarchy and Indians' "appropriate place" in the lower rungs of American society (Hoxie, 1984/1989).

This chapter traces the intersections of legal and social definitions of Native status, the extension of federal powers, the diminishment of economic and social opportunity for Natives, and the implementation in schools of practices designed to prepare young Indians as menial laborers and domestics. In this process, notions of gender and childhood were strategically employed to sort out safe from dangerous cultural difference, as attempts were made to selectively integrate certain categories of music and women's "craft" production into the curriculum.

Lullabies sung to soothe children and decorative baskets or pottery intended for sale to generate cash were deemed safe, and the "preservation" of a few Native arts served federal purposes. Assimilation into the American working classes assumed religious, linguistic, political, and economic transformation and obliteration of those systems within Native cultures. A few controlled expressions of Native difference, however, served to mark Native peoples' distinctive cultural status, which linked with and, to a degree, justified their legal status as diminished wards under federal "protection."

INDIANS AS CHILDREN: "INSENSIBLE WARDS"

On January 15, 1820, Secretary of War John C. Calhoun reported to Congress on the missionary societies' educational work among American Indians. In his view, Indians

> must be gradually brought under our authority and laws, or they will insensibly waste away in vice and misery. It is impossible with their customs that they should exist as independent communities in the midst of civilized society. . . . They should be taken under our guardianship; our opinions and not theirs ought to prevail in measures intended for their civilization and happiness. (U.S. Department of the Interior, Office of Indian Affairs, 1927, p. 2)

Calhoun's remarks were reprinted 107 years later in an Indian Office report summarizing the history of Indian education. The report's authors selected an opinion from the available historical documents that reinforced their own ideology: Education equaled civilization and Indian opinions and wishes should be ignored. The authors might have chosen differently; more respectful views of Indian peoples existed, even in Calhoun's times. We can contrast his pronouncements with Chief Justice John Marshall's articulation of the distinctive status of Indian nations in an 1832 Supreme Court decision:

> The Indian nations had always been considered as distinct, independent political communities, retaining their original natural rights, as the undisputed possessors of the soil, from time immemorial. . . . The very term "nation," so generally applied to them, means "a people distinct from others." (*Worcester v. Georgia*, quoted in Prucha, 1984, p. 211)

In this decision, Marshall appeared to back away from an opinion he had expressed only a year earlier when he declared tribes to be "domestic, dependent nations" whose "relation to the United states resembles that of a ward to his guardian"—the opinion shared by Calhoun (quoted in Wilkins & Lomawaima, 2001, p. 68).

The two Marshall decisions beautifully illustrate the tension between views of American Indians as dangerous or safe. Are tribes nations or wards?

Are Indian people insensible children or self-governing adults? These questions persist to the present day. Clearly Native nations composed of self-determining adults exercising dual or multiple citizenships have been perceived as much more threatening than groups defined as wards, marked by the mental, moral, and legal deficiencies linked to the status of children. Children belong in school, and the premise of school as the paramount Americanizing institution depends on the perception of "different" peoples as immature.

Federal Powers as Parental Powers

The view of Indians as insensible wards dominated the early 1900s, when they were characterized as willful, dangerous children. Voluminous correspondence between Charles Burke, Commissioner of Indian Affairs from 1921 to 1929, and Mrs. Stella Atwood of Riverside, California, clearly expressed this shared view of Native peoples. Burke was Indian Service "old guard"; Atwood, chair of the Indian welfare committee of the General Federation of Women's Clubs, was a critical reformer. Despite their differences of opinion, they developed a close working relationship. In 1921, Atwood wrote Burke that she wished to work *for* but not *with* the Indians, whose passions were so easily aroused by their misfortunes, making them ready "for almost any deed of violence" (National Archives & Records Administration [NARA], Entry 177, 1921). Neither Burke nor Atwood could envision Indians as responsible adults who might work for themselves.

Federal employees and reform-minded citizens held extraordinary powers over Native peoples, who were expected to be quiet, polite, and obedient, replicating the power imbalance and social rules of the adult/child relationship. In 1918, for example, a young Omaha student enrolled at Genoa Indian School in Nebraska wrote home to her agency superintendent, requesting that he forward her money—from her own bank account, which he administered, a customary power of superintendents at the time. He chided her for her "disrespectful" attitude, and told her she could threaten all she liked to run away from school or to write to the Indian Office; he would not send her any money until she wrote him respectfully (NARA, Entry 121, CCF Omaha 820, 1918).

Federal Powers Override Parental Powers

The federal assumption of guardianship powers over Native wards turned the American model of community control of schools on its head. Indian parents, classified as children themselves, were denied the rights of choice in their children's education. On September 30, 1896, in a Circular Order to Service personnel, Commissioner Daniel Browning answered the question, "Do Indian parents have a right to decide where children go to school?" with a resounding "No." His categorical annulment of Indian parental rights, known as the Browning Ruling, was harsh enough to draw public criticism even in an era when Native political and civil rights were arguably at their lowest ebb. By 1902 the Secretary of the Interior had abrogated the Browning Ruling, but this softening of policy did not reform practice (NARA, Entry 718, 1902). Despite new directives to off-reservation boarding school superintendents that they must "in every case" of student enrollment have "the parents, guardians, or next-of-kin sign a consent blank" (NARA, Entry 718, 1902), Native memoirs testify that forced enrollment remained common through the 1950s, and it never entirely disappeared from the federal school system.

Reservation and school superintendents forcefully objected to the abrogation of the Browning Ruling, and within a few months the Secretary of the Interior clarified that Native parents were allowed some choice *among* schools but could not keep their children *out* of school. Instructions in 1908 reiterated, "You will allow Indian parents the largest latitude in their choice of schools"; educating children at home lay far outside the allowable latitudes (NARA, Entry 718, 1908). Federal powers, as usual in this period, trumped the powers of parents over their own children's lives. Children had to attend school, and federal debates centered on what kind of school was best to train Indian children and young adults.

BOARDING SCHOOLS VERSUS DAY SCHOOLS

In the late 1800s, off-reservation boarding schools were seen as the ideal facility to Americanize Native individuals. Off-reservation boarding schools included Carlisle (Pennsylvania), Chilocco (Oklahoma), Genoa (Nebraska), Haskell (Kansas), Phoenix (Arizona), Salem (later known as Chemawa) (Oregon), and Sherman (California); the federal Indian school system also included on-reservation boarding schools and day schools. A small number of Indian children attended public schools, but little is known about early Indian experiences in public schools, and many public schools denied Indian enrollment until well after World War II. The federal government did establish a contract system to channel monies from the Indian Service to public schools to support Indian students (since Indian reservations, like military reservations, are federal trust lands and exempt from the local property taxes that support public education). According to federal records, only 118 children were publicly schooled under contract in 1900. The number rose to 1,900 by 1910, to 26,000 by 1915, and to slightly more than 37,000 by 1927 (U.S. Department of the Interior, Office of Indian Affairs, 1927).

[handwritten: Boarding vs. Day Schools]

Richard Henry Pratt, the Army officer who established Carlisle in 1879 under authority of the Secretary of the Interior, was convinced that Native people only required equal educational and vocational opportunities in order to excel as American citizens. Pratt believed Native capacities equaled those of White Americans. By the early 20th century, however, the optimistic views of Native capabilities espoused by Pratt and others were being pushed aside by less generous judgments (Hoxie, 1984/1989). As Clyde Ellis (1996) argues in his history of the Rainy Mountain Boarding School for Kiowa students, "New interpretations labeled Indians as racially backward, culturally deficient, and intellectually feeble" (p. 130).

By the early 1900s, these limiting ideas of Native deficiencies had defined day schools and on-reservation boarding schools as the appropriate institutions to uplift whole communities to the lower levels of American social and economic life. Francis Leupp, Commissioner of Indian Affairs from 1905 to 1909, spelled out the perceived advantages of the day schools:

> The day-school system far outstrips any other in stimulating interest among the Indians at large—parents as well as children—and in presenting our civilization to them in the most natural and attractive way. . . . The personal contact and example, as well as the more formal instruction, of the teachers are enormously powerful factors in raising the intelligence and the moral tone of the whole tributary community of Indians. (NARA, Entry 718, 1907)

[handwritten margin: Like the HT model]

Under Leupp's direction, the number of federal day schools increased from 138 in 1905 to 167 in 1908.

Whether schools were located on or off reservation, organized as day or boarding, they shared pedagogical and disciplinary practices. Schools provided elementary academic training (equivalent to the public schools' lower elementary grades) alongside explicit, well-developed moral, manual labor, and domestic training.

A POLITICAL ECONOMY OF SCHOOL PRACTICES: THE "DIGNITY OF LABOR"

[handwritten margin: NP for taking their land]

Recent scholarship analyzes Indian schooling as an exercise of national powers, instilling new practices and habits into American Indian citizens. In his groundbreaking article about the "deep meaning" of Indian schooling, Adams (1988) recognized that a "fundamental consideration" was the transfer of real estate from Indian to White hands. School practices, which fit hand-in-glove with congressional passage of the 1887 General Allotment Act, were designed to condition Native people to surrender tribally controlled lands and accept individual land allotments.

Littlefield (1989, 1993), working from a political economy perspective, describes the goals of federal Indian schools as "proletarianization" rather than assimilation (1993). Littlefield (1993) and Lomawaima (1993, 1994, 1996) emphasize that educational practices were designed to train Indians for subservience, making them amenable not only to surrendering tribal lands but also to entering the manual/domestic labor market. Native individuals, as well as particular cultural traits or practices, were being fitted into an American "safety zone" of obedient citizenry and innocent cultural difference. Parameters of the safety zone corresponded to relations of power: Safe citizens were part of a subservient proletariat, and safe cultural differences were controlled by non-Native federal, Christian, and social agencies that could proclaim themselves benefactors dedicated to "preserving" Native life.

Indian school industrial training was designed to *prevent* Native economic competition in the American workforce, just as low-level academic training precluded aspirations to professional schools or careers. An Office of Indian Affairs (OIA) Education Division publication at the turn of the 20th century stressed that "higher education in the sense ordinarily used has no place in the curriculum of Indian schools" (NARA, Entry 718, 1900). "Higher" education meant work beyond the sixth grade. The circular specified that girls should be trained to serve "good wholesome meals at tables of moderate means" but not to aspire to hotel or restaurant style (NARA, Entry 718, 1900). The Indian Office gave occasional lip service to the notion that students "should not be placed in the fields merely for drudgery, or manual labor alone" (NARA, Entry 718, 1903), but school records and alumni memories document that drudgery in work details dominated student life through the 1930s and never receded far into the background after that.

Alumni memoirs attest that Native people did desire education beyond the six grades offered in the reservation schools; their enrollment in off-reservation boarding schools might not have fit current definitions of *voluntary,* but it was not entirely coerced, either, despite the flaws in these schools that were well known to Native people (Child, 1998; Lomawaima, 1994). Native students and parents frequently protested the low academic standards of the Indian schools and limited job opportunities after graduation, but policymakers were not inclined to take their concerns seriously. One example of alumna dissatisfaction can be found in a letter from Miss Priscilla LaMote (Menominee), of Neopit, Wisconsin, responding to an inquiry from the OIA about her life after graduation from Hampton Institute:

> When I left Hampton I intended to return in the fall but conditions have changed my plans. . . . The agent here wished me to teach in this government school. The principal said that Indian teachers were forbidden to teach members of their own tribe. . . . The Tomah Indian School superintendent asked me if I'd

accept the position of assistant laundress if it was offered to me. . . . It seems queer though when I've been to school so long . . . that I can['t] get a better place than that of an assistant. (NARA, Entry 761, 1910)

Miss LaMote came face to face with the practical reality of proletarianization, not the rhetorical ideal of assimilation. Allowing tribal members to teach children of their own community was entirely too dangerous to be countenanced; and the laundry room, not the classroom, was judged her proper place in the Indian school job marketplace. Whether searching for jobs within the federal school system, in their local community, or beyond, American Indians in the early 20th century struggled to find a safe place.

JOBS NOT AVAILABLE OUTSIDE THE SCHOOLS

The poor economic status of Native populations and abysmal job opportunities on and near reservations generated the frequently referenced "plight" of American Indians. Some critics blamed the federal schools for inadequate job training, but some federal workers, such as Charles Buchanan at Tulalip Reservation in western Washington, recognized that employment opportunities for Native people were limited by more than poor educational preparation:

I regret to state that there is a very serious, deep and positive prejudice, general throughout the Northwest, against the Indian. This makes it difficult if not impossible for Indian boys, trained in trades, to secure employment side by side with white men. (NARA, Entry 761, 1914)

As late as 1937, Bureau of Indian Affairs (BIA) Education Director Willard Beatty found it "prudent" to discontinue the Pima dairy herd since the "evidence is overwhelming that the racial prejudice of white toward Indians in southern Arizona makes impractical the development of an Indian dairy as a commercial proposition" (NARA, Entry 121, CCF Pima 800, 1937).

The challenges of placing Native alumni of the federal school system into the job market led Commissioner Leupp to create the Indian Employment Bureau in 1905, hiring Charles Dagenett (Peoria), a graduate of Carlisle Indian School, as the first supervisor (Adams, 1995). Dagenett surveyed job possibilities across the country and arranged outing contracts. "Outing" was developed by Pratt at Carlisle; during the summer months and after graduation, students were placed with prosperous White families to learn the skills of farming and small trades, as well as the social, cultural, and material habits of "civilized" living (Lindsey, 1995; Pratt, 1964). As time passed, however, prejudice narrowed the outing system. Work was not seen as a mechanism enabling social mobility; "job opportunity" meant summer work gangs of boys were hired to pick beets in the Colorado fields, and girls became domestic laborers in Phoenix and the San Francisco Bay area (Lomawaima, 1994; Trennert, 1988).

Federal Indian schools provided such an exquisitely controlled laboratory to exercise federal powers that they could not produce graduates well trained to work in the real world. One job market for which Indian school graduates were quite well trained, however, was the lower ranks of positions within the schools themselves. Upper-level positions, such as teacher or administrator, were not usually open to Indian school graduates who had been trained in subservience, with minimal skills. Even Charles Dagenett struggled against discrimination in the Indian Service before he was employed as supervisor of Indian employment. In 1898 he was the disciplinarian in the boys' dormitory at Chilocco Indian School, where the superintendent wanted to replace him with "a white man who has been trained in military tactics in the regular army" (NARA, Entry 91, 1898). Dagenett achieved remarkable success in the Indian Service; he was its highest-placed Native employee in his time, but we know little about his experiences. He was one of the six Native founders in 1911 of the American Indian Association, the precursor of the Society of American Indians (Nabokov, 1991; Olson & Wilson, 1984), but his story remains to be told, one of the many Native lives of which we catch only a glimpse.

RACE AND THE SAFETY ZONE: FINDING THE RIGHT LEVEL

Academic achievement and professional success were not possible outcomes for American Indians because they lay too far outside a safety zone that allocated social rankings by race. The Indian Office struggled to demarcate an appropriate level for American Indians; the struggle was complicated by their ambiguous position in America's racial hierarchy. Many Americans viewed Indians as less objectionable than Blacks, but views varied by class and region. In Virginia at Hampton Institute, the training school for African American teachers where Pratt had enrolled young Native men and women before founding Carlisle, Black Americans (not Africans) were ranked higher on the ladder of human achievement than Indians because of the allegedly uplifting effects of slavery (Adams, 1977; Lindsey, 1995). In any case, a great deal of federal ink was spilled in the quest to delineate the "right level" of social, moral, educational, and economic achievement for American Indians. In the schools, debates focused on curriculum, vocational training, and the accoutrements of civilized living—wallpaper or whitewash?—that fit the right level.

Estelle Reel, Superintendent of Indian Schools, instructed all matrons and teachers in 1904 that students' "dormitory rooms must be clean and cheerful, but no useless hangings and few pictures or ornaments should be employed, as these collect dust" (NARA, Entry 719, 1904). Born in Illinois, Reel had migrated to Wyoming, where she worked as a teacher and county superintendent; in 1894 she successfully ran for State Superintendent of Public Instruction. An active Republican, she was credited with carrying the state for McKinley in his presidential bid, and he rewarded her with nomination for the position of Superintendent of Indian Schools within the Office of Indian Affairs. Reel was the first woman nominated for a federal post high enough to require Senate ratification; as an ardent suffragist, her nomination drew intense public and media scrutiny. Her nomination was ratified, and she served as superintendent from 1898 until 1910. Through her brother, Wyoming's governor, and family ties to ranching interests, Reel was connected to politically powerful westerners who leased vast tracts of federal lands, including vast tracts of Indian reservations (Lomawaima, 1996).

Like others of her time, Reel believed that different capacities were bred into the blood of different races through centuries of civilization or barbarism, and she had a low opinion of the Indian "race."

> Allowing for exceptional cases, the Indian child is of lower physical organization than the white child of corresponding age. His forearms are smaller and his fingers and hands less flexible; the very structure of his bones and muscles will not permit so wide a variety of manual movements as are customary among Caucasian children, and his very instincts and modes of thought are adjusted to this imperfect manual development. . . . In short, the Indian instincts and nerves and muscles and bones are adjusted one to another, and all to the habits of the race for uncounted generations, and his offspring cannot be taught like the children of the white man until they are taught to do like them. The children of our aboriginal land holders are now wards of the nation, and in the minds of most right thinking people, they are entitled to kindly consideration. (Reel Papers, 1900)

Reel felt the schools should prepare Indian girls to become "mistress of a log cabin" and she discouraged her teacher corps from fostering students' "erroneous ideals" of living above their station (Reel Papers, 1908b, p. 20). The dust-magnet clutter of high-fashion Victorian homes was ruled off limits to Native home decorators.

In the national debate over education—should it be liberal arts or practical?—Reel advocated practical training for most American citizens and *extremely* practical training for Indians and other minorities. A "practical course of study" for White public high school graduates would prepare them to pass the entrance exam to any college, technical school, school of law or medicine, West Point or Annapolis; to pass the civil service exam; or to take any business position requiring knowledge of bookkeeping, typing, or stenography (Reel Papers, n.d.). The "intensely practical" course of study developed for the Indian schools, on the other hand, did not have such lofty goals. Reel's *Uniform Course* is filled with minutiae calculated to fit Natives to the right level in America's laboring classes. Reel emphasized physical training as a spiritual leavener for a race she deemed "too dull" to excel intellectually. Hoxie (1984/1989) points out that it took 5 years to teach students how to plow.

By 1918, the Commissioner's annual report continued to stress vocational education "along practical lines"; "nonessentials" such as powers and roots, ratios, foreign currencies, and stocks and bonds were eliminated from arithmetic classes. The elimination of nonessentials from the "academic" curriculum freed up 3 to 4 hours a day for Indian students to apply to "productive industrial work," although the mechanics arts classes were specifically designed *not* to produce "experienced master craftsmen" (ARCIA, 1918, pp. 21, 25).

Although Reel advocated "kindly consideration" toward Native people, they were not welcomed as equal citizens, as Pratt had hoped. The question of integration versus segregation did present a quandary, however. On the one hand, Commissioner Leupp argued against separate status: Indian education aimed "to preserve him from extinction, not as an Indian, but as a human being. As a separate entity he cannot exist encysted, as it were, in the body of this great nation" (Reel Papers, 1907). On the other hand, Reel believed that Indian–White intermarriage in Oregon led to "a state of degeneracy among the offspring" (Reel Papers, 1899). Why were the offspring of Indians and Whites considered degenerate? Racial "theory" held that racial mixing was never a good thing. Here we can see federal insistence that Indians surrender "separate" status as sovereign nations coming to loggerheads with racist insistence on segregation to maintain racial purity. Resolving the dilemma of integrating Indian individuals into a racially segregated society meant destroying tribes as "encysted" nations and incorporating racially defined individuals into their proper place in society.

Even in the severely assimilationist setting of the Indian schools, then, it made sense to preserve some "safe" markers of Indian identity that marked or defined racial difference. The challenge was how to find adequately safe differences.

A PLACE FOR NATIVE SONGS: "INNOCENT IN THEMSELVES"

In 1899, fresh to her appointment as superintendent, Estelle Reel encouraged Indian Service teachers to use song and music to make their schoolwork cheerful and attractive and to imbue Indian students with patriotism.

Reel imagined teachers would use English songs, with Western melodies, retraining Native vocal cords to correctly articulate English (NARA, Entry 719, 1899). Reel's emphasis on the English language and European American musical traditions fit perfectly with federal policy goals. Native languages and music were scarcely recognized as meaningful media of communication or artistry. Perceptions of Native peoples and expressive media as simple, childlike, and therefore innocent, however, facilitated the introduction of "safe" Native songs into the curriculum. In 1907 Commissioner Leupp wrote:

> I have . . . made special mention of the successful practice of one of our teachers in the Southwest, of inducing her pupils to bring to the classroom the little nursery songs of their homes, and sing them there in concert, in their own tongue. . . . As everyone who reads this letter probably knows, I have none of the prejudice which exists in many minds against the perpetuation of Indian music and other arts, customs, and traditions, provided *they are innocent in themselves and do not clash needlessly with the new social order.* (NARA, Entry 718, 1907; emphasis added)

Leupp believed "little nursery songs" were culturally innocuous. Childhood pastimes—defined as innocent by Victorian sensibilities—were not seen as threats to the new social order. A 1908 education division circular repeated Leupp's call for "tribal songs" plucked from domesticated realms: "the home, the fireside, the nursery" (NARA, Entry 719, 1908).

As we have noted before, the schools were an extreme expression of the range of federal powers over Native peoples. Native cultural expressions rendered safe there might still seem too dangerous in other locales. In the only slightly less rigidly controlled environments of reservations, federal authorities did not tolerate Native music and songs, which were often central to religious life.

Just a few years after John Lolorias's challenge to the Lake Mohonk conference, Akimel O'odham neighbors (then known as Pimas) to the north of his Tohono O'odham homeland in southern Arizona tried—unsuccessfully, as it turned out—to stretch the boundaries of the musical safety zone. In the fall of 1912, reservation Superintendent Thackery admonished Mr. Anton White, a Pima, "that the holding of his Indian dances and the singing of his foolish, meaningless songs are forbidden." Thackery explained to the Indian Office he would not object if White sang "present day Indian dances or songs," but "particularly bad" influences were involved with "Indian songs and dances of the old style" (NARA, Entry 121, CCF Pima 752, 1913).

Presumably anything that predated federal control was "bad" and "present day" was a code for federally sanctioned dances and songs that could not involve Indigenous religion. Anton White's defense of his songs is preserved in a transcript in the National Archives; he argued his "singing, and a little dancing" were harmless. White explicitly removed any religious associations and compared his gatherings to the social "amusements of a different class of people like the white people, Chinese and Mexicans" (NARA, Entry 121, CCF Pima 752, 1913).

> Why, there is no drinking, there is not anybody shot, there is nothing bad when I sing. Now, look here: the white people have their circus. During the circus there are a lot of Indians drunk, there is lots of gambling going on, there are lots of bad things I have seen with my own eyes. (NARA, Entry 121, CCF Pima 752, 1913)

White reassured the superintendent that his songs were safe, turning to Indian school policies and practices to support his case.

> Young men have gotten interested in my singing and they have come over to listen to me. . . . I continue my songs and still the young men sit around listening to my singing. I suppose it is because they have heard American songs in school and they were interested in those songs because it was for their education and for their amusement. (NARA, Entry 121, CCF Pima 752, 1913)

White strategically sought the assistance of Pima alumni fresh from boarding school to support his arguments. What was going on in the schools that these savvy young men could use to *support* the performance of O'odham songs?

Leupp and Reel were encouraging "innocent" children's songs and lullabies that posed no threat to the "new" social order. Thackeray, as an agent in the field, was very concerned with the preservation of his power over social order. The lyrics and melodies of songs were not their most dangerous components; the greatest danger lay in social gatherings outside the control of the federal agent. Thackeray stressed the necessity of closely regulating all social gatherings on the agency—including those among federal employees —for the good of the community. White lost the contest, despite mobilizing an argument for the "educational" use of songs that was drawn directly out of the boarding schools. Power was the key variable setting the boundaries of the musical safety zone.

A PLACE FOR NATIVE WOMEN'S ARTS: "MOST ATTRACTIVE JARDINIERES"

Early in the century, Estelle Reel (1901) experimented with Native arts in her standard curriculum, *The Uniform Course of Study*. The federal schools employed Native women to teach economically viable crafts such as basketry, pottery, and rug-weaving. Historian Paul Prucha (1984) views Reel's encouragement of select crafts as an example of "occasional breaks in the absolute ethnocentrism" of the *Uniform Course* (p. 829). Prucha also credits Commissioner Leupp for "systematically hop[ing] to save instead of crush what was characteristically Indian. He promoted a revival of Indian music and plastic arts in the schools" (1984, p. 829).

We have already seen how Leupp's ideas about music were constructed within the boundaries of a safety zone; close examination of Reel's experiment in Native arts instruction reveals a similar story. Imagining that Native peoples possessed no sophisticated philosophies or arts, federal officials could also imagine that "simple" arts or lullabies, under strict federal control, were safe. Putting their ideas into practice, however, brought federal employees face to face with the real cultural knowledge and power embodied in Native arts and music, and that reality was entirely too dangerous to handle. Leupp's and Reel's ideas were not a break in ethnocentrism or a true valuing of Indian-ness, but rather part of the ongoing struggle of sorting safe from dangerous difference.

Despite her belief in the lower physiological and intellectual development of the Indian "race," Reel recognized Indian women's skills in the arts of basketry, sewing, netting, and weaving. She deemed these arts worthwhile because they represented the stages of technological development through which civilized peoples had passed.

> Sewing: All civilized nations have obtained their culture through the work of the hand assisting the development of the brain. Basketry, weaving, netting, and sewing were the steps in culture taken by primitive people. (Reel, 1901, p. 450)

Indian women's mastery was not a sign of their civilization but resulted from untold generations of habit.

Reel integrated two ideas into her plan for domestic education: (1) manual, physical training in the civilized domestic arts, including cooking, sewing, and housekeeping; and (2) instruction in tribally appropriate arts such as pottery, basketry, and textile weaving. Both arenas were seen as essential for Native families' economic development. Teaching sewing to Indians in the federal schools entailed more than mere assistance to "profitable occupation," however (Reel Papers, Report of the Superintendent of Indian Schools, 1901). Instruction—formulated to regiment in every detail the sewer's attitudes, values, even posture—was an exercise of power.

> In the first year: Never permit sewing without a thimble. . . . See to it that all sit in an erect position, never resting any part of the arm on the desk. . . . Drill

in use of the thimble, length of the thread, threading needle, motion of arm in taking stitches, fastening thread. (Reel, 1901, p. 452)

Exercises were also devised for "marching, breathing, calisthenics, and games," all for "requisite muscular exercise" (Oklahoma Historical Society, 1906). Why the emphasis on muscular exercise and "motion of arm in taking stitches" in the "civilizing" process? Ideology of the times postulated an inescapable relationship between racially inherited "physical" traits, manifested through skin color, posture, "industry" or "laziness"; "mental" traits such as intelligence; and "moral" traits such as virtue, monogamy, and thrift. The *Uniform Course* was an excruciatingly detailed blueprint for total physical, mental, and moral control of Indian people.

Soon after distributing the *Uniform Course*, Reel invited "agents and superintendents representing the weaver and potter tribes of Indians [to recommend] native teachers in these arts" (Reel Papers, Report of the Superintendent of Indian Schools, 1901). Indian Office support of Native craftspeople in the name of economic self-sufficiency assumed a characteristic paternalism. White aesthetic values would improve the artistic merit of "declining" Native arts, school training would improve their technical quality, and federal management was necessary for success in the marketplace.

The Woman's National Indian Association (WNIA), a prominent reform group of non-Native women, eagerly allied with the government. The WNIA envisioned modern uses for traditional crafts—ecclesiastical beadwork, for example—and not surprisingly had some condescending ideas about the way Indians did things. In a promotional leaflet endorsed by Commissioner Jones and Superintendent Reel, *Two Ways to Help the Indians*, Mrs. E. N. Doubleday of New York City observed that Pueblo pottery could make "most attractive jardinieres for palms and houseplants, affording unspeakable relief after the high glazed Vienna and majolica pottery seen in the department stores ad nauseum" (Reel Papers, 1901). Doubleday reiterated that all Native arts would profit from White oversight. Pueblo pottery was too fragile but "we, their white guardians, know how to harden paste"; and Navajo weaving might yet be saved from the "awful" effects of Germantown worsted yarns and aniline dyes (Reel Papers, 1901).

By 1911, the year after Reel's retirement, the Indian Office was split by "differences of opinion" over Native arts as a source of livelihood. Navajo blanket weaving was recognized as a viable industry, and a weaving instructor was employed at the Navajo boarding schools, but demands for beadwork and basketry were not so reliable, and the work was so slow it might generate only 25 cents a day (NARA, Entry 722, 1911). External critics also doubted the potential for economic stability based on Native crafts. In 1922, the Commissioner inquired of various "Indian policy" experts their opinions on the preservation of the Indian arts and crafts industry. Dakota physician and Carlisle graduate Charles Eastman dismissed the idea as impractical (NARA, Entry 761, 1922).

The Native arts programs never appear to have been particularly well integrated into the schools, reflecting the difficult challenges posed by dangerous difference. Only hints suggest their sporadic survival after Reel's tenure. A number of photographs preserved in the National Archives provide tantalizing glimpses of the ways that federal staff tried to domesticate Native cultural expressions within the confines of the schools. We believe their ultimate failure stemmed from the fact that arts and music presented a fundamental Indian-ness that schools simply could not control.

ATTEMPTS TO DOMESTICATE DIFFERENCE

Figures 3.1 through 3.5 compellingly illustrate the federal determination to domesticate and render safe Native material culture. They also provide clues to the challenges that stood in the way.

Figure 3.1 shows a typical exhibit of boarding school and "traditional Indian" crafts presented in Boston in 1903. Public exhibits of the Office of Indian Affairs's "good works" appeared in public expositions and county, state, and world's fairs. The Boston exhibit safely domesticated Navajo rugs, Pueblo pottery, beaded bags, a Tlingit (Chilkat) dance cape, and an array of western baskets. Artfully arranged in the piles reminiscent of the "Indian corners" of well-off Victorian family parlors, the "primitive" arts are stitched into and constrained by a tableau of civilized arts. A handmade harness is draped on the right, while a miniature wagon and examples of fine carpentry anchor the left side of the exhibit. Home-canned products of Chilocco's fields and orchards nestle between the pottery and beaded bags, while ranks of artifacts firmly affixed to cardboard poster backs ascend to the ceiling. Fine lace and minutely crafted baby clothes abut Navajo textiles and photographs of expansive agricultural industry. Bands of beadwork, cutwork and appliqué doilies and antimacassars, miniature baskets, baby moccasins, and baby layettes form a tightly regimented mosaic backdrop for a fanciful Victorian doll house, the type of school project assembled from balsa and decoupaged with kidney beans, rice grains, and macaroni shells. Extracted from Native contexts of Indigenous meaning and social control, "traditional" artifacts take their regimented places as props in a story of race development.

Similarly, Figure 3.2 of the clothing class at Phoenix Indian School juxtaposes civilized and primitive arts in school workrooms. At the left and center, girls cut, sew, and fit tailored clothing. At the far right, we see a hooked

Figure 3.1. "Boston Exhibit, July 6, 1903." Photo in the collection of Estelle Reel Papers, Northwest Museum of Arts and Culture/Eastern Washington State Historical Society, Spokane, Washington.

rug with "Indian" design arranged between a Navajo woven textile and Navajo-style weaving in process on a loom.

The beautifully posed photograph of Elizabeth Walker, a 16-year-old "Piute" sixth grader at Carson Indian School, in Figure 3.3, was taken during Estelle Reel's tenure to illustrate Elizabeth's artistry. Walker's bead necklace, however, is thoroughly subjugated by the emphatically documented markers of civilization: the stock portrait photographer's backdrop; Elizabeth's carefully coiffed pompadour hairstyle; and the impressively starched, pressed, and gleaming contours of her government-issue school dress.

The contrasts between Figures 3.4 and 3.5 reveal, perhaps, the difficulties of domesticating Native culture that doomed Reel's experiment to failure. Figure 3.4, another photograph from the Estelle Reel collection, depicts Native basket weaving surgically inserted into, and confined within, the standardizing classroom of the Uintah Boarding School. Sample work, produced either by students or by Native women, is captured in the display cabinet

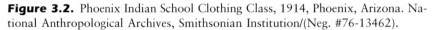

Figure 3.2. Phoenix Indian School Clothing Class, 1914, Phoenix, Arizona. National Anthropological Archives, Smithsonian Institution/(Neg. #76-13462).

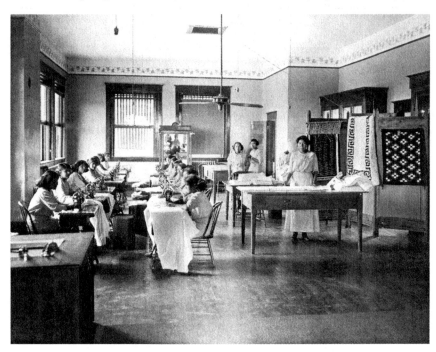

hanging on the back wall. The girls, slotted into school desks bolted to studs on the floor, are primly dressed in identical, government-issue sailor-style dresses, with identical braided hairstyles. A rank of the students' English names marches down the blackboard on the left wall.

Each girl holds a basket, but the untidy bundles of materials necessary to their construction are conspicuously absent. Not a shred of wayward willow, sedge, junco, sumac, or yucca litters the well-swept floor. Figure 3.5, on the other hand, reveals some of the messy reality that the Uintah school classroom so assiduously denies. The photograph, captioned "Teaching Native Industries, Phoenix Indian School, Arizona," shows these Indian girls more realistically "at work," seated on the floor with their materials and the tin cup of water necessary to keep the materials moist and pliable close at hand. Tellingly, the students are clustered on the floor of the hallway, not a classroom, outside the confines of structured "instruction." They have escaped, at least temporarily, the strictures of civilizing space and furniture,

Figure 3.3. "Bead Necklace—Made by Elizabeth Walker, Piute. Age 16. Sixth Grade. Six years in school. Carson Indian School." Photo in the collection of Estelle Reel Papers, Northwest Museum of Arts and Culture/Eastern Washington State Historical Society, Spokane, Washington.

just as their handiwork has escaped the curio cabinet to hang, rather haphazardly, along the hallway.

These photographs are intriguing glimpses into the difficulties federal authorities faced in trying to domesticate and contain Native arts. The challenges, we believe, proved too daunting and prevented Native crafts instruction from gaining a firm foothold in Indian schools.

Finding and recruiting acceptable instructors to teach Native arts must have exacerbated the challenges. Native teaching personnel were hard to come by, since they had to combine considerable skill in a Native technology, which

Figure 3.4. "One of last year's basketry classes at the Uintah Boarding School."
Photo in the collection of Estelle Reel Papers, Northwest Museum of Arts and Culture/Eastern Washington State Historical Society, Spokane, Washington.

often meant Native language and cultural fluency, yet be considered progressive enough to fit Indian Office employment requirements. An Indian Office report on the Casa Blanca Day School in central Arizona refers to one of these scarce Native employees (although not by name):

> They are fortunate at this school in having an Indian housekeeper who understands the hand work of the Pima Indians and can teach the pupils to make baskets, etc. I suggest that they make small baskets, cradles, and other hand work that may be sold as souvenirs to tourists, or curio stores. I also made the following suggestions: that the housekeeper talk English to the pupils, and that the pupils all be required to talk English at school, on the playground as well as in school. (NARA-LN, Pima Indian Agency–Subject Files of Superintendents 1918–1927, 1921)

Here we see the safe culture of "hand work" on a collision course with the dangerous culture of Native language. Reel's programs for practical household instruction and the "practice cottage" model for domestic training she borrowed from Tuskegee Institute were firmly integrated into fed-

Figure 3.5. "Teaching Native Industries, Phoenix Indian School, Arizona." Photo in the collection of Estelle Reel Papers, Northwest Museum of Arts and Culture/ Eastern Washington State Historical Society, Spokane, Washington.

eral curricula in the boarding schools and lasted long after she left office. Instruction by Native women in Indigenous arts, however, was not secure, precisely because it brought girls into contact with the kind of tribal women whose authority and respectability the schools were determined to under-mine. It is also important to note that the school encouraged these craft pro-ductions not as part of technologies to be used within viable Native economies but to make items for sale to Whites, to generate cash, and to knit Indian families into the dominant economy.

Apparently school officials found it impossible to neatly excise subsets of Native skills and knowledge from their cultural contexts and the languages that expressed them. Every so often a reference appears to Native arts in the schools, for example, in this snippet of a 1933 annual report from a school in Oklahoma: "Basket making is again being stressed as a method of increas-ing the family income of the families able to do this work" (NARA, Entry 758, 1933). In the years after Reel's retirement, these references are few and far between. It was not until the 1940s, when boundaries around the safety zone shifted dramatically, that Native arts were once again "revived" in the schools.

We can only speculate what the classes initiated by Reel meant to the Native women who taught or enrolled in them. Federal records are largely mute about these women's identities, motivations, opinions—or the outcomes of craft production after they left the schools. Has another set of stories slipped, perhaps, beyond reach? We hope not. We imagine that young Native women must have found a refuge in these classes, a small space carved out of an oppressive institution where they could express, or at least feel, the precious presence of Indigenous identity, knowledge, language, and daily practices.

AN UNPRECEDENTED POSSIBILITY: "TO REMAIN AN INDIAN"

Estelle Reel developed her notion of an intensely practical education for Indians in a national climate of low regard for Native abilities, but federal Indian policy and Reel's curriculum were not without critics. Elaine Goodale taught at Hampton Institute as a young woman and worked in the schools on the "Great Sioux Reservation" until she gave up her career to marry Dr. Charles Eastman. She responded acidly to Reel's claims that instilling respect for "the dignity of labor" in Indian pupils was a nobler calling than academic instruction or professional training.

> It is perfectly clear to everybody, including those who flatter the workingman with fair words, that the comforts and refinements of our civilization, the higher pleasures of art, literature, and travel, the society of cultivated men and women —all that the world calls success and honor—are the rewards of the *mind*, not muscle. (Eastman, 1900, pp. 413–414; emphasis in original)

Eastman and other advocates for Native rights never ceased their critique of federal Indian policy in the first decades of the century. In the 1920s, after World War I, progressive education and other social reform movements gained momentum as the Western world became disillusioned with industrialized, urbanized, "civilized" society. Social critics turned their attention to the rural and the natural world, and to American Indian societies, as sources of inspiration.

Mounting criticism of corruption and mismanagement within the Indian Office resulted in several investigations and reports. The U.S. Senate mounted one investigation in the mid-1920s, and Secretary of Interior Hubert Work commissioned another by a nongovernmental research organization, the Institute for Government Research, chaired by Robert S. Brookings (the organization still exists as the Brookings Institution. The Institute organized and funded a research team, led by staff member Lewis Meriam, which included prominent social and health scientists as well as Winnebago educator Henry Roe Cloud, who was listed as the project's "Indian advisor."

After extensive field research, the team wrote an excoriating critique of the Indian Service, *The Problem of Indian Administration*, commonly known as the Meriam Report (Meriam et al., 1928). Faulting the government for substandard efforts in health, management of assets, and social services—in fact, in all areas of responsibility—the report targeted boarding schools as the most severely deficient institutions.

Despite the "grossly inadequate" care offered by the boarding schools (Meriam et al., 1928, p. 11), the Report identified education broadly as the keystone to effective administration of "Indian affairs" and offered an alternative to the long-standing assumption that assimilation was the only option for Native people:

> *Recommendations.* The fundamental requirement is that the task of the Indian Service be recognized as primarily educational, in the broadest sense of that word, and that it be made an efficient educational agency, devoting its main energies to the social and economic advancement of the Indians, so that they may be absorbed into the prevailing civilization *or be fitted to live in the presence of that civilization at least in accordance with a minimum standard of health and decency.* (1928, p. 21; emphasis added)

The "or" after "may be absorbed into the prevailing civilization" was an unprepossessingly radical word. The survey team proposed a profound departure from established federal policy and practice when they proposed that Native people had an option besides absorption and that they possessed rights to decide how they might wish to live.

Even more radical was their proposition that those wishing to pursue a "Native lifestyle" had a right to do so "in accordance with a minimum standard of health and decency." This was such a radical notion that the report staff carefully explained exactly what they meant. The work to fit Indians into the prevailing civilization, they wrote, "is apparently so clear on its face as to require no further explanation. The second [option], however, demands some further explanation":

> The position taken, therefore, is that the work with and for the Indians must give consideration to the desires of the individual Indians. He who wishes to merge into the social and economic life of the prevailing civilization of this country should be given all practicable aid and advice in making the necessary adjustments. He who wants to remain an Indian and live according to his old culture should be aided in doing so. The question may be raised "Why aided?

Just leave him alone and he will take care of himself." The fact is, however, as has been pointed out, that the old economic basis of his culture has been to a considerable extent destroyed and new problems have been forced upon him by contacts with the whites. Adjustments have to be made, economic, social and legal. . . . Both the Indians and their white neighbors are concerned in having those Indians who want to stay Indians and preserve their culture, live according to at least a minimum standard of health and decency. (Meriam et al., 1928, p. 86)

CONCLUSION

Remain an Indian? Preserve Native cultures? These were unprecedented federal goals in Indian country, although Native people like John Lolorias had been fighting for generations to exercise these rights. We use the Meriam Report to mark a transition period when boundaries around a safety zone of tolerable cultural difference were redrawn, but not as radically as policy historians have believed. The safety zone was not abandoned, and the issue of federal power remained firmly at the crux of federal–Indian relations in the next few decades, but the shifting boundaries around the safety zone can be traced through the trajectory of Indian education through the 1930s and 1940s, which we chart in the next chapter.

CHAPTER 4

How to "Remain an Indian"?
Power Struggles in the Safety
Zone, 1928–1940

In May of 1935, Jeff Mouse wrote to the Commissioner of Indian Affairs, protesting proposed changes in the high school program at Chilocco Indian Agricultural School. Mouse was a Chilocco graduate, president of the Alumni Association, and a school employee. Supported by letters from Will Rogers, then Chairman of the Commission on Indian Affairs in Washington, D.C., and Oklahoma Congressman Wilbur Cartwright, Mouse and the Alumni Association adamantly opposed a plan to replace Chilocco's academic high school curriculum with a vocational-only program: "We respectfully request that the present academic program of accredited high school work be retained as it is in connection with the vocational training, since we believe academic training furnishes a foundation for all vocational training and for higher education" (NARA, Entry 121, CCF Chilocco 810, 1935).

In 1928, the Meriam Report had excoriated the off-reservation boarding schools for inadequate academic training and menial "drudge" work masquerading as vocational training. A new administration under President Franklin D. Roosevelt had replaced much of the Washington office "old guard." Charles Rhoads became Commissioner of Indian Affairs in 1929 and was succeeded in 1933 by activist John Collier. In 1930 the progressive educator and Meriam Report researcher W. Carson Ryan Jr. was named Director of Education. But Jeff Mouse and Chilocco alumni were fighting to keep the academic program painstakingly built from 1928 through 1934 from being eradicated by a "new" vocational program that was as regressive as the old manual labor system. Commissioner Collier's response to Mouse did not chart a new course for Indian education but reiterated long-standing policies that students desiring college preparatory coursework belonged in public schools, despite the well-documented resistance of public schools to Indian enrollment (NARA, Entry 121, CCF Chilocco 810, 1935).

What went wrong? How could New Deal "reforms" be used so perversely to overturn the hard-won possibility of accredited high school degrees for Indian school graduates? The Meriam Report had boldly articulated a new possibility for federal Indian policy: to assist Native people who wished to "remain an Indian." Under John Collier's leadership (1933–1945), many Indian Service employees worked to redraw the boundaries of the safety zone, but it was an arduous task. Even well-intentioned reformers had difficulties entrusting power and decision making to Native peoples. In this chapter, we trace developments in Indian education during this period to show how the promise of reform bogged down in practical battles as people tried to reconfigure—or to maintain—power relations.

Commissioner Collier advocated for Native religious freedom, self-government, and cultural survival, but he has been criticized for replacing federal paternalism that denigrated Native societies with a paternalism that romanticized them (Philp, 1977; Szasz, 1974). Both versions of paternalism elevated federal over tribal powers, and we see federal control as a critical continuity linking educational policy and practice across the earlier decades of the century through the "Indian New Deal." In this chapter, we examine debates over a "new" vocational education; attempts to develop Indian History and Lore classes; the role of Native teachers; and the much-touted "revival" of arts and crafts instruction. In all arenas, power relations continued to define the federal–Indian relationship, reinforcing the boundaries of the safety zone even as Native and non-Native reformers worked to expand them.

Native people persevered in their determination to "remain an Indian," however, and took strategic advantage of the windows of opportunity opened during and after the Collier years. The bottom-up efforts of Native communities, students, and teachers met with the top-down policy directives of the Collier administration to build a mid-century foundation for significant developments in tribal self-determination. Indian people used the Bureau's rhetorical support for "remaining an Indian" even as they resisted alleged reforms that perpetuated old ideas in new guises, such as the "new" vocational education.

THE "NEW" VOCATIONAL EDUCATION

Given past emphasis on the "dignity of labor" and the thousands of hours Indian students spent on their knees polishing hallways with old gray sweaters wrapped around bricks, one might think that reformers would have stressed academics when envisioning a new era of Indian education. One might have expected Collier and Ryan to support schooling that, in Elaine Goodale Eastman's words, developed "the rewards of the *mind*, not muscle" (1900, pp. 413–414; emphasis in original). Interestingly enough, a movement away from vocational toward academic education is not what happened next.

Reformers did hope to replace the schools' repetitive toil in laundries, power plants, and fields with meaningful, job-focused training. Native peoples, however, were still not seen as fit for academic or professional higher education. In fact, new Bureau guidelines stripped accreditation from the few off-reservation boarding schools that had painfully evolved into high schools. A coherent logic was at work in New Deal policies that moved some Indian schools backward. A new idea—schools should serve the needs and interests of Native students—was wedded to an old idea—federal policymakers were best qualified to define those needs and interests. Stiff resistance confronted Native students and parents who protested the "new" vocationalism and demanded accredited academic high schools.

The Native Quest for High School Education

From 1900 to 1920, the Indian Office had been secure in its position that the federal Indian school system had no business offering "higher education" above grade 8. Pressures mounted, however, to remake the off-reservation boarding schools as high schools. More children were completing the lower grades at on-reservation schools, and students and parents petitioned for high school grades; given widespread prejudice against Indians, federal schools were often the only "higher education" option available. At Chilocco Indian School, for example, "enrollment in grades seven through ten more than doubled in the five years between 1920 and 1925" (Lomawaima, 1994, p. 39).

Superintendents of the off-reservation schools also lobbied to add high school grades, struggling to keep their schools open in the face of declining congressional support and the restriction against recruiting students for the lower grades, the turf of on-reservation schools. Through the mid-1920s the Washington office denied requests from Chilocco to add grades 11 and 12, but after publication of the Meriam Report the higher grades were added. The report explicitly recommended that boarding schools should function as accredited high schools.

> Although the boarding school must be distinctive in the emphasis on the special needs of the Indians, it should not be so distinctive that it will not dovetail into the general educational system of the country. . . . The faculties and their courses of study should be such that they can meet the standards set for accredited high schools. (Meriam et al., 1928, p. 35)

By 1934, the Chilocco superintendent proposed to the central office that the seventh and eighth grades be eliminated as soon as students in those classes moved up (NARA, Entry 121, CCF Chilocco 810, 1934). Other off-reservation boarding schools followed a similar pattern.

Meriam Report critique intersected with Native demands, and the federal system slowly developed accredited high schools. That hard-won accomplishment was threatened when the Indian Office reorganized the high schools in the mid-1930s. The "new plan" appears to have been designed to take advantage of Roosevelt's 1934 Executive Order (No. 6750-c), "which provided for an apprentice-training program . . . to provide opportunities for boys and girls to learn trades and enter skilled occupations" (NARA, Entry 724, 1935). The Office of Indian Affairs's vocational and education divisions cooperated with the U.S. Office of Education to channel federal dollars for apprentice training into the Indian schools. Officials at Haskell were optimistic about the new funds: "If the proposed plan of apprentice training is worked out, then the future of Haskell Institute as a vocational school is indeed bright" (NARA, Entry 724, 1935).

"New" Vocationalism Motivated by Economic Depression

Haskell administrators had reason to be concerned about their future. The depressed economy generated hot debates over the fate of off-reservation boarding schools. In June 1933, the Commissioner suspended all activities at Chemawa Indian School in Oregon. The order was rescinded in the fall but the "accredited four-year high school course" was discontinued and a "two-year vocational program was hastily mapped out." Students and staff at Chemawa, and other schools, were deeply unsettled by the precipitous and haphazard sequence of orders and counterorders, and the school year was chaotic (NARA, Entry 724, 1934). By February 28, 1935, the staff at Haskell, under the direction of their new superintendent Dr. Henry Roe Cloud, quickly pulled together a proposal to train young Indians "for worthy participation in home and community life" (NARA, Entry 724, 1935; NARA, Entry 723, 1935). The goals of training in community life included "civic, social, and economic efficiency," and it appears that economic efficiency dominated other concerns. The schools' hastily contrived "new vocationalism" was created to tap into federal funds, not to develop locally relevant curricula.

Students at Haskell and Chilocco were outraged that the new plans resulted in their schools' loss of accreditation, and many agitated to transfer. The Commissioner tried to reassure staff that the new program simply needed to be adequately explained to the students. "These changes are being made solely in the interests of a sounder education. . . . The new Haskell program is designed primarily to serve the great majority of students for the work which they will do and the life which they will lead better than does the present program with its academic emphasis" (NARA, Entry 724, 1935). Of course the federal Indian schools had never been highly academic, but the Commissioner's language hints at the slippage between Roosevelt's executive order—intended to create opportunity through training for "skilled occupations"—and the implementation in Indian schools that limited opportunity by stripping away the hard-won chance for a high school diploma.

The Pretense of "Locally Relevant" Education

The Meriam Report called for a "locally relevant" curriculum to replace a "uniform" course of study. Educational methods, the report stated, "must be adapted to individual abilities, interests, and needs." (Meriam et al., 1928, p. 32). Federal educators, however, defined locally relevant education to fit entrenched notions of Indians' lesser abilities and circumscribed opportunities, stressing vocational training at the expense of Native communities' requests for accredited academic high schools.

By January 1936, Native communities were in an uproar. Chilocco Superintendent Correll let the Washington office know how difficult things were in the field. "I have talked to every superintendent in the state of Oklahoma and to most of the educational field agents and social workers and have tried to explain the new set-up." (NARA, Entry 121, CCF Chilocco, 800, 1936). Correll hoped to send them copies of the new courses; the curricular plan was still unformed. A "big group of students went home in a rush at the opening of school," Correll reported, complaining that "they were not going to get a diploma showing that they had graduated from an accredited high school" (NARA, Entry 121, CCF Chilocco, 800, 1936). Native students were making their voices heard, and some were voting with their feet.

The controversy attracted press attention. The *Wichita Eagle* reported: "Departing from the former policy of preparing students for college, the Chilocco Indian school is now teaching undergraduates how to operate farms, with the idea . . . they can return to their land and use it to the best advantage" (Engle, 1935, p. 32). Chilocco's principal defended the change, asserting that Indian education was shifting from national uniformity to local specificity and diversity, no longer aiming to imitate White schooling (as if it ever had). He evoked the Meriam Report's language condemning standardization to cloak the same old approach to educating Indians. In an eerily perfect echo of Estelle Reel, he explained the school would now devote "less time . . . to teaching the girls how to prepare fancy dishes. . . . They learn how to cook nice, plain foods, and how to can food properly" (quoted in Engle, 1935, p. 32).

Resistance to "Higher Education" for Indians

In 1936, Chilocco Superintendent L. E. Correll tried to persuade the Indian Office to support Chilocco graduates enrolled at Arkansas City Junior

College. Director of Education Willard W. Beatty replied: "I can see no reason whatever why we should over-urge any student to go on to junior college. . . . Our Indian boys and girls need . . . practical vocational training" (NARA, Entry 121, CCF Chilocco 850). Beatty objected to the government "coddling" young Indian people. A few years later, Pima parents in central Arizona were "agitating" to accredit the local high school so their children could apply to college. Beatty wrote to the agent: "I am glad that you and I agree that this hullabaloo about college preparation is largely a waste of time" (NARA, Entry 121, CCF Pima 806, 1939).

As Americans turned their attention to the war, the "hullabaloo" over low academic standards and forced vocational training subsided, but never entirely so. In 1945, concerned parent and tribal council member David Johnson addressed school personnel at the Pima Agency:

> I have a son who graduate [sic] in Phoenix. I took him to Tucson to enter college. He could not because he did not have the necessary credits. My boy cried all the way home. . . . It makes me feel that there is something lacking in Indian schools because . . . students are not accredited so that they can go on to college without losing two years. (NARA/LN, Entry 121, CCF Pima Indian Agency, 1945)

Johnson was unsuccessful in the short run; the Indian Service did not extend the local school at Sacaton, Arizona, through the twelfth grade. He was successful in expressing his dissatisfactions with the federal Indian schools, as did the students who protested at Haskell and transferred from Chilocco. Even when Native people could not immediately divert the course of federal intentions, they built moments important to those individuals involved and those who came after them. Jeff Mouse enlisted prominent allies in the service of Indian students; tragically, his life was cut short in the service of Indian schools. The assistant coach at Chilocco, he was killed when the bus carrying the boys' basketball team was struck at a railroad crossing in southern Kansas in 1937 (NARA/FW, Entry 45, Records of Chilocco Indian School, 1937).

Tracing the route from harsh criticism of manual labor to a "new" vocational education that sabotaged high school accreditation illuminates exactly how dangerous Native self-determination has appeared. The threat that a high school degree might enable access to higher education and economic development, possibly economic competition, trumped the promises of Native participation in defining "locally relevant education." This example highlights the dual nature of the safety zone: It outlines safe expression of Native cultural distinctiveness—what is allowable in "remaining an Indian"— and simultaneously delineates tolerance levels for equal opportunity in education and employment within the national society.

Limitations of New Deal Reforms

Collier-era reforms cannot be understood as a simple swing of the pendulum of federal policy toward more "liberal" attitudes celebrating Native cultures, promoting local control, and creating opportunities. The vocational education example demonstrates that certain ideas persisted: Indians were suited for manual labor, and higher education should be reserved for select classes who would lead in the marketplace. New ideas were added to the mix: Indians had a right to "remain an Indian," as long as they remained on their reservation or allotment land and did not compete for jobs. The lines around the safety zone were being redrawn not to liberate Indian-ness but to suit American social, cultural, and economic realities.

Despite the evolution of a "new" vocational education that bore remarkable resemblance to earlier manual labor regimes, the Indian Bureau was forced to respond to the growing need and call for accredited high school education on reservations (although they never kept up with demands; the Hopi Junior/Senior High School, for example, was finally constructed in 1986 after 40 years of lobbying). In 1936, there were 13 high schools in the federal school system for Indians, none of them accredited. By 1951, there were 33 fully accredited high schools; the number reached 42 in the 1940s, but shifting enrollments into public schools reduced the number (Beatty, 1953).

INDIAN HISTORY AND LORE COURSES

The Meriam team saw a special curricular opportunity in Indian schools to develop locally meaningful materials based on tribal, social, and civic life. Under Collier and Ryan, schools incorporated Indian geography, history, arts, and experiences into coursework. These courses engaged educators and students in a mix of obstacles and opportunities as they struggled to reconfigure the safety zone within the schools. In 1935 Chilocco instituted its first course on Indian History and Lore; teachers appealed to Washington for books, maps, and information, but the central office had no such resources. Teachers actually asked students what they would like to study—design on "costumes," homes, sign language, dances and ceremonials, legends?—while asserting that students' knowledge of their own background was "pitifully meager" (NARA, Entry 121, CCF Chilocco 810, 1936). Sadly, this judgment was sometimes true. Two, three, or more generations of federal and mission schooling in partnership with powerful assimilative pressures (including endemic poverty and poor health) had eroded Indigenous knowledge—but not student interest in learning it. Nearly 300 students signed up for the elective course designed to enable students to learn about other tribes and "to inspire a deeper sense of appreciation of his ancestors so that he can say with pride, 'I am an Indian.'" (NARA, Entry 121, CCF Chilocco 810, 1936). Given the paucity of materials and the novelty, accomplishing these goals proved difficult for both teachers and students.

Many Chilocco students were second- or third-generation boarding school attendees; their parents and grandparents had either taken to heart the harsh punishment they had suffered for speaking their language or expressing Native identity or were understandably skeptical of the Bureau's new approach. Teachers asked their students to "find out all they could about their tribal history and lore from elderly relatives and friends," but some students reported, "My father told me not to write anything about our tribe. He doesn't want me to" (NARA, Entry 121, CCF Chilocco 810, 1936). Parents, teachers, and administrators were uncertain, suspicious, or outright opposed to curricular innovation.

Teachers and students in Chilocco's Indian History and Lore course did their best. Teachers read creation stories culled from the anthropological literature. Students "memorized some sayings of great chiefs," studied southeastern removal, and discussed the Bureau publication *Indians at Work*. They read "Let's Help Ourselves" by Esther Burnette Horne, a Shoshone teacher in the federal schools; they searched newspapers for articles about Indian issues; they read Stanley Vestal's "Indians Dance in Oklahoma," and a Cheyenne boy described a Sun Dance he had once seen. Native content at Chilocco was not confined to the Indian History and Lore course. In American History, students studied Native domestication of crops, and in Rural Sociology they studied the Okmulgee and Muskogee Constitutions alongside the U.S. Constitution (NARA, Entry 121, CCF Chilocco 810, 1936).

Chilocco staff made sincere efforts to implement new curricular goals. Students had an opportunity to study topics never before allowed within their classrooms and to connect to their heritage in ways that would have prompted strict punishment in the past. Other schools in the federal system experimented with curricular reform, organizing "home rooms" that included "Indian Lore," for example, at Haskell Institute:

> The young Indian of today, as he absorbs more . . . of the white man's culture . . . is prone to lose interest in the story lore, customs, and superstition of his forefathers unless he is made to feel that these are . . . worthy of preservation. (NARA, Entry 724, 1935)

Haskell rhetoric characteristically shifted the blame for loss of Native culture to Native people; just as earlier generations of White women took credit for preserving and improving Native arts, federal school personnel bore the burden of preserving a "worthy" heritage.

"Safe" Topics in Indian Lore

At Haskell, the outline of "Indian lore" topics reveals the parameters of the safety zone. Treaty rights and Indigenous governments were not discussed, but we find theories of Native origins in North America; the early locales of tribes; language groups; tribal social, civic, and economic organization; religion; social customs; mythology; games; music; and arts and crafts. These topics were rendered safe by overlapping strategies that corralled difference. Terminology such as *origins* and *early locales* placed Native societies firmly in the past. Western classificatory systems organized cultural traits as the subjects of study; one studied "language groups" but did not use a Native language day to day. Native students were not a source of meaningful knowledge but were the lucky recipients of federal guidance defining what was "worthy" in their heritage.

The "simple" topics of Commissioner Leupp's day—divested of danger by being stripped out of their cultural context—survived to be included as "stories," games, "mythology," music, arts, and crafts. All were packaged within the frame of a home room organized on parliamentary procedure. The inclusion of religion appears the only anomaly in this group, even in the highly controlled frame of the home room; no documentary evidence indicates, however, any substantive study of Native religion in a federal school during this era. A few years later, Haskell's home room was a 1-hour period including administrative announcements, campus conduct, vocational guidance, and "tribal customs, Indian lore, superstitions, etc." to serve students from 63 tribes in 27 states (NARA, Entry 724, 1933). The Meriam team's vision of a "special curriculum opportunity" did not come to fruition at Haskell.

Local Control but Not Community Control

Different schools developed quite different programs in "Indian lore" in part because of a concern for locally relevant curriculum, but also because the regulations authorizing the new programs gave local jurisdictions wide latitude to implement coursework—or not. The Indian Office drew up a "General Statement of Policy Relating to Indian Secondary Schools" (NARA, Entry 724, 1935) that called for a locally developed course of study to "help [students] to appreciate and perpetuate those elements of Indian culture which hold real values for the present and future generations" (NARA, Entry 724, 1935). All the boarding schools were required to submit a planned course of study that fit a general template.

The plan of study developed by the Charles H. Burke School at Fort Wingate, New Mexico, illustrates the possibilities for local control—by federal employees, not Native parents—enabled by the new general policy. School staff assumed their students would live in (Navajo) hogans; they appreciated the values of a Navajo diet but wanted to add milk and green vegetables; they assumed a pastoral economy but wanted to develop student appreciation for "the present depleted condition of the range." Navajo arts and crafts were appreciated for their economic value, but Navajo students required instruction in the nature of personal and communal property under Indian custom and American law; the curriculum explicitly addressed the meaning of stealing, honesty, and the care of government property. An extensive section in the proposed study plan was devoted to "Navajo Indians and the American government" (NARA, Entry 724, 1935). The Burke School curriculum embedded Navajo cultural elements within a framework of American, not Navajo, cultural meaning.

Indian Lore in the Day Schools

In the day schools, such as those scattered across the Pima Agency, schoolwork was often even less progressive than in the boarding schools. The 1936 BIA annual report described text-focused instruction in these small, overcrowded, and understaffed schools. In at least one Arizona day school, "minor units on the Casa Grande ruins and on Home Life in Colonial Days were attempted with meager results" (NARA, Entry 121, CCF Pima 800, 1936). The day schools were closely tied to community life in many ways, however; all were heavily used for women's club gatherings, garden work, and access to showers (NARA, Entry 121, CCF Pima 800, 1936). Perhaps as a result of close community ties, the day schools were felt to be less controlled and thus less safe environments than the large off-reservation schools to introduce Native-focused curriculum.

At the Pima Central School in Sacaton, Arizona, staff struggled to integrate Pima history and culture into social science courses (NARA, Entry 121, CCF Pima 800, 1936). "Adult Indians" were invited to talk about the reservation; the agency farmer discussed the cultivation of Pima cotton. Students collected Pima foods and used the museum collection attached to the classroom, including "pottery, grinding stones, beads, headdresses, and baskets . . . all of which have been brought in by the students" (NARA, Entry 121, CCF Pima 800, 1936). Elsewhere in the curriculum, however, Pima subjects were less evident. The sewing class stressed the production of plain clothing, curtains, bath towels, and patchwork quilts, although all Wednesday sewing periods were set aside for basketry. Cooking classes developed the skills of basic American cooking such as breads and cookies, and children raised onions, carrots, lettuce, and spinach in the school gardens rather than traditional, desert-adapted crops (a few years earlier the annual report admitted that the students were totally "fed up" with lettuce) (NARA, Entry 724, 1931).

Innovative curricular development in the day schools was also hamstrung by the quality of the teacher corps. Low salaries and extreme isolation thwarted recruitment and retention. In 1900 the superintendent of the Colorado River School in Parker, Arizona, stressed the importance of thanking the day school teachers for the "little kindnesses" that "make all forget for a time the dreary wastes surrounding them and the utter isolation of our field of labor" (ARCIA, 1900, p. 187). The Meriam staff blasted the Indian Bureau for low hiring standards and low teacher pay scales; these problems were worst in the day schools. The "uniform elementary salary of $1,200 in the Indian Service" did not compare favorably with a national range for public school teachers of $2,000–$3,400. Expecting poorly trained, poorly paid teachers to develop radically new curriculum did not augur for success.

Despite these obstacles, the Indian Office teacher corps contained creative, dedicated individuals. There were not many Native teachers in the system before World War II, but Native teachers could and did significantly impact students' lives. Teachers often spent their lives chipping away at the walls around the safety zone.

NATIVE TEACHERS IN THE FEDERAL SCHOOLS

Esther Burnett Horne (1909–1999) was a Shoshone teacher whose work was incorporated into the Indian History and Lore course at Chilocco. Horne attended Haskell, where she was greatly influenced by her teachers Ruth Muskrat Bronson (Cherokee) and Ella Deloria (Dakota), and she taught for many years at the Wahpeton Indian School in North Dakota. We compare her career to that of equally innovative Hopi educator Polingaysi Qoyawayma (1892–1990; also known as Elizabeth Q. White) in the day schools of the Hopi reservation in northeastern Arizona. These women struggled within the constraints of an often oppressive, and sometimes rewarding, federal school system to create and nourish spaces for Native children to safely express their identities, experiences, and knowledge. They originated many of the curricular reforms of their day and significantly impacted the lives of Native students.

"Essie": Esther Burnett Horne

Esther Burnett Horne collaborated with scholar Sally McBeth to write her life story, *Essie's Story: The Life and Legacy of a Shoshone Teacher* (Horne & McBeth, 1998). Horne, who attended Haskell from 1923 to 1928, quickly developed a reflective insight about her place within the federal schools that served her well throughout her life. A student officer, she realized that "we officers were being used by the school, but like student governing bodies today, we were aware that we were being taught self-discipline. . . . We nurtured a sense of community among ourselves" (p. 34). Horne credits two Native teachers for helping her find a place of Native community at Haskell. Ella Deloria (Dakota) earned a graduate degree at Columbia University under the mentorship of Franz Boas; at Haskell she taught the girls' physical education class and drama. Cherokee educator Ruth Muskrat Bronson, who had graduated from Mt. Holyoke College, taught English. According to Horne, both women possessed a healthy sense of humor; they "had a very strong respect for Indian culture, and they were clever enough to integrate it into the curriculum" (p. 41).

Deloria and Bronson taught their students self-respect, pride, and a sense of Indian values. Horne recalled that they "listened to us. They were interested . . . in our lives" (Horne & McBeth, 1998, p. 42). These two inspiring teachers helped their students keep a positive attitude while pointing out the biases that surrounded them. Horne noted that they "taught us how to disagree without being disagreeable. They taught us how to defend ourselves, as Indian people, without getting angry or defensive" (p. 42). Horne praised them for teaching their students "to be receptive to new ideas," reminding them that they did not "know it all," especially in the arenas of American Indian issues (p. 42).

Ruth Muskrat Bronson is perhaps best known today for her 1944 publication, *Indians Are People, Too.* In that work she walked the tightrope that Horne described, actively criticizing some government policies at the risk of being dismissed as "disagreeable." *Indians Are People, Too* presents a complicated picture of Bronson's own sense of identity. Although her father was Cherokee, she adopted the authorial position of a White person, reminding her readers "they [Indians], too, are persons like ourselves" (Bronson, 1944, p. 2). Bronson celebrated the rich Native "disciplines for living"—courage, endurance, patience, and personal dignity—and called for Native self-determination in education (p. 76): "What to prune and what to retain of the Indian way of life must in the end be decided by Indians themselves. . . . Educational goals for Indians advanced by the white man have often not been Indian goals" (pp. 80, 160).

In 1929 Esther Burnett assumed her first teaching position at the Eufaula Boarding School in Oklahoma, where she followed Bronson's and Deloria's examples and worked diligently to learn about her students' heritage. She used peer tutors among her first and second graders to help the Creek speakers, and she stomp danced with her Creek compatriots from Haskell days, knowing that if her superiors found out, she would be fired on the spot. After she married Bob Horne (Hoopa), the power plant foreman for the Indian school at Wahpeton, the Service allowed her to join him in North Dakota in 1930. Esther Horne was the only Indian teacher at Wahpeton, and she greeted her first class with characteristic forthrightness: "We're all Indians in this room so let's make our classroom the best classroom at Wahpeton" (Horne & McBeth, 1998, p. 63). In the early 1930s the schools still discouraged Indian-ness, but Horne persevered. "When B.I.A. supervisors came along, I was very adept at sweeping the Indian components under the table" (p. 67). The atmosphere of the school service had become more congenial under the direction of Willard Beatty (1936–1951), and Horne felt he shared a deep respect for Native cultures. She was able to teach openly what she had taught secretly in the past, and she combated the stereotypes that pervaded school textbooks.

Horne shared the uncertainty many Native people felt about Commissioner Collier and his unprecedented approaches to Indian policy. "Many of us thought, 'Lo, the poor Indian' . . . once again the government is using us as guinea pigs" (Horne & McBeth, 1998, p. 76). Despite her initial skepticism, by 1936 Horne was enlisted at an in-service summer school "to 'demonstrate' how a fourth-grade teacher could incorporate Native American materials into the subjects that we teach" (p. 83). In her teaching at Wahpeton, Horne invited Lakota parents into the classroom; when she focused on dance she sought help from knowledgeable community members as well as school employees Martha Voight (Hidatsa, on the dorm staff) and Albert Howle (Turtle Mountain Chippewa, the bus driver). "Those days were so exciting! Finally, we no longer had to hide the fact that we were incorporating our cultural values into the curriculum and student life" (p. 86). Throughout the 1940s and 1950s, Horne taught in the summer school in-services for teachers, leading workshops on effective methods to teach arts and crafts. Her career at Wahpeton flourished, especially when a new superintendent arrived in 1955 who was deeply committed to providing Indian students with "a school with a home atmosphere . . . community and social life" (1998, p. 95).

By the time Horne retired in 1965, she had devoted most of her life to Indian students and schools. In 1966, the Bureau recognized her achievements with its Distinguished Service Citation. One of her former students, Dennis Banks, called Horne the "mother of AIM": "You used to tell us, 'Keep your heads up. Don't smell your knees. And don't be a puppet on somebody else's string'" (Horne & McBeth, 1998, p. 129). Horne summed up her philosophy of education as follows:

> I attempted to incorporate Indian values into every sphere of instruction—classroom, scouting, Indian Club, sports, everything! The five values that I focused on in particular were bravery, generosity and sharing, respect for elders, individual freedom, and respect for the environment. (p. 130)

"Bessie": Elizabeth Q. White

When Horne began teaching in 1929, Elizabeth White, as she was then known, had been working in the Indian Service off and on for a decade. In many ways, the two women traversed parallel journeys through the Indian Service. Polingaysi Qoyawayma/Elizabeth White worked with long-time newswoman Vada Carlson to produce her life story, *No Turning Back: A Hopi Indian Woman's Struggle to Live in Two Worlds* (Qoyawayma, 1964). Born in the Third Mesa village of Oraibi, Qoyawayma as a young girl defied her mother and allowed herself to be caught by the Navajo policemen who were rounding up Hopi children and removing them to the federal school in Keams Canyon, several miles east of Oraibi. Qoyawayma, rechristened "Bessie," attended the Keams Canyon School, Sherman Institute in Riverside, California, and the Mennonite Bethel Academy in Newton, Kansas. When Bessie returned home a staunch Christian, determined to teach her family the errors of their ways, she met determined resistance that forced her to reconsider her position.

In 1924 Qoyawayma was offered the position of housekeeper at the Hotevilla Day School (on Third Mesa), but when it was discovered she had substitute teaching experience, she was immediately promoted to teacher for the first grade and beginners. As she entered her classroom, she remembered "her first days at school when she obeyed instructions as best she could, not understanding a word the teacher spoke. At least she knew the language of these children. That, she reasoned, would make it easier for them and for her as well" (Qoyawayma, 1964, p. 125). To her dismay, Qoyawayma soon discovered that she was forbidden to speak Hopi in her classroom. Much as Esther Burnett Horne would do a few years later, Qoyawayma ignored her superiors' instructions and began with what her students found familiar. She developed her own teaching methods using the language in "familiar Hopi legends, songs, and stories" (p. 125).

Qoyawayma's unorthodox methods were not immediately understood or appreciated by Hopi parents, who protested that they sent their children "to school to learn the white man's way, not Hopi. They can learn the Hopi way at home" (Qoyawayma, 1964, p. 126). Qoyawayma persisted; working from their knowledge base in their own language and culture, her students made unprecedented progress in the "authorized" school subjects; by the Christmas holiday, they were forming whole sentences in English, spelling simple words, and learning numbers. With her colleagues' help, Qoyawayma passed the Indian Service test and became a "bona fide employee of the government" (p. 131).

During the Meriam survey, Henry Roe Cloud visited Qoyawayma's classroom, where her students had built a small replica of their village in the sandbox. Cloud praised Qoyawayma for her techniques, and his approval made a deep impression. She treasured the letter he sent her:

> I want to say that . . . I admire you very much for your work and want to en-
> courage you in your personal life and endeavors for the uplift of your people.
> I am keenly conscious of the struggles each one of us has . . . in loneliness to
> keep up the high standards which we have learned . . . in the fine schools we
> have been privileged to attend. I hope that you will never get discouraged and
> feel that the work is not worthwhile. It is infinitely worthwhile. (quoted in
> Qoyawayma, 1964, p. 144)

Qoyawayma was soon transferred to the Navajo schools; stationing Native teachers among their own people was not the norm in the Indian Service, and, like Horne, she had to find her satisfaction working with students from other tribes.

Qoyawayma yearned to return home, however, and was fortunate to be posted to the Hopi school at First Mesa in a few years, where she was teaching when the Collier administration began to redirect education policy. Qoyawayma was recruited, as Horne had been, to demonstrate her teaching methods at a 1941 summer in-service held at Chemawa School in Oregon. Her belief in teaching the familiar, in the language of the home, had proved successful. Qoyawayma retired in 1954, when she was presented with a bronze medal of commendation and a certificate of honor for commendable service from the Department of the Interior. After her retirement, she continued to counsel teachers in the Indian Service:

> Educate [the Indian child] from what they already know, not from a totally
> new, strange field of experience. . . . Lead them, guide them, but don't try to
> whip them into education, and don't make the mistake of thinking education
> can be superimposed upon them, like plaster on a wall. (Qoyawayma, 1964,
> pp. 174–175)

Native teachers were scattered throughout the Indian Service from the early years of the century, and their numbers grew as the century progressed. Some, like Qoyawayma, were able to teach in their home communities, but many taught among the communities of other tribes, as Horne did throughout her career. The majority of students in the system never experienced a classroom with a Native teacher, but the few who did might remember their influence as long as they lived, just as Essie remembered Ruth Bronson and Ella Deloria. Despite working within a system that continued to enforce federal powers and impose federal decisions, these courageous and innovative teachers, in alliance with non-Native colleagues, were able to implement, in a few schools, a more locally relevant federal Indian education.

THE REVIVAL OF ARTS AND CRAFTS INSTRUCTION

By the 1930s the Bureau's institutional memory seems to have retained no trace of Estelle Reel's introductions of Native arts to the federal schools. Central office personnel presented their plans as curricular innovations, although some local schools had kept the earlier classes going. The Burke School taught Navajo weaving until 1929, when the instructor married and resigned. The central office typically cast its development of Native arts and crafts curricula as a noble but difficult effort to revive "real" Native culture that was fast disappearing or already extinct. In a 1933 radio broadcast, Director of Education Ryan stated the "one or two general principles of Indian education": to educate children "where they are" in their own setting; and "wherever there are any possible survivals of Indian life and culture we are trying to maintain them" (NARA, Entry 177, 1933).

Federal authority and expertise were reinforced even as Native art was accorded a place—again—in the schools. Carrie Lyford, Associate Supervisor of Indian Education, authored several pamphlets in the Bureau's Indian Handcrafts series. In "The Use of Indian Designs in the Government Schools" (1931), she opined that "in a very few cases" students might be able to produce designs of their own tribe, but she was "certain" if the teacher gave them this opportunity before teaching "some of the good designs that are already available," they would be disappointed. Government experts, working from anthropological texts, could produce a finer array of design possibilities than Native students, and federal control was assumed essential to the continued life of Native crafts production. Figure 4.1 graphically illustrates the non-Native authority and the literal "oversight" over Native arts production felt necessary to render it safe.

The Indian Handcrafts Series included pamphlets on Navajo dyes, Seneca basketry, Ojibwe and Iroquois crafts, and Pueblo embroidery. The introduction to the series acknowledged that the "neglect" of Native arts was in part due to deliberate federal attempts to destroy all "pagan" expressions but celebrated current federal efforts to "revive" and "perfect" the arts.

If Native arts were going to survive as viable cultural expressions, the federal government made sure the credit did not go to Native ingenuity or persistence. Authors such as Lyford drew on museum collections, "supplemented by such information as could be provided by the older Indians on the reservations" (Lyford, n.d., p. 9). Museum experts and anthropologists, not Native people, reviewed the manuscripts for accuracy. The pamphlets reproduced line drawings of design elements (by Bureau employee Albert van

Figure 4.1. "Basketweaving Competition." Bureau of Indian Affairs *Annual Report* 1932, p. 86. National Archives & Records Center.

der Loo) but provided no Indigenous design names, aesthetic principles, or cultural context or meaning.

Despite the federal penchant for centralized control, local practitioners of Native arts did find allies in the schools. The Native basketry classes begun on the Pima Agency in the 1930s provided a window of opportunity for local weavers. As late as 1946, Women's Club members and girls from the Salt River Day School set out on a three-day "Willow Trek" to gather willow for basket-making. The reservation superintendent at Sacaton requested the school farm to butcher a small pig to help feed the group on their outing (NARA/LN, Entry 121, CCF Pima Indian Agency, 1945–1946).

[handwritten: Revival of Native Arts + Crafts]

[handwritten margin notes: ① Success in the southwest; 6 year program; Why the SW have Arts + Crafts and not other tribes/ones]

The "Special" Tribes of the Southwest

Bureau staff viewed a few southwestern tribes as authentically gifted artists with authentic connections to culture. As selected lullabies and crafts had stood for the safe expression of Indian culture in earlier eras, selected tribes represented "authentic" Indian-ness. As a result, southwestern schools were often the most successful in integrating arts and crafts into their curriculum.

In 1935 the Albuquerque Indian School's home economics department submitted a proposal for a 6-year program, including Indian arts and crafts, open to all students. From offerings in Pueblo weaving and embroidery, Pueblo pottery, kitchen pottery, and Navajo weaving, each girl could select "the craft which is native to her tribe" (NARA, Entry 724, 1935). Examples of the curricular integration found here but not typical at other schools included using yucca roots to wash wool and goat skins in the laundry classes; using Native foods and cooking techniques; and the construction, care, and cost of Native clothing.

The recognition of the Southwest as a "special" region rested on perceptions of culture and economic realities. At a meeting of southwestern reservation superintendents in the late 1940s, Robert L. Bennett, then training specialist for the Veterans Administration, reported on congressional intent to terminate the federal trust responsibility and relationship with tribes. Bennett voiced a concern over differential impacts on tribes based on their perceived Indian-ness: "We have the Pueblo people and others who have a culture; then we have Indians like the Dakotas," who by clear implication had none (NARA/LN, Entry 121, CCF Pima Agency Files, 1926–1946).

Bennett was not the only federal employee to privilege southwestern Native "authenticity." The Bureau's Salt Lake City home extension office in the 1930s employed seven women as home extension agents on seven reservations. These seven field agents provided "exhibits, photos, film strips, and drawings" to help revive high-quality Native crafts, since they had noticed that the majority of Indian people were too poor to keep valuable pieces and so had never seen "good specimens" (NARA, Entry 785, 1931). All sample photos and program materials came from the Southwest, including Pima baskets; Maricopa pottery; and Navajo weavings, silver jewelry, and sand paintings.

Community Reaction to Arts and Crafts Instruction

Documentary evidence from the 1930s and 1940s provides few clues to the reaction of Native students, parents, or communities to the arts and crafts classes introduced during this period. We know students enrolled; we know some Native artisans found employment for a time in the schools. They may have been aware of difficulties that remained invisible to most Bureau employees. Ruth Muskrat Bronson (1944) recalled this from a conversation with a Native friend who taught at a mission school:

> They asked me to teach tanning here at the school. But I don't feel that I ought to do that because I never had the tanning ceremony. . . . Of course, I know how to tan, but they [my people] gave the tanning ceremony to my sister. To me they gave the beading ceremony. That is why I am able to do beadwork so well. (p. 179)

Teaching NA arts + crafts a tribal ceremony issue

The instruction in Native arts developed by the Bureau during this era did not recognize this kind of conundrum. Schooling, even in allegedly Native content, was too decontextualized from Indigenous frameworks of meaning and transmission of knowledge, too much a product of non-Native experts accustomed to isolating "traits" for study, too subject to the control and power of even the most well-intentioned federal employees.

THE KEYSTONE OF CONTROL: REFORMS VERSUS BUSINESS AS USUAL

Even as Collier encouraged some aspects of Native political self-government and economic self-determination, the presumed efficacy of federal control over Indian social and cultural lives remained in the forefront of federal policies and practices. Collier valued some Native cultures he viewed as "intact," such as that of the southwestern Pueblos, but did not recognize "authentic" culture elsewhere. In a 1934 memo, Collier reminded Indian Service employees that economic depression devastated Indians even more than Whites because "Indian life, in most areas, is practically without organization and is dependent on the government services if it is to become organized" (NARA, Entry 723, 1934). He referred to the Indian Reorganization Act (IRA) he was muscling through Congress, which would enable tribes to form federally recognized governments if they were willing to "organize" themselves on the constitutional model Collier found most appropriate. It is clear, however, that the rest of the Bureau did not share Collier's vision of self-determining tribes.

The introduction of the IRA

Education Director Ryan argued that "the Indian can not and should not remain the concern of the National Government. Sooner or later all Indians . . . will become participating citizens of the state and local community as well as of the United States" (NARA, Entry 723, 1931). It is impossible to tell from the context if Ryan meant Indians would exercise the multiple citizenships we see today—as tribal, state, and federal citizens—or whether he felt Indian individuals should surrender tribal citizenship and tribes should surrender their government-to-government relationship with the U.S. government. In either case, it appears Ryan was walking a fine line between federally mandated responsibilities for Indian affairs and the "normal" responsibilities of states to provide for public education.

Within the federal Indian school system, the centralizing control of the Washington office remained paramount, despite the Meriam Report's call for locally meaningful school curricula. The off-reservation and larger on-reservation boarding schools were required to submit plans for "reorganization" (tribes were not the only entities Collier was intent on restructuring), and those plans had to be cleared through a committee in the Indian Office (NARA, Entry 724, 1935).

Field staff often proposed to continue old practices, not institute new ones. Faculty from the Pima Indian Agency used the rhetoric popular among Collier's staff to argue against, not for, Native language use in the schools. "We don't want him [the student] to forget anything that belongs to the tradition of his people," but the students' only chance to practice English is in school, where English use must be insisted upon (NARA/LN, Entry 121, CCF Pima Indian Agency, 1945). Faculty across the Service negotiated between policy directives and the practices they felt "must" carry on. At Chilocco, graduates were offered leases on small homes and agricultural plots in the Subsistence Homestead Project. The superintendent persuaded Washington that the leases must include understandings about "hangers-on or visitors" in order "to protect the homesteader from being a victim of the accepted pattern of Indian hospitality" (NARA, Entry 121, CCF Chilocco 360, 1934). The "understandings," he continued, would have to be handled delicately, as "we must not squelch this fine social trait entirely; but it must be controlled" (NARA, Entry 121, CCF Chilocco 360, 1934).

Indian Cultures as Pathological, not Productive

Control was key, masked in the guise of protecting Native people from their own "fine" social traits; the four homestead wives who spoke little English had to be guarded against "clanning" together, which they would "naturally" do because of their "language handicap and the consequent feeling of inferiority" (NARA, Entry 121, CCF Chilocco 360, 1934). There was no sense that Native language fluency might contribute to a productive community or a sense of superiority. Chilocco's plans to control young Native families on homestead plots were pursued at other reservation venues (NARA, Entry 121, CCF Pima 800, 1939). A principal at Salt River Consolidated School in Arizona suggested to the reservation superintendent in 1939 that they start a homestead "colony" similar to the ones at Chilocco and Phoenix Indian School. His rationale reminds us how useful the schools were, as controlled environments, for accomplishing federal goals. He noted that setting up homesteads as a school project made it possible to avoid the tribal consent process.

Indian Service field personnel more often than not projected a jaundiced view of Native life. A report from the Pima Agency told the tale: "Life on the Indian reservations is usually barren to the point of social desolation because of the restrictions on traditional activities and the breaking down of such without the opportunity or direction for building up others more appropriate" (NARA, Entry 724, 1931). "Traditional activities," according to this report, *had* to be broken down and replaced.

Indians as Unfit Parents

In the Pacific Northwest, poverty was "due to lack of resourcefulness rather than to lack of resources" (Stewart, 1934). A report on schooling on the Siletz Reservation in Oregon blamed the "retardation" of students who fell behind on

> irregularity of attendance. The reasons for this are as numerous as the ills and weaknesses that beset our whole social structure on the Indian reservations. . . . The economic handicaps, the moral and social irresponsibility, the entire lack of ambition for the children . . . that now characterizes the average Indian family. (NARA, Entry 724, 1934)

Clearly this employee did not share Collier's rosy view of the strengths and resources of select Native cultures. Natives who had been raised in boarding schools were defined as unfit parents when their children were to be enrolled in day schools and allowed to live at home. Corroboration came from Lac du Flambeau, where the superintendent hired a social worker to help the women get ready, since "for the first time in their lives they will have to undertake the responsibility of the care of children of school age throughout the year" (ARCIA, 1932, p. 5).

Military Discipline Replaced by "Character Education"

Social life within the schools continued to be highly regimented, in direct contravention of Meriam Report recommendations, even though military uniforms and drills were phased out. The "character education" that had dominated the schools in the early decades of the century continued to set the standards of civilized living to which Indian students should aspire. Haskell's overall goals remained "the development of the thousands of little courtesies that so make an individual as a lady or a gentleman . . . health and sanitation . . . use of leisure time . . . good sportsmanship . . . wise thrift habits and self-reliance" (NARA, Entry 724, 1933).

The Haskell matrons, newly renamed "housemothers" in 1933, sent out "reminders" to the Haskell girls about the "little courtesies" necessary to the development of young ladies, along with lists of questions to be considered at the students' weekly lodge meetings. Reminders for the week of November 20, 1933, asked "Whom shall I call friend?"

> Do I owe friendship to girls who are unworthy?
> What type of girl is a friend of Haskell?
> What shall my attitude be toward a girl who is common, cheap, vulgar, and unreliable?
> Shall I extend my courtesies to girls who have forfeited their rights to stay at Haskell?
>
> (NARA, Entry 724, 1933)

Reminders in early December lamented the "let-up in the tone of the dining room" because the girls had not stood dutifully and quietly in their assigned places—and a week later forcefully put the girls in their place:

> There are pending some revisions in the rules with regard to your privileges. Whether you are granted more rests entirely with you. The attitude you take in the next few weeks with regard to those you already have will be the deciding factor. Just how much liberty can you stand? (NARA, Entry 724, 1933)

That same year the Haskell guidance reports included a copy of "our Bible of courtesie [sic] and manners observed in dining halls," submitted by "the young men of Keokuk and Osceola Halls" (NARA, Entry 724, 1933). More than four pages of legal-size, single-spaced typed pages listed meticulous, rigid instructions regarding seating, placement of silverware, arrangement of food on the plate, and this nursery rhyme about table manners:

> The goops they lick their fingers,
> And the boops they lick their knives;
> They spill their broth on the tablecloth—
> Oh, they lead disgusting lives!
>   (NARA, Entry 724, 1933)

The rhyme was followed by the reminder that "eating is not very attractive, but a good time for meeting and greeting your friends. . . . The unattractive part of eating should be made as inconspicuous as possible" (NARA, Entry

724, 1933). Students were instructed to behave in the most modest, quiet, decorous, formal, and controlled way, with 25 minutes to complete their meal. Remarkably, alumni of the federal boarding schools enrolled during these years recall with great relish the loosening of military discipline and transformations in the dining halls; boys and girls were now allowed to sit together at table, rather than on opposite sides of the room!

Native People Persevere

Despite the denigrating paternalism of the federal bureaucracy, Native peoples soldiered on, using every bit of leverage and sliver of opportunity to determine their own lives. The first high school graduates of the Salt River Community Vocational High School in Arizona, one of the community-based high schools constructed under Collier's tenure, spoke clearly in support of local concerns. The graduation speeches of Harvey Schurz, Ernest Antone, Joseph Thomas, and Leonard Juan all focused on water (NARA, Entry 121, CCF Pima 800, 1939). The Salt River reservation is shared by Pima (Akimel O'odham) and Maricopa (Xalychidom Piipaash) peoples; their water had been diverted by dams and White farmers, and by 1939 the government was promising a new irrigation canal to restore the agricultural prosperity that Salt River had enjoyed before the diversions.

In the service of Salt River, these young men strategically employed the schools' curricular emphases on Native history and culture instituted in the Collier years. Leonard Juan highlighted American Indian contributions to world civilization, such as domesticated crops and outstanding Indian Americans, such as Will Rogers, Dr. Charles Eastman, and Jim Thorpe. Ernest Antone focused on the agricultural heritage of Native peoples in southern Arizona, stretching from the ancient Hohokam to the contemporary Pima. He vigorously asserted the rights and responsibilities of Indian people to work out ensuing challenges themselves:

> The water is ours. It is only up to us to use that water to the best possible advantage. How will we distribute the water? Shall we go against hundreds of years of traditions and allow some people to become huge land owners while others go practically landless? Although we have had much good advice on this problem from our good friend, Mr. Shipe [Special Assistant to the Director of Irrigation], it is still our problem to solve as we see fit. (NARA, Entry 121, CCF Pima 800, 1939)

Joseph Thomas enumerated the school's contributions to the community, concluding with this stirring statement of the benefits possible from a mutually enriching school–community relationship:

Joseph Tomes
Grad. Speech

Is there anyone here who has not felt proud when someone has said, "You're from Salt River? Fine school you have out there. Nice group of people, too." Do you realize how much the school has done to advertise your reservation? Do you realize how much it does daily in increasing the pride of your people in their reservation? Do you realize that it helps to make you proud that you are a Pima or a Maricopa? (NARA, Entry 121, CCF Pima 800, 1939)

CONCLUSION

We have seen that Collier's vision of tribal self-determination was flawed by his inability to see the true strengths of many tribal communities; it was also hampered by resistance from Bureau personnel and by the persistence of entrenched stereotypes about the pathologies of Native cultures and deficiencies of Native individuals. Despite these limitations, boundaries around the safety zone were substantially redrawn during the 1930s and early 1940s, as expressions of Native identity, language, and heritage gained a toehold in the schools and in limited arenas of reservation politics.

Native students, teachers, parents, and community members sustained a vision of cooperation between family and school through many decades of federal paternalism and control. They carved out spaces of Indian-ness when and where they could, stood ready to take action when opportunities presented themselves, and strengthened the resources they would draw upon in future battles. The next chapter examines the "window of opportunity" for bilingual education the Indian Bureau created under the direction of Commissioner Collier and the ways that Native communities built upon the promises embodied in early federal attempts to utilize Native languages in the schools.

CHAPTER 5

Control of Culture: Federally Produced Bilingual Materials, 1936–1954

As progressive educational policies and ideals of cultural pluralism increasingly influenced the work of the Bureau's education division in the 1930s and 1940s, the boundaries between safe and dangerous cultural difference shifted, although the tension between the two remained.[1] Close examination of the remarkable bilingual *Indian Life Readers* produced by the Bureau through the 1940s reveals the shifting values of policymakers and the windows of opportunity for Native-language use that were opened and then closed as far as policymakers were concerned.

By the 1950s, Native people had taken advantage of those windows of opportunity; we will see in the Navajo example later in this chapter and in Chapter 6 how Native educators were producing materials that expressed authentic Indigenous voices and perspectives long after federal policy had changed. Once again we catch glimpses of the creative and persistent efforts of Native peoples and their allies to indigenize schools. Their efforts have percolated throughout the last century of Indian education and led in circuitous, often barely recognizable or documented ways, to the better-known trends in Indian educational self-determination of the last few decades.

Two key players in the production of the *Indian Life Readers* were Willard Walcott Beatty, director of the education division from 1936 to 1952, and Ann Nolan Clark, the Indian Service teacher who wrote many of the readers in collaboration with Native translators and illustrators. The books are fascinating amalgams, bits and pieces of Native cultural practices, settings, and values embedded in a matrix of a persistently colonial, Eurocentric worldview that for many of these books organizes the narrative and reinforces the ongoing messages of assimilationist education that never completely disappeared between the Meriam Report and World War II. Analysis of the ambivalent nature of the Pueblo, Navajo, and Lakota *Life Readers* shows the difficulty encountered by well-meaning proponents of cultural pluralism as they charted their course through the unfamiliar territories of bilingual education in American Indian languages.

In attempts to value and preserve "worthy" aspects of Native cultures and languages, the Bureau veered and tacked between shifting notions of safe and dangerous cultural difference, just as earlier colleagues had searched for innocent lullabies and salable crafts to elevate as safe markers of Indian identity. As in earlier decades, issues of power and control over cultural production firmly grounded federal experiments in bilingual education. Native language was made safe by the thorough control of non-Native employees and academic experts who dictated storylines and evaluated translations.

Gloria Emerson (Diné), former director of the Native American Materials Development Center, has astutely noticed the "refined forms of colonization" embodied by the *Life Readers*, books that were "blatantly intended to acculturate Indians 'humanely' by gently guiding them away from the values of their own society and toward the Protestant work ethic" (2004, pp. xi–xii). Some examples from the readers were more blatantly assimilationist than others; we believe the range of cultural attitudes expressed in the various volumes can best be understood by examining the readers as milestones of Beatty and Clark's journey as they tried to track "safe," "worthy" aspects of Native cultures through the then-uncharted wilderness of Native bilingual education.

We carefully describe and compare the themes of each reader, the "tone" of the English in bilingual and English-only versions, and the character of the translation in a few select examples. Most of the readers were first composed by Clark in English and then translated into Navajo, Lakota, or Spanish; the Hopi readers were an exception to this rule and merit special attention as vibrant expressions of Hopi literature. We conclude by tracing the continued production of Navajo-language materials through the 1950s, after the Bureau had backed away from the sympathetic attitudes of the New Deal era and its immediate aftermath.

The 1950s have long been seen as a decade of significant federal policy changes, when the so-called policy pendulum swung back toward cultural intolerance and Congress legislated termination of tribal status and relocation of Native populations to urban areas. In the small arena of Navajo-language materials, however, local practice passed under the radar of national policy shifts, and the team of Robert Young, an academically trained linguist, and William Morgan, a native Navajo speaker and equally gifted linguist, produced materials that were profoundly Navajo in style and content and radically different from the readers of the Beatty/Clark era.

WILLARD WALCOTT BEATTY AND ANN NOLAN CLARK

In 1936, Beatty, a "dynamic and forceful personality," replaced Will Ryan Jr. as director of education within the Indian Service (Prucha, 1984, p. 978). Like Ryan, who authored the Meriam Report education chapter, Beatty was nationally prominent in the progressive education movement, serving as president of the Progressive Education Association in the 1930s (Prucha, 1984). Under several commissioners beginning with John Collier, Beatty pursued the goals articulated by Collier and Ryan, closing down boarding schools where possible, shifting resources to day schools, upgrading teacher training, and working with public schools (Prucha, 1984; Szasz, 1977). Two particular achievements were Beatty's institution of a bimonthly newsletter, *Indian Education*, for BIA teachers and staff, and development of bilingual readers (although a few were produced in English-only versions) for targeted Native communities: Navajo, Hopi, Lakota, and Pueblo. (At the time of extension of U.S. jurisdiction over the Southwest in the 1850s, the Native pueblos [Spanish for "towns"] of New Mexico spoke different languages—Tiwa, Tewa, Towa, Zuni, and Keres—as well as Spanish; the readers in the series were produced in English and Spanish.)

Beatty seemed to respect many aspects of Native life, even religious practices, at least the Puebloan practices that had attracted many reformers of the 1920s. He termed Zuni prayers "poetry" and compared Pueblo ritual favorably with the European pageantry of the Middle Ages (Beatty, 1950). Beatty (1950) believed that decades of overly paternalistic federal control had sapped the initiative of Native peoples and that the education division bore a particular responsibility to "make self-supporting and self-respecting citizens out of the young Indians in the Federal schools," especially those "handicapped" by a lack of fluency in English (p. 45). In the *Indian Education* newsletters, Beatty (1953) articulated his vision of American Indian education: It should not require Native people to sacrifice racial pride or identity but assist them to master the intellectual and manual skills, as well as the necessary "elements in [Anglo American] cultural behavior," to successfully transition into White society (p. 11).

In some ways Beatty (1953) extended earlier goals of transforming Native citizens into generically "Americanized" ones; in other ways, he espoused radically different ideals of humane treatment of students and "full appreciation of the Indian view point and Indian culture, including native arts and crafts, music, and religious ceremonials" (p. 13). The articles published in *Indian Education*, many by Beatty's own hand but also written by teachers, public school administrators, anthropologists, and lawyers, sent unfamiliar messages to Indian Service personnel. Newsletters stressed the importance of maintaining federal responsibilities in Indian affairs because the states had been hostile to Indian nations and argued that assimilation did not justify dispossessing Native peoples of their lands.

Beatty's Progressive Ideals

Beatty proposed other new ideas in Indian education. Indian families possessed the rights of all Americans to raise their own children. Education should build on a child's experiences and not criticize or constantly correct what the child knows. Mutual respect was necessary for cultural pluralism domestically as well as internationally—"Internationalism cannot mean submission to one major culture" (Beatty, 1953, p. 116). In the pages of the newsletter, linguist Robert Young wrote that "native languages have come to be recognized, not as encumbrances and impediments to . . . progress . . . but as definite tools already at hand to be fitted into the educational program" to "facilitate and accelerate the learning of the English language" (quoted in Beatty, 1953, p. 409).

Young's assertion reveals the tension that remained at the core of federal educational policy. Beatty eschewed the necessity, demanded by earlier policymakers, that Native identities, languages, and cultures be erased. His safety zone was considerably larger and did not demand the eradication of Indigenous life. He could appreciate Zuni prayer as poetry, but he envisioned a Zuni bilingual education designed to lead to English fluency and inevitable transition into White American life. Beatty and progressive educators of his time did not envision a "maintenance" bilingualism and biculturalism that would actively preserve, vitalize, and renew Native cultures into the future.

The safety zone espoused by Beatty and his compatriots was a nostalgia-infused arena in which selected Native traits were "respected," even admired, but were not a basis for guiding Native life into the future. The key concept that did strengthen during Beatty's administration was a demand for humane treatment of Native students and peoples; it was a critical advance and a legacy for future generations.

Innovations in BIA Classrooms: Bilingual Readers

Beatty envisioned a series of third-grade bilingual readers illustrated by Native artists, and he recruited Indian Service teachers, linguists, Native translators, and non-Native "experts" on Indian cultures to help realize his dream. Dorothy Dunn, art instructor at the Santa Fe Indian School, agreed to help find young artists. Ann Nolan Clark, an Indian Service teacher with experience at Zuni and Tesuque Pueblos in New Mexico, wrote many of the readers.

Influenced by progressive education ideals of building on children's knowledge and responding to the policy goals endorsed by Commissioner Collier and his appointees, teachers and administrators in the Indian Service experimented in the 1930s with "booklets written and illustrated by their students" (Benes, 2004, p. 25). Clark's day school students at Tesuque Pueblo put together such a book, *Third Grade Home Geography*, and Beatty helped convince Viking Press to publish it as *In My Mother's House* (Clark, 1941a), illustrated by Velino Herrero (Zia), an accomplished Native artist then teaching painting at Albuquerque Indian School (Benes, 2004).

Ann Nolan (1896–1995), born and raised in New Mexico, graduated from New Mexico State Highlands University in 1919 with a degree in education. In 1920 she married Thomas Clark and they had one son, who tragically was killed in World War II. A substitute teacher working at Tesuque Pueblo, she was recruited in 1920 to teach in the Indian Service, and she spent 42 years as a teacher, an agency supervisor, and a writer, producing 20 books, many during Beatty's tenure. She continued an active publishing career in children's literature after her retirement in 1962 (Clark Papers). The year she retired, she spoke at a meeting of the Texas Association of School Librarians, describing the "treasures" she had learned from Indian peoples, the "priceless valuables of heritage," including tolerance, courage, and faith.

Tolerance, Clark related, she learned as a young teacher at Tesuque, where her small son and his cousin desecrated a shrine. She described her horror when she realized what they had done and the trepidation with which she approached the Pueblo's governor. To her surprise, she and her son were forgiven the transgression, given their ignorance and her sincere apology. The generosity and kindness she experienced at Tesuque profoundly affected Clark:

> I believe that acceptance of people by people is not built with words nor treaties nor resolutions for coexistence. It is built upon tolerance—tolerance for other people's values. It is built upon respect—respect for the traditions and customs of other nationalities, races, and culture. It is built with sharing—sharing of experiences of the tangibles and intangibles of everyday living among the peoples of the world. (1969, p. 115)

Clark dedicated much of her life to the Indian Service, to Indian children, and to the Indian communities who welcomed her with kindness, generosity, and tolerance. She scratched together resources at Tesuque Day School so her five third graders could print their own book—they called themselves the Tesuque Printers—because she joined Beatty in his firm belief that "Indian children have the right to identify with children in books. But there had been no books" (Clark, 1969, p. 11). Like Beatty, Clark expressed both progressive and traditional notions about Indian people and Indian education through her work.

Assimilation: Business as Usual in BIA Classrooms

Clark's books jumbled and juxtaposed Native settings, experiences, and values with assimilationist messages stressing cleanliness and submission to federal authority, the importance of school, and English fluency. Clark invented plot lines and used Anglo American narrative structures rather than turn to Indigenous literatures; she wanted to write stories from an Indian point of view but consulted non-Native anthropologists, linguists, and "experts" as authorities. Our analysis of her books (and those by other authors) that follows is not intended to fault Beatty or Clark or to judge them by the standards of another era. The *Life Readers* are, however, instructive barometers of their time, indicators of where the boundary lines between safe and dangerous cultural difference were being drawn.

PUEBLO LIFE READERS

In *Sun Journey* (Clark, 1945/1988; published as an English-only reader), illustrated by Percy Tsisete Sandy, Clark presented the heartwarming, but quite unlikely story of a 10-year-old Zuni boy, Ze-do, who was released from government boarding school so he could spend a year being trained by his grandfather in Zuni life and values. Clark's storyline may have reflected progressive educational ideals, but bore it no resemblance to the political reality of Native lives.

Given her false premise that a young boy would be released from school to learn at home, Clark took an interesting tack in framing her story. She presumed that the 3 years Ze-do spent in boarding school would obliterate the 7 years of Zuni socialization that came before. The first several chapters began with Ze-do comparing home conditions unfavorably with those of the school. As Chapter 1 unfolded, Ze-do thought "longingly of the big Government school. He thought of the warm beds there, where he could now be sleeping" (Clark, 1945/1988, p. 1). By Chapter 3, Clark moved Ze-do along the path to greater appreciation of home. He still missed school terrifically, but now "How important he had felt! Being excused for a whole year to receive Zuni training!" (p. 9).

Clark presented the government school, rather than Ze-do's Zuni home, as the "default environment" credited with shaping the child's expectations and sense of normalcy. This assumption makes no sense in light of what we know about Native peoples' experiences with boarding schools, and it raises the question of whom Clark saw as her primary reading audience. To think that a 10-year-old boy would be so estranged from home and so enchanted with boarding schools after 3 years seems much more a federal fantasy than a Native reality. Clark used this same framing mechanism of "moving" her central character from a primary identification with "school as home" to "home as home" in several books (Clark, 1940a, 1945/1988). Perhaps it was Clark's and Beatty's way of persuading the teachers, rather than the students, to value Native homes as highly as schools. In later years, Clark characterized the Navajo series as "my plea for teachers to understand small Navajo children. . . . I really wrote these books for teachers" (Clark Papers, "Ship's Treasures").

By Chapter 4, Clark moved Ze-do even more dramatically into his journey away from school. Walking back to the village from a shrine, Ze-do
thought longingly again of "bread and meat. He was thinking of Government School. There one ate and slept first and used the time that was left for
doing things" (Clark, 1945/1988, p. 14). Distracted, he slipped and injured
his ankle; immediately he recognized his just punishment for thinking of food
when he should be fasting. While seriously misrepresenting the schedule of
boarding school life as arranged around the comfort of students, Clark successfully led her readers toward validating Zuni home training.

By Chapter 5, "Ze-do did not think of school. It dropped from him like
a blanket not needed. Ze-do was Indian" (Clark, 1945/1988, p. 17). Clark's
imagery seems calculated to shock teachers rather than reach young Indian
students, by reversing the old Indian Service cliché of the student "going back
to the blanket"; here he drops the blanket of civilization.

In Chapters 6 through 17, Clark immersed Ze-do in Zuni daily life, recounting activities that Zuni children surely could identify with: planting time,
caring for baby eagles, and the harvest. In Chapter 14, however, she inserted
a reminder of the appeal of government schooling. As the fall harvest season
approached,

> The Boarding School children went back to school. . . . Many of them cried
> when the bus came, but there was an undercurrent of excitement. . . . Even the
> youngest knew that school had its advantages. At school there was always
> enough food, and school was warm in winter. (Clark, 1945/1988, p. 53)

Children often did view school with a mixture of excitement and trepidation, but alumni tell us the excitement was more about reuniting with friends
than with the "advantages" of school life (Archuleta et al., 2000; Lomawaima, 1994). Asserting that the alleged physical comforts of school trumped
the comforts of family and home, Clark recognized one reality (the excitement of setting off for school in the fall) while imagining another, that even
the "youngest" children saw school's advantages. Boarding school histories
reveal that separation was hardest on the youngest children and that intense
homesickness often lasted much longer than "a few days" (Child, 1998;
Lomawaima, 1994).

On one level *Sun Journey* seems to welcome a broad range of Zuni life
into the fold of the safety zone, including religious beliefs and practices. We
assume the book would have afforded young Zuni readers much to enjoy
and remember (for those enrolled in boarding schools). We must remember,
however, that the premise of the book, that a young Zuni could "stop out"
from government school and return home for a year of home schooling, was
false. Even as Clark attempted, perhaps successfully, to lead her readers,

especially teachers, from valuing school to valuing Native homes, surely veteran teachers could recognize the comfort Clark offered them by promoting the advantages of school. They knew that Clark's vision of Zuni home training could not be experienced by their students. Part of what made Clark's safety zone feel safe to non-Indian readers was its political impossibility. Students would read about Zuni life presented in a positive, culturally inclusive way, but they would read about it in school; they would not have Ze-do's opportunity to live it.

The conclusions Clark drew (1945/1988) about Ze-do's year of "home schooling" reflect the circumscribed views even progressive educators had of Native cultures:

> Ze-do was happy. . . . His thoughts and his acts were fitting the patterns of Zuni living. Children in other parts of the world may receive praise for thinking differently than those about them . . . but this was not true of Zuni children. Zuni life is patterned, and Zuni children early learn to live in harmony with that pattern. They learn to think as the ancients have said they must think. . . . Ze-do did not, now, fight against things which were so. He accepted them. (p. 67)

Zuni life patterns are distinctive, encouraging cooperation, social harmony, and engagement with traditional values, but it was an error to mistake the conservatism of some Native cultures for a static pattern of unthinking, rote repetition over the ages. Cultures—or institutions—that inculcate only acceptance and submission are not viable, generative, or resourceful, and Native cultural systems are all of the latter.

Recognizing that Native cultures might hold the promise of nurturing viable life into the future lay outside the safety zone. Zuni culture could be admired as long as it was portrayed as unchanging and static—categorically of the past, not the present or future. Change and dynamism could only be associated with modern American cultural forms. Ironically, it was the federal schools, not Native homes, that trained Native people in unquestioning submission to authority (Littlefield, 1989; Lomawaima, 1994). Themes of obedience to federal authority, as well as obedience to specific policies such as livestock reduction, were repeated in the *Life Readers*, as we will see.

SIOUX LIFE READERS

In June 1943 Willard Beatty wrote a rationale for bilingual education in Native languages, and for the production of written bilingual materials, that was printed in the back of many editions of the Sioux *Life Readers*. He presented a more forceful argument for language preservation than was the norm in Indian Bureau publications, even as he clearly indicated arenas of political controversy in which the Bureau was pursuing specific agendas, such as livestock reduction and the approval of tribal governments under the 1934 Indian Reorganization Act, that were meeting resistance. About the persistence of Native languages, he wrote:

> Under ordinary conditions this need not be a matter of great concern, for it is a tendency of minority peoples everywhere who feel their culture threatened. However, at the present time, there are changes of great magnitude taking place in the Indian country. Conservation of natural resources is a vital issue in many areas, where overgrazing, water and wind erosion are rapidly destroying the fertility of the soil. In many other areas, understanding of new opportunities for Indian self-government and credit is blocked by difficulties of translation. . . . Therefore, at long last, the government which for many years made efforts to stamp out the native languages has reversed its policy, and is endeavoring through the Indian schools to increase familiarity with the written form of the languages spoken by large numbers of Indians. (Beatty, 1943, p. 90)

Although Beatty repeated that schools would remain places to learn and emphasize English, he allowed the possible survival of Native languages in the home. "The emphasis in the school will naturally be upon the English—in the home upon reading the native tongue. In this way, the young people may help educate their parents in the use of English, while the new readers assist the adults in preserving the use of the native language among their children" (Beatty, 1943, p. 91). The transmission of Native languages across generations was not often invoked as a federal goal during this era; more frequently it was assumed children would bring the readers home and they would become instruments for the older generations to learn English.

Lakota "Just-for-Fun" Stories

Beatty recruited Ann Nolan Clark as the lead writer for the Sioux *Life Readers*, even though she was not as closely acquainted with Lakota as Native conditions in New Mexico. Clark made up the stories and presented them as examples of "just-for-fun stories." Each story began:

> Just-for-fun stories
>   These are stories
>   told just for fun.
>   Teton Lakota call them
>   'Ohuŋkakaŋ.
> They are not true.
> They never were.

They never could be.
But what does it matter
in just-for-fun stories?
(Clark, 1941b, p. 1)

Harvey Markowitz, scholar of Lakota history and language at Washington and Lee University, points to Ella Deloria's *Dakota Texts* as the probable source for Clark's understanding of this class of stories, and a postscript in the readers identifies Deloria's texts as a source. According to Markowitz, Deloria described 'Ohuŋkakaŋ as tales "intended to amuse and entertain, but not to be believed" (Markowitz, personal communication, 2004). Markowitz describes an ongoing debate in Lakota studies over the "truthfulness" of these stories versus their status as profound repositories of Lakota values, but Clark probably accepted Deloria's description and appropriated 'Ohuŋkakaŋ to include her own creations intended to amuse and entertain. As Beatty's discussion of bilingual education points out, however, there was much more than simple entertainment folded into the readers. The Bureau intended them to inculcate values, especially the value of adhering to federal directives.

Clark incorporated elements of Lakota daily life and landscape into storylines that sprang from her imagination. The just-for-fun stories she created with animal characters are the most fanciful; they tell about the Pine Ridge porcupine, Slim Butte raccoon, Grass Mountain mouse, and the hen of Wahpeton. All were illustrated by Andrew Standing Soldier (Lakota) and translated by Emil Afraid of Hawk (Lakota). The two earlier stories about porcupine (Clark, 1941b) and raccoon (Clark, 1942a) are not particularly political or didactic, but the mouse (Clark, 1943a) and hen (Clark, 1943b) stories are quite explicitly so.

The raccoon from Slim Butte liked Indian farmers better than his own family, so he left home to live by their garden, imitating their clothing, speaking Lakota, and keeping time to their music. When he imitated a give-away by stealing their watermelons to give to his friends, however, the Indian farmers scolded the little raccoon, who ran home in shame. The moral of the story is to be true to one's self, concluding, "It was good to be home again, and to be a raccoon, with the other raccoons" (Clark, 1942a, p. 72).

Instructive Morals: Stay Home and Work!

Clark folded more serious agendas into her stories about the mouse and the hen. The story of the mouse from Grass Mountain addressed a concern of federal agents supervising western reservations—their wards' tendency to use federally endorsed social gatherings such as rodeos and Fourth of July celebrations to meet, mingle, and enjoy themselves. Originally proposed by federal agents to replace Indigenous social and religious dances, by the 1940s fairs and rodeos were seen as a serious threat to the Protestant work ethic that was supposed to keep people at home, toiling in fields and gardens.

The little mouse began her story as a model Lakota woman, from a federal perspective. She was quiet, always happy as she worked ceaselessly to gather and store food. Life was fine, until her relatives invited her to the rodeo. Her response could have been dictated by the reservation agent:

> Of course
>   she would not listen to them.
> She said, "Why how terrible
>   to go off rodeoing
>   when there is work
>   to be done."
>   (Clark, 1943a, p. 37)

The temptation was too great, however, and off she went.

In delightfully humorous passages, mouse underwent a transformation into a rodeo groupie, shedding her cotton housedress, moccasins, and shawl as she fashioned a paper sack into a ten-gallon hat and a leaf into a bandana. Her relatives were appalled at her decidedly unladylike behavior, from a Lakota perspective. Grass Mountain mouse followed the rodeo circuit all summer long. Finally, exhausted, she headed home, but retribution was severe: Caught in a winter storm, she fell ill. Would she freeze or starve first? Mouse was saved by a generous Lakota neighbor who nursed her back to health:

> The Grass Mountain Mouse said
>   over and over,
> "I have learned my lesson
> I am through with rodeos.
> Unless they should have them in winter."
>   (Clark, 1943a, p. 99)

Clark skillfully wielded her storytelling talents and humor to reinforce the lessons being driven home in schools and reservations, even as she described settings and relationships with which Lakota children could feel at home.

Markers of "Civilized" Living in the Life Readers

An even more outrageous character, the hen of Wahpeton, drove home similar moral lessons. An unusual incubator chick—yellow among the other white or black chicks—she was given special privileges, which turned her head. She discovered a book, *How to Be an Opera Singer in 5 Easy Lessons,* and a dream was born! Her assiduous opera practice was interpreted by her owners, the War Bonnet family, as the cackling of a hen who must be producing many, many eggs. When they invited all the neighbors to see, but no eggs were found, the proud little hen was destined for the stewpot. The other chickens tried to warn her, but she scurried around searching for a book to teach her *How to Lay an Egg in 5 Easy Lessons.*

Clark's humor helped her weave an entertaining tale; the moralizing was embedded in her descriptions of the War Bonnet family. They kept the milk cows and hens and used the technology—incubators and root cellars— promoted by agricultural agents. Root cellars, in particular, had been classified as premier markers of "civilized living" since the early 1920s. In Clark's (1943b) words, "The War Bonnet family, were very fine people. They did as they should do, and they bought what was good for them" (p. 8).

The safety zone housing Lakota activities and values promoted "civilizing" Bureau practices: raising milk cows and incubator chicks, digging root cellars, staying home and working, and supporting the new governments created under the Indian Reorganization Act, Commissioner Collier's brainchild. Beatty directed Clark that in addition to instilling "respect for Native cultures . . . the stories should reflect positive values such as hard work, thrift, frugality, and loyalty to one's identity." Beatty wanted each story to be "laid around some character of Sioux life which is in conflict with a successful economic adjustment" (Benes, 2004, p. 84). Hence the raccoon was brought low by his give-away, the mouse by her neglect of gardening, and the hen by "the tendency to live in a dream world to the neglect of reality" (Benes, 2004, p. 84). Federal policymakers still held the keys to successful economic and political adjustment on reservations.

NAVAJO LIFE READERS

Clark's *Little Herder Stories* followed a young Navajo girl through the seasons, from autumn (1940b) through winter (1942b), spring (1940c), and summer (1942c). These low-level readers presented simple, stripped-down English on the left-hand page, matched with a Navajo translation on the right-hand page. Set in Navajo country, the stories describe landscapes, family members, and daily activities familiar to Navajo children, rarely delving beneath the surface to examine religious beliefs, cultural values, or personal motivations.

When deeper issues were introduced, they usually promoted federal values and practices. In the spring reader, for example, sheep are tended, without commentary, except when the little herder's "Father says, that next year, He will try the white-man's way, of breeding the sheep. Then the lambs, will be born later, when summer has come to stay" (Clark, 1940c, p. 58). Just as no Navajo knowledge about caring for sheep is presented, land use is discussed only in terms of federal concerns over soil erosion. Her father attended agency meetings, so that "when I come here again [home], then I will know, if it is best to have many sheep, or few sheep. To use the land, or let it sleep" (p. 58). Benes (2004) found evidence that the "education division hoped, through the *Little Herder* series, to use literacy as a way to introduce this controversial subject [stock reduction] to the next generation" (p. 62).

NATIVE TRANSLATORS AND INTERPRETERS

Attending to the English portion of the *Life Readers* tells only part of the story. Larger questions remain of how the Lakota-, Navajo-, Spanish- (for the Pueblo *Life Readers*), or Hopi-language portions were translated or constructed by Native speakers and how the books were read and interpreted by Native students. These questions are much more difficult to answer, although we can catch glimpses of the ways Native peoples contributed to the creation and use of these readers. Partial as they are, the glimpses afford us clues to a developing appreciation of materials written in Native languages that provided important foundations for later Indigenous production of literacy materials.

Short commentaries by Beatty and others, published inside the readers, afford clues to the identities and roles of Native translators and illustrators. In the *Little Herder* series, Beatty described how the Navajo manuscripts were first prepared by linguist John P. Harrington and his assistant, linguistic graduate student Robert W. Young, then were checked for "colloquial correctness" by a number of Navajo speakers, including Willetto Antonio, Adolph Bitanny, Hoke Denetsosie (who illustrated the series), George Hood, Albert Sandoval, and Howard Gorman. The Sioux *Life Readers* were translated by Emil Afraid of Hawk, described by Beatty (1943) as "an experienced interpreter of the older generation" (p. 90).

The Navajo, Lakota, and Hopi *Life Readers* were produced under the supervision of Dr. Edward Kennard, who had been trained in anthropology and linguistics at Columbia, where he earned his Ph.D. studying Mandan and Siouan linguistics. According to Benes, Kennard and his wife Helen moved to Pine Ridge in 1941, where they became close friends with Ann Clark and Emil Afraid of Hawk. Edward and Helen Kennard also lived intermittently for several years at the village of Sipaulovi on the Hopi reservation, where they became close friends with the Secakuku family (Hartman Lomawaima, personal communication, 2004).

The Pueblo *Life Readers* were translated by Mrs. Jenkins, a Puerto Rican–born Spanish speaker who had lived in the Southwest "for a number of years." Her translations were "written in a simple but expressive idiom which will be clear to all who read Spanish" (Clark, 1943c, p. 55) and were reviewed by Professor Heberto Sein of Mexico; Esquípula Jojola of Isleta Pueblo, one of the original proponents of the readers; and George Sanchez, Professor of Latin American Education at the University of Texas (Clark, 1943c).

The Indian education division invested considerable time and care to ensure the accuracy and "authenticity" of its translations. All the players were involved in a complicated process, given the numbers of people involved, the groundbreaking character of their work, the widely varying experience of the English speakers with Native languages, and the difficulties of translating stories conceived in English.

Pitfalls of Word-for-Word Translation

To our knowledge, no systematic analysis of the translation processes used in the readers has been attempted. Detailed analysis across all the Native languages involved is a daunting task, which we only begin to address here. Harvey Markowitz (personal communication, 2004) does say of the Sioux *Life Readers* that "the pattern of discourse and language structure in her [Clark's] Lakota works . . . are *very* un-Lakota. In fact, the strain of the Native translator struggling to render Clark's prose into Lakota is almost palpable."

Markowitz's diagnosis of the difficulties experienced by Emil Afraid of Hawk should not surprise us, if we remember that Clark created these stories out of her own imagination and wove in elements of Lakota life, a culture with which she was not well acquainted. Translation is never a mechanical process of matching word to word. Translation is an intellectual and aesthetic challenge to reconcile unique concepts, traverse divergent ways of categorizing experience, and illuminate the unfamiliar.

The Flag of My Country: Didactic Moralizing Prevails

The following analysis of one Navajo reader, *The Flag of My Country* (King, 1956), reveals some of the ways Navajo translators were hampered by the word-for-word translation strategy that appears to have been standard Bureau practice and illustrates some of the creative ways the translators met and transcended the challenges at hand. This analysis is the work of Professor Mary Willie, Department of Linguistics, University of Arizona. Professor Willie is bilingual and biliterate in Navajo (her first language) and English. Her insights give us precious glimpses into the constraints and opportunities faced by the original translators of these stories.

Flag of My Country was produced at a later time (King, 1956) and under quite different circumstances from the readers of the Beatty/Clark era. In the 1940s the Bureau's education division established the Special Navajo Program to reach the approximately 26,000 Navajo children who had limited access to schooling. Designed to educate students 12 years and older with less than 2 or 3 years of schooling and minimal fluency in English, the program used the facilities available in the off-reservation boarding schools, such as Chilocco in Oklahoma and Carson in Nevada.

Bilingual teacher aides were important members of the teaching team in every classroom, and the Bureau realized the need to develop readers pitched to an adolescent audience rather than to the lower elementary students for whom Clark's readers had been designed. The result was the Navajo *New World Readers*, *Away to School: 'Ólta'góó* (King, 1951) and *The Flag of My Country: Shikéyah Bidah Na'at'a'í* (King, 1956). Both were authored by Cecil S. King, lead teacher in the Special Navajo Program, with Navajo translations by teacher-interpreters Ramona Smith and Marian Nez and illustrations by Franklin Kahn and Henry Bahe, students at the Carson Indian School.

By this time federal policy had shifted dramatically from the reform ideals of the post–Meriam Report era of John Collier and Willard Beatty. Collier resigned in 1945, Beatty in 1952. The former education director for the Navajo agency, Hildegard Thompson, replaced Beatty as national director of education, where she served until 1965 (Prucha, 1984). Although Thompson shared many of Beatty's progressive values, she faced a changed climate in Indian affairs. In the aftermath of World War II and the onset of the Cold War, American tolerance for cultural difference waned. Congress passed legislation, House Concurrent Resolution 102 or the Termination Bill, which aimed to terminate the federal trust responsibility and tribal entities. Commissioner of Indian Affairs Dillon S. Meyer, fresh from his assignment as director of the Japanese-American internment camps during the war years, implemented congressional programs to relocate Native populations into urban areas in a further effort to dissolve tribal identity.

The Navajo *New World Readers* reflected the tenor of their times. They lacked Clark's humor, liveliness, and details of Native life and landscape, retaining only dogmatic messages emphasizing individual and cultural transformation and obedience to federal dictates. *The Flag of My Country* chronicled the thoughts of a young Navajo man away at school, in a singularly heavy-handed attempt to foster patriotic feelings, at least in the English text. As we shall see, the Navajo text fostered a strikingly different tone and message.

In the original publication, the English text was printed first on the page, with Navajo text beneath and following it. We have tried to reproduce here the way phrases were printed on the page, but we have put the Navajo text to the right of the English to facilitate comparison.

"I am a Navajo boy	"*Naabehó 'ashkii nishłí*
This is my home	*Díí shighan 'át'é*
My home is in Arizona	*Arizona bii' shighan*
Arizona is in the United States.	*Arizona 'éí kéyah dízdiin dóó ba'aan tseebíí sinilígíí bii'.*
The United States is my country."	*Kéyah dízdiin dóó ba'aan tseebíí sinilígíí shikéyah'át'é."*
	(King, 1956b, pp. 1–2, 4–5)

The penultimate Navajo phrase translates as "Arizona is one of the 48 things," establishing an immediate dichotomy of tone between English and Navajo texts that permeates the entire reader. The English text is unrelenting, almost strident, in its essentialized patriotism, asserting one-to-one connections between national homeland and family, possessions, and personal identity.

The Navajo text lacks all connotations of patriotism and in comparison seems flatly descriptive. Several Navajo words and phrases utilized throughout the text, however, are deeply evocative of a Navajo sense of identity and of sacred landscape as homeland. We can only imagine how, why, and by whom these words were chosen, but one wonders if there was a conscious translation of the Bureau's inculcation of national patriotism into a more locally and personally meaningful sense of "Navajo-ness."

Navajo Country Versus "My Country." The translation of "The United States is my country" is illustrative of this process. "*Shi kéyah*" can be broken down into *shí*, first-person possessive, and *kéyah*, "land," but in normal usage, the latter term does not mean "nation-state." "*Shi kéyah*" is the common term for "my land" or "my country," from a very personal perspective, thinking of one's own property or immediate surroundings; in common usage, *Diné bikeyah* would refer to "Navajo land" or "Navajo country," the landscape ordained in the creation stories, whose boundaries are demarcated by the four sacred mountains central to Navajo philosophy and life. Neither term would ordinarily be used to refer to "the outside," the rest of the country outside "Navajo country."

"I look at my flag. (p. 7)	"*Shi dah na'at'a'í nish'į́.*
I think of my home." (p. 8)	*Shighan baa nitséskees."*

In the second couplet reproduced above, the English carries no under-tone of patriotism or emotion in the act of "thinking," but the Navajo verb translates "I am thinking and wondering about my home, as if from a lonely distance." The word for "my home," *shigan*, is a very literal reference to a person's physical home dwelling—their *hooghan*—not to a nation-state or geographical area. Just think of the young person reading this book in board-ing school, far away from home and lonely. Surely these word choices would resonate with their situation.

④ **Assertion of Native Knowledge and Rights.** In the next example, the Navajo verb carries profound implications of Navajo knowledge and mas-tery of herding skills.

"I think of the sheep.	"*Dibé baa nitséskees.*
I take care of the sheep.	*Dibé baa 'áháshyá.*
I can herd the sheep." (p. 10)	*Shí na'nishkaad yiishchííh.*"

The English verb *can* might imply either the freedom or permission to do something or the personal ability to do something. The Navajo verb *yishchííh*, however, means much more. *Yishchííh,* "knowing the craft of something," implies mastery of a set of knowledge, that one knows well a method for doing something. In the case of herding sheep, the herder knows where the grass is, when and where to move the sheep, the sheep's nature and their personalities. The translator appears to have carefully chosen a word that foregrounds the depth and complexity of knowledge a young Navajo herder would be expected to have mastered.

On the next page, the Navajo text makes a veiled criticism of the re-moval of children from home to attend school; of course the criticism was invisible to English readers.

"My school is far from my home.	"*Ííníshta' dóó 'éí shighan doo deeghání da.*
My school is off the reservation." (p. 19)	*Naabeehó bikéyah bits'ą́ą́di 'ííníshta'.*"

Bits'ą́ą́di, the word used to translate "far" off the reservation, away from it, indicates a place so far away that one would not ordinarily attempt to go there. An analogy in English would be for an Arizonan to refer to France rather than Phoenix; it is outside the range of normal travel. It also is a "malefactive" word in Navajo; while a "benefactive" word implies a beneficial effect, *bits'ą́ą́di* implies a loss or negative effect. It is used in constructions in which something is being taken away from someone, with a sense of loss or being lost, and could conceivably have been chosen to criticize the removal of children from their homes.

LEGACIES OF THE FIRST TRANSLATORS

Perhaps future research will uncover the strategies and intentions of translators such as Marian Nez and Ramona Smith. Hopefully we will one day learn much more about the reasons Emil Afraid of Hawk and other translators chose or were constrained to make awkward, word-for-word translations. Perhaps we will never know; their stories may be among the many Native stories that have slipped beyond our grasp (Scott Momaday, personal communication, 2004). Even so, the texts give us clues to cherish and ponder as we endeavor to trace the presence of Native speakers, thinkers, collaborators, and educators through the decades when documentary records tell us less than we would wish to know.

The Special Navajo Program employed dozens of Native speakers who gained valuable experience as teachers, interpreters, writers, and Indian Bureau employees. Even those Native people peripherally involved with production of the Indian *Life Readers*—the boys working in the print shops of Chilocco and Phoenix Indian Schools—might have been inspired by the possibilities for Native languages indicated by the readers. The bilingual education materials produced by the Bureau in the 1930s and 1940s may seem dated or flawed to us now, but in their time they were remarkable harbingers of new possibilities, new visions for Indian education. They laid a foundation that later generations built on, directly or indirectly, as Native people increasingly "took hold" of the local processes and mechanisms of Indian education, important steps in the journey toward increasing self-determination at the levels of educational policymaking and control.

The story of the Hopi *Life Readers* and the story of the continued production of Navajo-language materials after Beatty, during the Cold War era of Hildegard Thompson's tenure as education director, are important pieces of what came next in this century-long story of American Indian education.

NEW DEVELOPMENTS IN BILINGUAL MATERIALS

When Hartman Lomawaima was a young boy growing up on the Hopi reservation at Sipaulovi village, Second Mesa, he attended Toreva Day School.[2] His mother, Elsa Setima Lomawaima, taught there part time. In the early

1950s, the 2 years she had completed at business college in Phoenix provided the credentials necessary to be hired as a teacher. Elsa read her students the Hopi stories published by the Indian Office education division in the 1940s' Pueblo *Life Reader* series, *Little Hopi Hopihoya* (Kennard, 1948) and *Field Mouse Goes to War* (Kennard, 1944). Hartman laughs as he recites from memory, in Hopi, what he recalls as the first line of the field mouse story: "*Ephaqam Musangnup sinom kyahak yeese*"—"At that time in our history, the people of Misongnovi were living very rich!" He remembers his disbelief hearing that remarkable statement about rich Hopis. The storyteller had done the job; the listening children were caught up.

We do not know the full story behind the production of the Hopi readers, but Hartman's memories afford insights into the circumstances that may have contributed to their distinctiveness, compared to the Navajo and Lakota readers. The Hopi books lack the heavy-handed assimilationist moralizing embedded in the Lakota readers (Avoid rodeos!) and the Navajo readers' inclusion of earnest experts' advice (dip sheep!). The Hopi readers also appear to have been constructed as two parallel stories—one in Hopi, one in English—rather than using the painstaking (and sometimes painful) word-for-word translation that Markowitz and Willie perceive in the other readers. What might have made the difference?

Hartman Lomawaima was born in 1949, into the Bear clan of Sipaulovi village. When he was a small child, his parents, Harvey and Elsa Setima Lomawaima, ran a small store close to Toreva spring, just below the mesa's edge on the road leading up to the neighboring villages of Sipaulovi and Misongnovi. His mother's parents, Anna Mae Secakuku and Ben Setima, directed his upbringing. So, he recalls, his family was the typical multigenerational, multicultural Hopi family: "kid, parents, grandparents, and resident anthropologist—that was Ed Kennard." When Ed and Helen Kennard first came to Hopi, they lived at Misongnovi village, but quickly became close to a number of Bear clan Sipaulovis: the renowned storyteller Frank Masaquaptewa, who would become *kikmongwi* (village "chief") in his seventies, and the sisters Anna Mae and Elsie Secakuku, who helped Dr. Kennard learn the Hopi language. Hartman remembers that he did not know that Helen's (English) name was Helen until much later; he knew her by her Hopi name, the jokingly affectionate Kenahwùuti, a play on *Kennard* meaning "beautiful, attractive woman." As a professionally trained anthropologist, Dr. Kennard had a keen scholarly interest in Hopi culture; as friends who were welcomed into Hopi families, he and his wife respected Hopi people and their knowledge.

We do not know who originally narrated or created the field mouse story; perhaps it was Frank Masaquaptewa, or Frank and Ed Kennard working together. The publication credits Albert Yava as translator; a Tewa from First Mesa, Yava was a proficient linguist in his own right, fluent in at least three languages—Tewa, Hopi, and English. He is credited as translator in a variety of contexts, from the Hopi readers to printed transcripts of tribal council meetings.

Field Mouse Goes to War tells the story of the field mouse who is moved by the sorrow of his Misongnovi neighbors, distraught over a hawk's depredations of their chickens. Field mouse prepares himself as would a Hopi warrior and successfully slays the "monster hawk." Illustrated by Hopi artist Fred Kabotie, field mouse is arrayed in a warrior's face and body paint, kilt, and regalia, with an arsenal of bow, shield, and war club. Hartman Lomawaima offers this analysis of the Hopi title of the story, *Tusan Homichi Tuwvöta*. *Tusan* means "unwashed" or "unkempt," from *tusna*, the dirt that accumulates on skin; *homichi* is not a specific term for "mouse," but a generic term for "rodent"; *tuwvöta* conjures the image of brandishing a warrior's shield, issuing a challenge, the act of declaring war.

As the Hopi story unfolds, the storyteller employs several devices to engage the listener's attention. Although it is not in fact the first line, the assertion of "Rich Misongnovis!" that young Hartman found so unbelievable appears on the first page. The Hopi version, however, has an element of suspense that the English lacks. Both versions begin with extensive descriptions of the people's wealth—their store of corn, beans, squash, and melons—and their deep concern over the hawk killing their precious chickens. On page 15, the English version names the "little field mouse [who] lived on the south side of the village. He heard all about all the trouble the Mishongnovi people were having. He felt very sorry for them." The Hopi text does not name the mouse, but refers to some unnamed being who knew the whole story, who not only had heard about the trouble but who felt the Misongnovis' dismay so deeply that he made a plan to help.

> Pas amungem qahaalaitique.
> Pas yaw qahaalaitique
>   amungem kiisat niinaniqe
>   pasiwna.
>   (Kennard, 1944, p. 15)

The Hopi text sets the single word *pasiwna* apart, befitting its deep meaning in Hopi culture. *Pasiwna* refers to the life plan, in some sense prophesied for each individual. The little mouse was undertaking a part of his life plan in a way that resonated through Hopi philosophical and religious practice. Hopi "key words," such as *pasiwna*, convey deep moral instruction; *Field Mouse* is not a just-for-fun story or a story using familiar settings to further federal agendas; it is a meaningful Hopi story. Many examples can be found in the story, but we will conclude with the key word *tokwisni*.

When the "dirty little rodent" offers to kill the hawk, the village chief is skeptical but accepts the offer. He directs the village crier to announce the event and tell the people to prepare.

> The Crier smoked four times.
> When he had finished
>   the Chief said,
>   "Thinking only of this great event
>   let us go to sleep."
> The Village Chief went home.
> He went to bed.
>   (Kennard, 1944, p. 29)

The English "He went to bed" corresponds to the Hopi *Itam oovi tokwisni*. *Tokwisni* translates "to go to bed with a sense of hope, a feeling in your heart that things will get better." Hope, invested in prayer and ceremony, permeates a Hopi way of life as dry farmers in a demanding and arid environment.

Processes of Hopification

Hartman Lomawaima has used the word *Hopification* to refer to the age-old process of Hopi people learning and adapting from others useful ideas, practices, technologies, and material culture (H. Lomawaima, 1989). Whether dealing with peach trees, burros, sheep, or cattle; governors or elected councils; tribal constitutions or legal codes; writing systems or schools, the Hopi have endeavored to fit new things into an overarching system of Hopi meaning. It appears they successfully "Hopified" the Bureau's *Life Readers,* perhaps by successfully "Hopifying" the resident anthropologist, Edward Kennard, beginning a local publishing tradition of juvenile literature that resurfaced in later years (Balenquah, 1981). They were not alone in appropriating the mechanisms of literacy for their own purposes.

Publication of Authentically Navajo Stories

In other parts of Indian country where Native-language fluency was still the norm, opportunities for Native-language publishing took hold in the 1940s and 1950s. On the Navajo reservation, a monthly newspaper, *Adahooníłígíí* (*Events*), was published. Linguists Robert Young and William Morgan extracted stories from the paper and published, under BIA auspices, the Navajo Historical Series (Left-Handed Mexican Clansman, Gorman, & Young, 1952; Young & Morgan, 1954). A 1954 publication in this series, *Navajo Historical Selections*, like the Hopi readers, contrasted strongly with the Beatty/Clark publications. The stories that Young and Morgan printed in Navajo and English were recorded from real narrators, recounting the creation of the cosmos, explaining and reinforcing Navajo social mores, and actively criticizing federal policies, especially livestock reduction.

No one in these stories "did as they should do, and . . . bought what was good for them" (Clark, 1943b, p. 8). In versions of the origin stories, narrators asserted the truth, historical validity, and political potency of their oral tradition. "This isn't something of recent origin that I have told. These are our stories—our document" (Young & Morgan, 1954, p. 14).

> The white people all look to the Government like we look to the Sacred Mountains. You, the white people, hold out your hands to the Government. In accord with . . . [the Government] you live. But we look to our Sacred Mountains. . . . According to them we live—they are our Washington. (Young & Morgan, 1954, p. 17)

Scott Preston, in his story about the origins of the clans, asserted the powerful educational and intellectual purposes embodied in Navajo oral traditions:

> From time immemorial the old men . . . have always told their grandchildren [about things], and that is the way the traditions have been passed down. They tell short parts of stories as they keep the evening fires going. . . . The stories are told so the People will develop their minds. (Young & Morgan, 1954, p. 23)

Given the debates and struggles at the time over the extraction of Navajo children from families and communities in order to attend schools, it is not surprising that several narrators commented on the state of education. Some supported the necessity of school-based education but articulated the benefits of home-based education as well:

> As time goes by, a child develops his thinking from his mother and father. That's the Navajo way. . . . His grandparents are like teachers. . . . He asks them how the People need to live, and they tell him. It is akin to the textbooks of the white people. (Young & Morgan, 1954, p. 54)

The stories within this publication that recounted the extreme hardships accompanying livestock reduction could not be more different from the accommodationist tone of the Beatty/Clark years.

> It [stock reduction] is something akin to the dictatorial systems of government across the sea. We hear stories to the effect that, in those areas, anyone who speaks unfavorably about the Government is killed. That's where we're headed. Why should anyone be manhandled just because of his food and the things he lives from? (Young & Morgan, 1954, p. 69)

Scholars of American Indian history have tended to characterize the 1950s Cold War context, emphasizing federal moves to terminate tribes, abrogate treaties, and end federal trust responsibilities. These characterizations are accurate, but an emphasis on national political processes should not obscure the profound shifts in local and national beliefs and practices in Indian Country. Possibilities to "remain an Indian," articulated decades earlier in the Meriam Report and implemented, however incompletely, in federally controlled bilingual materials in the 1940s, were being appropriated and recreated by Hopi, Navajo, and other dedicated Native parents, educators, tribal leaders, and activists. In local places and local ways, they set the stage for the more sweeping national trends of the coming decades.

CHAPTER 6

Indigenous Bilingual/Bicultural Education: Challenging the Safety Zone

People were shocked when we suggested using Navajo in school. Nobody has ever suggested using Navajo in the school to learn, so how can you do that? School is to learn English.

—Agnes Dodge Holm, Navajo bilingual educator
and cofounder of the internationally acclaimed
Rock Point Navajo Bilingual Education Program,
in a 1996 interview (cited in McCarty, 2002a, p. 113)

Bilingual education. The concept is no less fraught with controversy today than it was in the 1960s when pioneering Indigenous educators such as Agnes Dodge Holm quietly but decidedly began to transform the medium of instruction in American Indian schools. Yet the story of bilingualism and bilingual education for Indigenous peoples of the Americas goes back thousands of years. Multilingualism was always highly valued in Indigenous societies and, indeed, was essential for trade and survival in one of the most culturally, linguistically, and ecologically diverse regions of the world. In the swirl of interests that engulfed North America following the European invasion, multilingualism continued to be both common and necessary, a tool of trade, of intertribal communication, and, for Europeans, of efforts to convert Indigenous souls. Yet even as the colonizing project took root, some Indigenous groups such as the Choctaws and Cherokees in the 19th century co-opted missionary literacies, operating bilingual newspapers and schools and developing autochthonous systems such as the Cherokee syllabary introduced by Sequoya in 1821. In fact, first-language literacy among the Cherokees in the early 1800s was higher than that of the local White population (Spack, 2002; see also Goddard, 1996; McCarty, 2002c, 2004; Noley, 1979; Spring, 1996.)

As we have seen, the boarding school system placed bi/multilingualism well outside the zone of safety, determining Native American languages to be unquestionably "unsafe." Perhaps the clearest statement of this policy was made in a 1887 report by then-Commissioner of Indian Affairs John D. C. Atkins. Nothing so perfectly stamps upon an individual a national characteristic as

language, Atkins observed, declaring that no Indian pupil would be permit-
ted to study any other language than our own . . . the language of the greatest,
most powerful, and enterprising nationalities beneath the sun" (quoted in
Crawford, 1992, pp. 49–50). Along with cleanliness and obedience, "No Indian Talk" was the first rule in government boarding schools (Spack, 2002,
p. 24). So began a language education policy that, notwithstanding brief for-
ays into bilingual education during the Collier and Beatty years (see Chapters
4 and 5, this volume), would remain in effect well into the 20th century.

The brutality and child-negating consequences of this policy have been
well documented, and we will only highlight them here. "We were forced
and pressured to learn English," Navajo educator Galena Sells Dick writes.
"It was confusing and difficult. . . . Students were punished and abused for
speaking their native language" (Dick & McCarty, 1996, pp. 72–73; see also
McCarty, 2002a). Numerous accounts describe students being beaten, placed
in solitary confinement, having their mouths "washed" with bar soap, or
being forced to stand for hours holding stacks of books on their heads for
speaking their Native language (see, e.g., Archuleta et al., 2000; Ellis, 1996;
McCarty, 2002a; Spack, 2002; Trennert, 1988). The English-only curriculum fit hand-in-glove with manual training intended to produce docile, low-
wage laborers. Indian school textbooks in the 1950s, for example, featured
titles such as *Shoe Repairing Dictionary* (Rhodes, 1953), *Please Fill the Tank*
(Benton & Kinsland, 1953), *Be a Good Waitress* (Payne, Wallace, & Shorten,
1953), and *I Am a Good Citizen* (Williamson, 1954), with instructions to
teachers that "all pupils . . . should understand the contents of this book"
and that each page "should be studied thoroughly and slowly" (Clark, quoted
in Williamson, 1954, p. ii). BIA Five-Year Program readers such as these were
written for students who had "chosen" a particular trade as their vocation
(Epley, Benton, & Bitsie, 1953, p. iv).

SEEDS OF TRANSFORMATION

What happened to challenge the entrenched English-only policies and practices in Indian schools? By the 1960s, a rising tide of political and cultural
activism was sweeping the nation, and Native people were flexing the political skills acquired through the social and political battles waged since the
turn of the century. Many of those battles had been fought on the turf of
education, and education was clearly a highly valued commodity among
Native people despite the inhospitable, even inhumane, school environments
endured by many students. As more American Indian people sought college
and advanced degrees through the 1950s and 1960s, the majority of those
degrees were in education (Lomawaima, 2003).

Local, tribal, and national Indian leaders and young people spoke up throughout the 1960s and early 1970s, and the American public seemed more receptive to their messages. Tribal leaders such as Stanley Smartlowit (Yakima), tribal educators such as Annie Wauneka Dodge (Navajo) and Esther Burnett Horne (Shoshone), political activists such as Dennis Banks (Ojibwe) and Russell Means (Lakota), scholars such as Vine Deloria Jr. (Lakota), Helen Scheirbeck (Lumbee), and Alfonso Ortiz (Tewa), and myriad, dedicated others pushed for tribal sovereignty: self-government, self-determination, and self-education.

The safety zone was, gradually but relentlessly, being expanded, and, in the context of wider civil rights reforms, Congress responded. In 1964, Congress passed both the Civil Rights Act and the Economic Opportunity Act, providing, respectively, legal protection from racial discrimination and funding for Head Start, Upward Bound, Volunteers in Service to America (VISTA), and Indian Community Action Programs. In 1965, Congress authorized the Elementary and Secondary Education Act, or ESEA, the most sweeping education reform to that time, which included a Title I amendment for compensatory English reading programs. Although focused on English and remedial in nature, Title I became a key resource for Indigenous literacy efforts, as we show in the sections that follow. In 1968, the Bilingual Education Act, calling for "new and imaginative programs" that used children's native language while they learned English, was authorized as a Title VII amendment to the ESEA. And in 1972, Congress passed the Indian Education Act, a Title IV amendment to the ESEA that supported Indigenous bilingual/bicultural materials development, teacher preparation, and parent involvement in schools. By the early 1970s, even some spokespersons within the BIA had begun to embrace bilingual education as one of "the most promising" approaches for educating Native students (Bauer, 1970, p. 223). Taken together, these initiatives nudged the boundaries of the safety zone, nurturing a new terrain for the exercise of choice in Indigenous education: Indigenous community-controlled schools.

A "WINDOW OF OPPORTUNITY"

The year 1970 has been portrayed as a turning point in American Indian affairs (American Indian Policy Review Commission, 1976; Fuchs & Havighurst, 1972; Szasz, 1974). In that year, President Richard M. Nixon delivered a message to Congress on Indian policy, promising "self-determination without termination" (American Indian Policy Review Commission [AIPRC], 1976, p. 111). "We believe that every Indian community wishing to do so should be able to control its own Indian schools," Nixon declared (AIPRC, 1976,

p. 111). Later that year, Nixon's Commissioner of Indian Affairs, Louis R. Bruce, outlined plans to implement the president's message to Congress. "For Indian educational programs to become truly responsive to the needs of Indian children and parents, . . . control of those programs should be in the hands of the Indian communities," Bruce maintained (AIPRC, 1976, p. 117).

Nixon's historic pronouncement did not emanate from sudden federal enlightenment or largesse. Rather, in an interesting twist on interpretations of "safe" versus "dangerous" policies and practices, this statement followed a widely publicized and highly negative assessment of failed federal policies and BIA mismanagement as well as equally well-publicized Native efforts to assert educational rights. Just months before, the Senate Special Subcommittee on Indian Education, chaired by Robert Kennedy and, after his death, by his brother Edward Kennedy, had released a report on a 2-year congressional investigation of Indian education. Condemning federal policy as "one of coercive assimilation," the report cited dismal statistics of Indian student failure and the denigration of Native languages and identities in federal schools, which "had disastrous effects on the education of Indian children" (U.S. Congress, Senate Committee on Labor and Public Welfare, Special Subcommittee on Indian Education, 1969, p. 21).

THE RISE OF INDIGENOUS COMMUNITY-CONTROLLED SCHOOLS

In counterpoint to the Senate Special Subcommittee report, a fledgling self-determination movement had taken root in several Indigenous communities. At Blackwater, a tiny Akimel O'odham (Pima) community on the Gila River Indian reservation in the central Arizona desert, a pre-K–3 BIA school was under the direction of a local board of trustees as early as the 1960s. More than 350 miles to the north, a Navajo bilingual/bicultural demonstration project jointly funded by the Office of Economic Opportunity and the Bureau of Indian Affairs was established at Lukachukai, Arizona. Relocated in 1966 to a new BIA school facility at Rough Rock, Arizona, the Rough Rock Demonstration School quickly rose to international prominence as a model of Indigenous self-determination (Johnson, 1968; McCarty, 2002a; Roessel, 1977). Other Native American communities watched these developments with great interest and in time, "activists within the [BIA] reestablished procedures for contracting Bureau schools" (Holm & Holm, 1990, p. 173). Those procedures later were incorporated into P.L. 93-638, the 1975 Indian Self-Determination and Education Assistance Act, enabling tribes and Native communities to contract to operate their own schools and other health and social services from the BIA and Indian Public Health Service.

By the late 1970s, there were 34 American Indian community-controlled schools. The Tribally Controlled College or University Assistance Act was passed in 1978, supporting tribes in operating their own community colleges, and the Coalition of Indian Controlled School Boards, a political lobbying force and clearinghouse on educational self-determination, had emerged as "the most important thrust in the education of Indian children today" (AIPRC, 1976, p. 257; see also Szasz, 1974, p. 162). The policy paradigm had shifted, as federal interests and those of Native communities seemed fortuitously (if momentarily) aligned. According to Wayne Holm, cofounder of the Rock Point bilingual program, Indigenous communities "had a window of opportunity . . . where we were allowed to do our own thing, and communities were willing to try [bilingual/bicultural education], and . . . the government was set up in a way that they weren't down on us so hard" (quoted in McCarty, 2002a, p. 113). Within a short period of time, Holm reflected, "if you were not attempting to have community-based curriculum, to use language, if you did not have something dealing with culture, the question was, why not?" (Teresa McCarty, from an unpublished interview, January 31, 1996).

TAKING UP THE CHALLENGE: "WHY NOT?"

In 1974, sociolinguist Bernard Spolsky counted 74 American Indian and Alaska Native bilingual/bicultural education programs. These programs owed something to the earlier BIA initiatives described in Chapter 5, but they were more immediately tied to the developing movement for local control and the availability of Title I, Title IV, and Title VII funds (Spolsky, 1974). The programs reflected the wide diversity of American Indian and Alaska Native languages, including language groups in Alaska (Aleut, Athabaskan, Haida, Inupiaq, Tlingit, and Yupik); Arizona (Navajo, Tohono O'odham [then called Papago]); California (Pomo); Colorado (Southern Ute, Navajo); Florida (Miccosukee); Maine (Passamaquoddy); Montana (Cheyenne, Cree, and Crow); Oklahoma (Cherokee, Choctaw, and Seminole); New Mexico (Keresan, Navajo, Tewa, and Zuni); South Dakota (Lakota); and Wisconsin (Chippewa, Menominee, Oneida, Potawatomi, and Winnebago). The range of language proficiencies in these contexts varied considerably, from situations of nearly 100% Native-language fluency (Miccosukee and Navajo), to situations in which the Native language was used primarily among adults (Seminole), to situations in which the Native language was in drastic decline and even Native teachers lacked proficiency in the heritage language (Pomo). Accordingly, the goals, content, and teaching methods in these programs also varied widely, from language maintenance to language revitalization to efforts that were "cultural rather than linguistic" (Spolsky, 1974, p. 32). But in all cases, Spolsky (1974) states, bilingual education was viewed as key to "a movement for tribal or community [education] control" (p. 25).

Bilingual/bicultural education continues to trouble the boundaries of the safety zone. Legally sanctioned and economically constrained, bilingual/bicultural education nonetheless became the lightening rod for Indigenous self-determination in the latter part of the 20th century. With the recent ascendancy of English-only policies in key states with large Native populations, the importance of this movement has been heightened.

In the remainder of this chapter, we examine four American Indian bilingual/bicultural initiatives that illustrate the development and significance of this movement. We select these programs for closer analysis because they are among the earliest and most long-lived initiatives in American Indian bilingual/bicultural education (and thus also are better documented); they were originally designed to serve students whose primary language was not English (we address heritage-language education for Native students whose primary language is English in Chapter 7); they represent a cross section of institutional arrangements, including community-controlled schools, a public school, and a university setting; and they are programs with which we have had some firsthand involvement. All are based in Arizona. Two—Rock Point and Rough Rock—serve Navajo-speaking communities; another serves the Hualapai community of Peach Springs; and the fourth—the American Indian Language Development Institute (AILDI)—is an international teacher preparation program for educators of Native American children and youth. The data on these programs come from the published literature, much of it authored by Native educators and program "insiders," and from long-term, firsthand research, particularly oral historical, ethnographic, and program development research conducted at Rough Rock, at Peach Springs, and with AILDI.

Initiatives & Locations of these initiatives.

In reading the program portraits that follow, it should be remembered that each program evolved over a period of many years. The programs are fluid, dynamic, and processual, and they continue to change and unfold. Our goal is not to portray them as static models, but rather to highlight both shared and unique experiences in the implementation of Native American bilingual/bicultural education, as well as program outcomes over time.

Rock Point: "A Navajo Way to Go to School"[1]

Rock Point is one of the better-documented American Indian bilingual education programs; "rigorous, ongoing evaluation of student learning" in Navajo and English has historically been a primary program concern (Holm & Holm, 1990, p. 178). Originally a two-classroom school for beginners through second grade built under Commissioner Collier's "New Deal," the school went through several metamorphoses until, in 1972, it became one of a handful of Navajo community-controlled schools. Agnes and Wayne Holm, who helped found the school's bilingual program and worked at Rock Point for 25 years, characterize Rock Point's 17-month struggle to "go contract" (i.e., to assume community control of what had been a BIA school), as the school board's "Long March";[2] until the passage of P.L. 93-638, they write, a few key people in the Bureau, resistant to self-determination, "could stall a board intent on contracting almost indefinitely" (Holm & Holm, 1990, p. 174; see also Reyhner & Eder, 2004).

A community of about 1,300 situated in the center of the high, arid plateau lands of northern Arizona, Rock Point at the time of contracting had only recently gained access to electricity and a paved road. "English in the Rock Point community at the time was essentially a foreign language," Holm and Holm report, with 90% to 95% of students entering school dominant or monolingual in Navajo (1990, p. 173). Not surprisingly, Rock Point students ranked near the bottom of all students in comparable Navajo BIA schools on English standardized tests (Rosier & Farella, 1976, p. 379).

In 1967, even before Rock Point "went contract," school leaders agreed to try something revolutionary: teaching Navajo students to read in their primary language first. Using students' first language for initial literacy learning is, of course, standard practice for native English speakers in U.S. schools. But this tried-and-true method, taken for granted in majority-language settings, was, as Spolsky and his associates in the Navajo Reading Study point out, a "new" approach to reading in Indigenous schools (Spolsky, 1975). The assumption at Rock Point, according to the former school director, Paul Rosier, and English-language evaluator Marilyn Farella, was that "a child learns to read only once . . . most easily in the language [s/he] speaks" (Rosier & Farella, 1976, p. 380).

> [S/he] can then transfer most of the skills thus acquired to another language. Learning to read in a second language may require learning new sound-symbol associations and some new rules, but the essential concepts of reading can be transferred. (Rosier & Farella, 1976, p. 380)

With Title I funds targeted for English reading, Rock Point "quietly set up its kindergarten as a bilingual classroom" (Holm & Holm, 1990, p. 173).

With the advent of the school's P.L. 93-638 contract, Rock Point developed a K–6 bilingual/bicultural program that subsequently extended to grade 12. "The design that emerged we called 'coordinate bilingual' instruction," Holm & Holm (1990) relate, involving one or more Navajo-language teachers (NLTs) and an English-language teacher (ELT) in each primary classroom

(p. 176). "NLTs were expected to teach and interact only in Navajo; ELTs were expected to teach and interact only in English" (Holm & Holm, 1990, p. 176). Externally imposed status distinctions between credentialed (primarily White) and noncredentialed (Navajo) teaching staff were dissolved, as both NLTs and ELTs planned, carried out, and evaluated instruction.

Using the Navajo literacy materials developed by Robert Young and William Morgan (see Chapter 5, this volume), as well as locally developed materials and methods, students learned to read first in Navajo, then in English. As students advanced to higher grades, "We did not replace reading in Navajo," Holm and Holm assert, "we added reading in English" (1990, p. 177). Students learned mathematics in both languages and studied science and social studies in Navajo, including Navajo clanship, history, social problems, government, and economic development. "Rock Point students were among the few students on the Reservation who left high school with some formal preparation for participation in the Navajo political process," Holm and Holm state (p. 178). A secondary-level applied literacy program engaged students in locally relevant research published in a bilingual school newspaper and broadcast on a school television station (see McLaughlin, 1995).

The Rock Point school board insisted that its students would perform at least as well as BIA students on BIA-mandated standardized tests, flawed and discriminatory as those tests are. The students did not disappoint. Longitudinal data from Rock Point demonstrate that Navajo-speaking children who learned to read first in Navajo not only outperformed comparable Navajo students in English-only programs, they surpassed their own previous annual growth rates and those of comparison-group students in BIA schools (Holm & Holm, 1990, 1995; Rosier & Farella, 1976). "More impressive," Holm and Holm (1990) state, "they did so by a greater margin at each successive grade," illustrating research findings from around the world on the cumulative benefits of bilingual education (pp. 182–184; see, e.g., Crawford, 1997; Cummins, 1989, 2000; Cummins & Corson, 1997; Garcia, 2003; Krashen, 1996; Ovando, Collier, & Combs, 2003; Skutnabb-Kangas & Cummins, 1988; Thomas & Collier, 1997). Students "who spoke only limited English were able to express themselves more fully and [grasped] higher abstract concepts when the vernacular was used" (Rosier & Farella, 1976, p. 380). In addition to learning English, of course, these students had the benefit of becoming literate in Navajo.

In a 25-year retrospective analysis of the Rock Point program, Holm and Holm (1990) describe the "four-fold empowerment" engendered through bilingual education there: of the Navajo school board, who "came to acquire increasing credibility with parents, staff, and students;" of the Navajo staff, whose pedagogical vision and competence were recognized by outside observers as well as community members; of parents, who for the first time played active roles in their children's schooling; and of students, who "came to value their Navajo-ness and to see themselves as capable of succeeding because of, not despite that Navajo-ness" (pp. 182–184; see also Holm & Holm, 1995). "The importance of the Rock Point data," Holm and Holm conclude, "was that they showed, contrary to the conventional wisdom, that being rural and speaking Navajo need not lead to doing poorly in school" (1990, p. 184).

Demonstration at Rough Rock[3]

On July 7, 1966, five leaders from the Navajo (Diné) community of Rough Rock, Arizona, met to chart the direction of the new school they had been elected to govern. The five newly elected board members had been chosen to inaugurate a school that would position parents and community members at the center of their children's schooling. The school was named Tsé Ch'izhi Diné Bi'ólta—Rough Rock The People's School (McCarty, 2002a). When it opened in September of that year, only one child in the two beginners' classrooms was reported as speaking English (Roessel, 1966).

Rough Rock at the time was one of the most economically impoverished areas in the United States. A community about the size of Rock Point located 40 miles to the southwest, Rough Rock was still recovering from government policies implemented decades before that had forcibly reduced their livestock holdings and attenuated their land rights. As one measure of the effects of these and other federal policies of containment, annual per capita cash income at Rough Rock in 1966 was $85 (McCarty, 2002a).

An outgrowth of federal War on Poverty programs, the demonstration school was established through a unique contract among the local Navajo board, a tribal board of trustees, the BIA, and the Office of Economic Opportunity (for more on the school's founding, see Johnson, 1968; McCarty, 2002a; Roessel, 1977). The privileging of local leadership and of Navajo language and culture in the school curriculum was intended not simply to aid children in learning English but to be a "terrain of knowledge and a field of possibilities for community action" (Rivera, 1999, p. 485). "Rough Rock's very existence," Dillon Platero, the school's second director, wrote, "fosters the hope of . . . other tribal groups to . . . realize greater control of their own destinies" (1970, p. 58).

Like Rock Point, the Rough Rock school board quickly set about "growing its own" bilingual/bicultural materials and Navajo-speaking teaching staff, efforts made possible by Title I, Title IV, and Title VII. As those funds waxed and waned from year to year, however, teacher turnover and curricular and financial instability became chronic problems. These conditions are directly linked to the economic and political marginalization of Indigenous communities and to institutional arrangements that make reservation schools dependent for their survival on fluctuating federal programs, policies, and funds. We take up these issues and their implications later in this chapter.

In 1983, a constellation of events set into motion processes that, for a time at least, ameliorated these problems. That fall, anthropologists and reading specialists from the Hawai'i-based Kamehameha Early Education Program (KEEP) came to Rough Rock for the express purpose of determining whether the reading comprehension strategies proven effective with Native Hawaiian children would work with Navajo students (Vogt & Au, 1995; Vogt, Jordan, & Tharp, 1993). The KEEP–Rough Rock collaboration lasted 5 years, during which a core group of eight bilingual teachers, assisted by KEEP staff, began implementing culturally relevant, comprehension-based English reading instruction. "At first," one teacher reported, "we thought we should follow KEEP strategies strictly. Then we started sorting things out for ourselves" (McCarty & Dick, 2003). The result was the Rough Rock English-Navajo Language Arts Program (RRENLAP), initially a K–2 then a K–6 program that, for the next decade, served 150–225 students each year identified as "limited English proficient" (see Figure 6.1). According to the project proposal, RRENLAP was "designed to provide the framework for basic developmental Navajo and English language arts" (RRENLAP grant proposal, 1989, p. 16).

The details of this program have been described elsewhere, and we will only outline them briefly here (for a fuller account, see Begay et al., 1995; Dick, Estell, & McCarty, 1994; Dick & McCarty, 1996; Lipka & McCarty, 1994; McCarty, 2002a; McCarty & Dick, 2003). Instructional practice in RRENLAP classrooms was based on the premise that students are more successful if they are able to learn in a context that is socially, linguistically, and cognitively compatible with the local culture. Classrooms were organized around learning centers and small-group instruction that included both Navajo and English. Curriculum content centered on teacher- and student-developed interdisciplinary units based on local content and themes. Complementing classroom instruction during the academic year were annual summer literature camps in which students conducted field-based research on such topics as animal husbandry, ethnobotany, and the archaeology and geology of Dinétah, the Navajo homelands in the Four Corners region of the U.S. Southwest. In these and classroom-based learning activities, parents, elders, school staff, and students jointly engaged in storytelling, song, drama, art, and research and writing projects related to locally relevant themes. The oral tellings from these experiences were recorded, providing new computer- and text-based curriculum resources.

Figure 6.1. Rough Rock Community School librarian Thomas Willetto, with elementary school student, 1983 (photograph by Fred Bia, courtesy of Rough Rock Community School).

Much like the fourfold empowerment described by Holm and Holm (1990) for Rock Point, RRENLAP empowered Rough Rock teachers, parents, students, and the local culture itself. "We came a long way," one teacher reflected after 10 years of program implementation. "RRENLAP gave us ways of *how* to develop appropriate materials and assessment," the program director, Galena Sells Dick, said; "it gave us that confidence and empowerment" (quoted in McCarty, 2002a, p. 159). "I thought only the Anglos wrote books," a parent remarked on viewing RRENLAP's teacher-developed storybooks in Navajo (quoted in McCarty & Dick, 2003, p. 114). Drawing on

Figure 6.2. Navajo schoolchildren on the playground of Rough Rock School, 1983 (photograph courtesy of Rough Rock Community School).

and validating the local culture, materials such as these allowed students and their parents to see local teachers as published authors—in Navajo (McCarty, 1993; McCarty & Dick, 2003; see Figure 6.3).

Longitudinal achievement data from RRENLAP show significant indicators of student success. After 4 years in the program, RRENLAP students' mean scores on locally developed measures of English listening comprehension rose from 58% to 91% (McCarty, 1993). On standardized reading subtests, the same students' scores initially declined, then rose steadily, although they remained below national norms. Similar patterns were observed in mathematics (McCarty, 1993). When individual and grade cohort data were analyzed for all RRENLAP students over 5 years, an overriding pattern emerged: Bilingual students who had cumulative, sustained initial literacy instruction in Navajo over 3 to 5 years made the greatest gains on local and national measures of achievement (McCarty, 1993, p. 191). RRENLAP students also were assessed by their teachers as having stronger oral Navajo and Navajo literacy abilities than their non-bilingual-education peers (McCarty, 1993, 2002a).

Figure 6.3. Examples of teacher-developed Navajo literacy materials (courtesy of Rough Rock Community School).

"The Thing Is Perseverance": Bilingual/Bicultural Education at Peach Springs

A few hundred miles west of the Navajo Nation, on the edge of the Grand Canyon, the town of Peach Springs straddles the main line of the Santa Fe railroad and U.S. Highway 66. The tribal seat for the 1,800-member Hualapai Tribe, Peach Springs has a K–12 school, a general store, a post office, two gas stations, a lodge and tribally-operated tourist facilities, and tribal government and U.S. Public Health Service offices. Clusters of homes built through the federal office of Housing and Urban Development line both sides of the railroad tracks. This is where the majority of the members of the Hualapai Tribe reside, although the reservation itself encompasses nearly a million acres of surrounding desert plateau and evergreen forest.

Hualapai is a Yuman language, related to the Hokan–Coahuiltecan language group whose speakers reside in what are now California, Arizona, the Baja Peninsula, and the Gulf of California in Mexico. Until the advent of the Peach Springs School bilingual education program, Hualapai lacked a practical writing system. Under the auspices of Title VII, Hualapai educators collaborated with academic linguists to develop an orthography, a grammar, and a corpus of children's literature, as well as to make Hualapai the co-medium of instruction in the local K–8 (now K–12) public school.

We have seen that the programs at Rock Point and Rough Rock evolved out of locally distinct circumstances, resources, and needs. This was no less the case at Peach Springs. In 1975, there was only one Hualapai certified teacher, Lucille Jackson Watahomigie. Returning to Peach Springs after completing a university degree, she began teaching at the local school. At the time, Watahomigie was told by the non-Indian principal that state law prohibited using the Native language in public schools. Yet 90% of the fifth-grade class had been referred to special education because they spoke Hualapai as their primary language. Watahomigie (1998) recalls: "Finally, one brave little boy asked me in Hualapai, 'Like this, teacher?' I began teaching the students in Hualapai even though the principal had forbidden it" (p. 6).

Recruiting academic linguists to assist in developing a writing system for classroom use, Watahomigie and other community members began the cultural and linguistic work to make Peach Springs a bilingual/bicultural school. Their participation in the Summer Institute of Linguistics for Native Americans (SILNA), founded by the Wycliffe Bible Translators, helped jump-start these efforts. According to program coordinator Philbert Watahomigie, "We decided we were going to learn linguistics—we were going to be our own linguists" (quoted in Watahomigie & McCarty, 1996, p. 103). Hualapai educators, parents, and elders continued to work with academic linguists to refine the orthography and develop a bilingual/bicultural curriculum that would become a nationally recognized and widely disseminated model (Watahomigie, 1995; Watahomigie & McCarty, 1994, 1996; Watahomigie & Yamamoto, 1987).

The Peach Springs curriculum included a series of teaching units on Hualapai cultural-environmental studies, literacy, mathematics, and science, as well as dozens of attractively illustrated Hualapai-language children's books (see Figure 6.4). The program also emphasized interactive technology, involving students in community-based research on such topics as the geology and petroglyphs of the Grand Canyon region. Student-produced videos from these projects, as well as their desktop publications, were used as teaching resources for younger children at the school.

Initially, Watahomigie reports, the Hualapai staff faced stiff opposition from non-Indian teachers, who viewed the Hualapai materials as irrelevant, harmful to children's academic progress, and a threat to the "regular" curriculum (Watahomigie & McCarty, 1994, 1996). Children's positive responses to the Hualapai materials and their improved academic achievement gradually defused these objections (project evaluations show consistent improvements in children's English-language achievement as well as high school graduation rates of 100% [Watahomigie, 1988; Watahomigie & Yamamoto, 1987]), as did the certification of more Hualapai teachers and thus the penetration of the school infrastructure by local people.

But bilingual/bicultural education was foreign to many in the community, a situation that must be understood in terms of the power relations that have shaped it. "When I was in grade school," one community member recalled, "I was punished because I spoke my language. I turned against my language" (quoted in Watahomigie & McCarty, 1996, p. 106). Helping community members "turn toward" their language required a public discourse Watahomigie (1995) describes as "reverse brainwashing." "We have had to re-educate our parents on the importance and priority of the values and knowledge embodied in our culture," she writes (1995, p. 191). In much the way that Freire (1970, 1993) describes, a dialogic process at Peach Springs made visible the problem the bilingual/bicultural program there faced: How could the school, historically an agent of Anglo American oppression, become an instrument of community empowerment?

At Peach Springs, critical reflection and public dialogue, as well as parents' observations of their children's academic growth with bilingual/bicultural schooling, gradually transformed community resistance into support. "We saw an opening," Philbert Watahomigie recalls. "The thing is perseverance . . . something Native people have been told they can't do." (Watahomigie & McCarty, 1996, p. 106)

Figure 6.4. Hualapai language instructional booklets (courtesy of *Common Ground: Archeology and Ethnography in the Public Interest*, Fall, 1999, p. 35; published by National Park Service, Archeology and Ethnography Program, 1849 C Street, NW [NC 210], Washington, DC 20240).

"It Made Me Proud to Be Indian": The American Indian Language Development Institute[4]

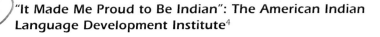

The American Indian Language Development Institute (AILDI) is one of the most far-reaching outgrowths of Native bilingual/bicultural education programs. When they were established in the late 1960s and early 1970s, these programs faced two immediate needs: Native-language teaching materials and Native-speaking teachers. To address those needs, Lucille Watahomigie and a group of academic linguists in 1978 launched the Yuman Language Institute, a university-accredited summer program that brought together parents, elders, educators, and linguists to develop Indigenous writing systems and teaching materials. As federal funding increased and the number of American Indian bilingual education programs grew, additional communities became involved, and the Yuman Language Institute grew into the AILDI, now an international teacher preparation program housed at the University of Arizona.

AILDI's primary goal is to integrate Indigenous languages and cultural content into school curricula in ways that affirm students' identities and academic achievement (McCarty, Watahomigie, Yamamoto, & Zepeda, 2001b). This 4-week summer residential program features an integrated suite of courses in American Indian linguistics and bilingual/bicultural curriculum development. The institute enrolls approximately 75 to 100 Native and non-Native participants each year from Indigenous communities throughout the Americas. Over the years the institute has prepared thousands of parents and educators to work as researchers, curriculum developers, bilingual teachers, and advocates for Indigenous languages (McCarty et al., 2001b, p. 372).

Like local bilingual education programs, AILDI has faced significant challenges. For years it had no permanent home. Continuity in program goals and curricula was maintained by the presence of a core group of faculty, most of whom worked outside the host institutions. The positioning of two key AILDI faculty members at the University of Arizona brought the institute there in its 12th year, and after 6 years of negotiation with the university administration, AILDI was awarded modest but permanent funding. The program continues to seek discretionary funds each year for participant scholarships and guest faculty salaries.

In addition to facilitating Native-language materials development, teacher credentialing, and the recruitment and retention of Native educators in higher-degree programs,[5] AILDI has created an international forum for language education planning, policy development, and activism. In 1988, AILDI faculty and participants drafted the resolution that became the 1990/1992 Native American Languages Act (NALA), the only federal legislation that explicitly vows to protect and promote Indigenous languages and cultural systems. (For the text of this legislation, see Cantoni, 1996, pp. 69–72; Hinton, 1991, also discusses the legislation's origins and provides a synopsis of it.) Perhaps for all of these reasons, AILDI has been adapted in Indian communities throughout the United States, including credit-bearing institutes for Arapaho, Cherokee, Chickasaw, Choctaw, Creek, Euchee, Lakota, Kickapoo, Northern Ute, Ojibwe, Omaha, Osage, Navajo, Potawatomi, Sauk-Fox, and Shawnee language groups (McCarty et al., 2001b, p. 376).

These represent AILDI's tangible outcomes. Other program impacts are less concrete but no less significant. As one program participant states:

> I used to wonder why the students would just sit there when the teacher gave them all these verbal directions [in English]. I know now that it was because they did not understand. . . . They were trying to tell us that there was not anything of meaning to them. This will give you an idea of what I've learned at the institute. (quoted in McCarty et al., 2001b, p. 372)

Another bilingual teacher-participant writes, "I've learned that I have many skills, and it made me proud to be Indian" (quoted in McCarty et al., 2001b, p. 373).

By facilitating new curricula, programs, and personnel able to make use of those resources, AILDI has helped to valorize the linguistic and cultural capital American Indian students bring to school. By simultaneously preparing and credentialing Native educators, AILDI has empowered its alumni in their local school systems. Finally, by building a network of Indigenous educators, AILDI has reinforced the collective power of its alumni. These educators have strengthened Native languages, built more effective school programs, and influenced federal policies such as the Native American Languages Act. "I would like to be an informed advocate for bilingual education," an alumnus writes, and "convince fellow teachers, administrators, the school board, parents, and community members about the need for our language." Another states: "I will be an inspiration and educator of language maintenance for my students" (quoted in McCarty et al., 2001b, pp. 375–378).

LESSONS LEARNED

At the time of this writing, some of the programs described in the previous section continued to flourish, while others had faded or been substantially transformed. Bilingual/bicultural education continues in some form at all three K–12 schools, although as we describe in Chapter 8, these efforts have been severely impacted by the ascendancy of the standards movement and English-only initiatives. In this section, we take stock: What lessons can be learned from these four illustrations of Indigenous bilingual/bicultural education?

School achievement data from Rock Point, Rough Rock, and Peach Springs, as well as that from other well-implemented programs for which there is long-term documentation (e.g., Native-language programs in Hawai'i; see Kamanā & Wilson, 1996; Romero & McCarty, 2006; Wilson, 1998), show students doing exactly what a larger body of research on bi/multilingualism predicts: They acquire the Native language without cost to their

English-language learning or academic achievement, performing as well as
or better than comparable peers in nonbilingual programs after a period of
4 to 5 years (see also Crawford, 2004a; Cummins, 1989, 2000; McCarty,
2002c; Thomas & Collier, 1997). Data from Native American bilingual/bi-
cultural programs also indicate that bilingualism enhances cognitive flexibility
and the development of critical thinking, a finding supported by research with
other populations (see, e.g., Bialystok, 1991; Cummins, 2000; Garcia, 2005).
These data support a 5- to 7-year timeframe for developing age-appropriate
levels of academic proficiency in a second language, providing further evidence for late-exit models (see, e.g., Crawford, 1997; Ramírez, 1992; Thomas
& Collier, 1997) and for consistent, long-term program funding. All of these
studies make clear that validation of children's natal culture and use of the
Native language for high-level intellectual engagement are essential components of a genuinely empowering and effective pedagogy.

But educational and linguistic outcomes, as important as they are, are
only part of the story. As Spolsky (1974) pointed out more than three decades ago, "To establish bilingual education is not just changing the curriculum. . . . It leads to basic changes, not just of philosophy but of *teachers
and control*" (p. 52; emphases added). Unlike English-as-a-second-language
instruction—the method historically favored, in addition to "sink or swim,"
in schools for Native students—bilingual education requires Native-speaking
teachers and administrators. "The threat of bilingual education is thus a direct
economic one to [non-Native] teachers and administrators," Spolsky (1974)
observes (p. 54).

To the extent that it challenges these dominant-group interests, bilin-
gual/bicultural education is inherently "unsafe." As an expression of and tool
for the exercise of self-determination, bilingual/bicultural education also
challenges historical relations of tribal–federal authority. A brief return to
the level of federal policy illustrates how complex these power relations continue to be.

CONFOUNDING FEDERAL FORCES

In 1988, just as many Native bilingual/bicultural programs were beginning
to demonstrate positive results, Congress passed P.L. 100-297, the Elementary
and Secondary School Improvement Amendments. Among other things, P.L.
100-297 provided a forward-funding system for American Indian community-controlled schools intended to mute the highly volatile federal funding
system with which Indigenous school boards had to cope under P.L. 93-638.
For example, at Rough Rock, it was typical for the school's financial contract with the BIA to be finalized months after the school year began. In the

meantime, no employee contracts could be signed, no supplies could be ordered, and the school board and administration were in negotiations with the BIA instead of at school when the school year began (McCarty, 2002a; Tonigan, Emerson, & Platero, 1975). P.L. 100-297 enabled Indigenous school boards to seek "grant status," an arrangement distinct from the contracting process under P.L. 93-638, which provides a lump-sum base budget each year. (Final school budgets must await enrollment counts and any discretionary funding schools might obtain.) Grant status thus appeared to offer welcome relief from chronic financial insecurity for Indigenous community-controlled schools.

Achieving grant status, however, requires schools to meet standards defined and regulated not by tribes or local school boards but by national or regional accrediting boards. Thus, Indigenous community-controlled schools have been plunged into the treacherous waters of English-only standards, accreditation, and high-stakes testing. Under these circumstances, many schools have been pressured to adopt "mastery learning," "outcome-based" instruction, and other remedial education programs. Rough Rock, for example, introduced an outcome-based education program in the 1990s as part of a required plan to achieve North Central Association accreditation. The philosophy of outcome-based education is stated in positive terms ("all students can learn and succeed," "success breeds success"), but a critical reading of the program's documents makes it clear that *some* students are guaranteed school-defined success, while others must be drilled and coaxed and even then are likely to fail. A program handbook, for instance, identifies "corrective activities" to ameliorate student "deficiencies," including reteaching and instructing students to reread their (English-only) textbooks. In contrast are enrichment activities for "fast learners" designed to "broaden their horizons" (Danielson, 1989, pp. 82–86).

When P.L. 100-297 was introduced, Senator Dennis DeConcini, Democrat from Arizona, reaffirmed the federal government's "special duty to the Indian tribes to assure the availability of the best educational opportunities," a duty he maintained "must be fulfilled . . . in a manner consistent with . . . Indian self-determination" (White House Conference on Indian Education, 1992, p. 6). Despite Senator DeConcini's pronouncement, P.L. 100-297 continues to lock Indigenous schools into a system of federal constraint and control. The fact that some Native communities have managed to work around these constraints, continuing to implement bilingual/bicultural education, is testimony to their imagination, perseverance, and commitment to self-determination. "Our people believe that control of education is a natural and inherent right," Dorothy Small, a member of the Rocky Boy Community School Board, testified before the American Indian Policy Review Commission in 1976 (AIPRC, 1976, p. 261). Three decades later, that fundamental human right is still under assault.

CHAPTER 7

"The New American Revolution": Indigenous Language Survival and Linguistic Human Rights

Teaching an Indian youth in his own barbarous dialect is a positive detriment to him. The first step to be taken toward civilization, toward teaching the Indians the mischief and folly of continuing in their barbarous practices, is to teach them the English language. The impracticability . . . of civilizing the Indians of this country in any other tongue than our own would seem to be obvious.
—Commissioner of Indian Affairs John D. C. Atkins in his annual report of 1887 (quoted in Crawford, 1992, p. 51)

It is the policy of the United States to . . . encourage and support the use of Native American languages as a medium of instruction in order to encourage and support . . . Native American language survival, educational opportunity, increased student success and performance, increased student awareness and knowledge of their culture and history, and increased student and community pride . . .
—Native American Languages Act of 1990 (Sec. 104[3])

A little more than a century after Commissioner John D. C. Atkins posted his 1887 annual report, Congress passed the Native American Languages Act (NALA), reversing more than two centuries of formal and informal language policy. Authorized for funding in 1992, NALA vows to "preserve, protect, and promote the rights and freedom of Native Americans to use, practice, and develop Native American languages" (NALA, 1990, Sec. 104[1]). It further makes it federal policy to "use the Native American languages as a medium of instruction in all schools funded by the Secretary of the Interior" (Sec. 104[5]). To paraphrase the words of the eminent sociolinguist Joshua Fishman (2002) in his commentary on decades of sociolinguistic research, what a difference 100 years make!

Was NALA simply another arbitrary, if fortuitous, pendulum swing in federal Indian policy? Utilizing the theoretical framework developed in previous chapters, we suggest a more complex analysis of this policy shift and its consequences.

INDIGENOUS LANGUAGES IN AND OUTSIDE
THE SAFETY ZONE

By the late 20th century, Native American bilingual/bicultural education programs had been in operation for more than three decades. Yet even as many of these programs were demonstrating effectiveness in improving student achievement and school–community relations, Native American languages were in drastic decline. At the end of the 20th century, the linguist Michael Krauss (1998) of the Native Alaska Language Center reported that of an original 300 languages indigenous to North America, 210 were still being spoken (see also McCarty, 2002c, 2003; McCarty, Watahomigie, & Yamamoto, 1999). Of those languages, only 34 (16%) were still being naturally acquired as a first language by children. Put another way, by the late 1990s, fully 84% of all surviving Native North American languages had no new speakers to pass them on. Language loss is now proceeding at such a rapid rate, Krauss (1998) writes, "that we stand to lose more indigenous North American languages in the next 60 years than have been lost since Anglo-American contact" (p. 10).

The causes of language loss are as complex as the history of colonization and are ultimately traceable to the policies of containment, dislocation, and genocide that characterized four centuries of Anglo European imperialism. Within this historical context, federal boarding schools and the policies called for in Commissioner Atkins's 1887 report were instrumental in eradicating Indigenous languages.[1] As Krauss (1998) points out, one does not simply "get over" the federally sanctioned abuse inflicted on children for speaking their tribal languages in school (p. 16; see also Svensson, n.d., p. 36). As one telling example, a Hualapai elder recalls being "thrown in the government boarding school," where teachers used belts and hoses "to knock out the Hualapai part of me" (quoted in Watahomigie & McCarty, 1996, p. 101). The lingering consequences of these experiences have been well chronicled (see, e.g., Adams, 1995; Dick & McCarty, 1996; McCarty, 2002a; Spring, 1996; Udall, 1969). "I was not taught my language," a Hualapai youth relates:

> My . . . dad didn't want us to learn, because when he was going through school he saw what difficulty *his* peers were having because they learned Hualapai first, and the schools were all taught in the English language. And so we were not taught, my brothers and I. (quoted in Watahomigie & McCarty, 1996, p. 101; emphasis in the original)

A Navajo teacher echoes this young man's sentiments: "What the boarding schools taught us was that our language is second-best" (quoted in Dick & McCarty, 1996, p. 70).

By the time of NALA's passage, then, Native American languages were, for all practical purposes, well within the federal safety zone. From the federal perspective, NALA was a symbolic gesture with little real consequence. As Schiffman (1995) points out, NALA's passage "can be described as 'locking the barn door after the horse is stolen'" (p. 245). This interpretation is buttressed by the legislation's meager funding—not authorized until 2 years after passage of the original legislation and only after voluminous congressional testimony by Native and non-Native educators and linguists. Since that time, annual NALA allocations have averaged $1 million, an amount that, if distributed equally among more than 560 federally recognized tribes, would amount to approximately $1,800 per tribe per year.[2]

Language, Identity, and Power

It would be misleading and inaccurate to leave our analysis of NALA here, however. As May (2001) notes in his treatise on minority-language rights, "language loss is not only, perhaps not even primarily, a linguistic issue," but is deeply implicated in issues of identity and unequal power relations (p. 4). As such, language loss and reclamation raise fundamental questions about the viability of cultural pluralism, self-determination, and democracy (Fishman, 1991, 2001; Hornberger, 1996; May, 2001; McCarty, Romero, & Zepeda, 2006a, 2006b; Nettle & Romaine, 2000).

Viewed in this light, NALA is a formal articulation of long-held Indigenous desires to retain their heritage languages and, by extension, Indigenous community distinctiveness and *choice*. "Embedded in [the heritage] language are the lessons that guide our daily lives," Northern Cheyenne educator Richard Littlebear (2004) writes; "we cannot leave behind the essence of our being" (p. 12). Language is the means through which parents and grandparents socialize their children and grandchildren, imparting all that a community and a people believe their children ought to learn and become. When that bond is broken, intergenerational ties and community relationships also are ruptured. Hence, rights to language are fundamental to collective and personal identity, and efforts to resist language loss cannot be decoupled from larger struggles for personal and communal well-being, self-determination, and cultural survival (McCarty & Romero, 2005).

NALA represents both a resource for and an expression of these linguistic and education rights. Like other hard-won victories seized through "windows of opportunity," NALA was the product of Indigenous vision, intent, and design (see discussion in Chapter 6, this volume). Indigenous educators, linguists, and their allies wrote the legislation and propelled it through Congress. They subsequently fought for amendments that would further the original legislation's goals by providing for Native American Language Survival Schools.[3]

Language, Svensson (1981) argues, "is the symbolic banner of [the] new American revolution":

> Language can no longer be taken for granted as an indifferent tool of communication; it becomes a tool of self-awareness and community identification . . . [that] stands out as a key point of attack on the trend toward ethnic extinction. (pp. 34, 40)

For Native people in the United States, the stakes in this revolution are extremely high, for, unlike immigrant minorities, Native communities have no other nation-state or homeland but their own to secure the future of their languages. "Our Native American languages are in the penultimate moment of their existence in this world," Littlebear (1996) writes (p. xv). "When an indigenous group stops speaking its language," Hinton (2001) points out, "the language disappears from the face of the earth" (p. 3).

Language Revitalization and Linguistic Human Rights

The remainder of this chapter examines the "new American revolution" being waged over, about, and around Indigenous efforts to protect and promote their languages. These battles are rightly conceptualized as struggles for fundamental human rights: at the individual level, the unconditional right to learn one's heritage language or mother tongue, and at the community level, the right to enjoy, conserve, and develop a heritage or community language as a protection against cultural and linguistic extinction (Skutnabb-Kangas, 2000; Skutnabb-Kangas & Phillipson, 1994). As Skutnabb-Kangas and Phillipson (1994) note, "People who are deprived of [linguistic human rights] may thereby be prevented from enjoying other human rights, including fair political representation, a fair trial, access to information and freedom of speech, and maintenance of their cultural heritage" (p. 2).

A key strategy for reasserting Indigenous rights to heritage/community languages has been heritage/community-language immersion, instruction that provides all or most content in the tribal language. "There can be no doubt that [heritage-language immersion] is the best way to jump-start the production of a new generation of fluent speakers," Hinton (2001) observes (p. 8). We focus on the Hawaiian, Fort Defiance Navajo, and Keres Pueblo cases—immersion efforts that are successfully producing new Native-language speakers.

As we will see, these projects continue to bump up against the safety zone, particularly as they begin to penetrate and challenge institutions of formal education. The most significant challenge for these and other language revitalization efforts, however, involves transforming the long-term effects of policies and practices that continue to condition language attitudes and choices in favor of English at the expense of Indigenous mother tongues. Restoring dignity and utility to tribal languages is at the heart of the "new American revolution." Because youth are central to these transformations, we conclude with a discussion of recent research on youth perspectives on their heritage languages and the issues for linguistic self-determination this research raises.[4]

HAWAIIAN IMMERSION: "I THINK THEY THOUGHT WE'D GIVE UP"

We begin this discussion with Hawaiian immersion. Although Native Hawaiians only recently were incorporated into the federal system for dealing with Native Americans, Native Hawaiians' experiences with U.S. imperialism and English-only schooling bear the same imprint and legacy as those of other Native peoples in the United States. Moreover, Hawaiian-language immersion may be the most dramatic success story in the "new American revolution" to date. It is a model that has been emulated by many Indigenous communities in their efforts to reclaim and restore tribal languages.

Beginning with Captain James Cook's arrival on the Hawaiian islands in 1778, the European invasion decimated the Native population, disenfranchising survivors from traditional lands. Following the illegal takeover of the Hawaiian monarchy by the U.S. military in 1898, Hawaii was annexed as a U.S. territory.[5] In 1959, it became the 50th state. From a long and rich tradition in which Hawaiian served as the language of government, religion, business, education, and the media, by the mid-20th century Hawaiian had become restricted to a few hundred inhabitants of a single island enclave.

Throughout this period, Hawaiian was formally and informally deemed by non-Native outsiders as inherently unsafe. Bans on Hawaiian-medium instruction and mandates that all government business be conducted in English further diminished the viability of Hawaiian as a mother tongue. According to Sam L. N. Warner (2001), a Native scholar and leader in the Hawaiian immersion movement, between 1900 and 1920, most Hawaiian children began speaking a local variety of English called Hawaiian Creole English. This continued into the 1960s, when a resistance or "Hawaiian renaissance" movement took root. "From this renaissance came a new group of second-language Hawaiian speakers who would become Hawaiian language educators" (Warner, 2001, p. 135).

In 1978, Hawaiian and English were designated co-official languages in Hawai'i. At the same time, a new state constitution mandated the promotion of Hawaiian language, culture, and history (Warner, 2001). Encouraged by these developments and the example of Māori preschool immersion "language nests" in New Zealand (Bishop, 2003), a small group of parents and language educators began to establish a similar program in Hawai'i (Warner, 2001, p. 136; see also Wilson, 1998, 1999).

The Hawaiian immersion preschools, or *'Aha Pūnana Leo* ("language nest gathering"; Wilson & Kamanā, 2001, p. 149), were designed to strengthen the Hawaiian *mauli*—culture, worldview, spirituality, morality, social relations, "and other central features of a person's life and the life of a people" (Wilson & Kamanā, 2001, p. 161). The family-run preschools, begun in 1983, enable children to interact with fluent speakers entirely in Hawaiian. "The original concept of the Pūnana Leo," program cofounders William H. Wilson and Kauanoe Kamanā (2001) write, was not "academic achievement for its own sake," but rather the creation of an environment "where Hawaiian language and culture were conveyed and developed in much the same way that they were in the home in earlier generations" (p. 151). Wilson and Kamanā describe a typical day as follows: The day begins with a circle involving "singing and chanting, hearing a story, exercising, [children] learning to introduce themselves and their families [or] cultural activities" (Wilson & Kamanā, 2001, pp. 151–152). This is followed by free time and structured lessons on reading, math, social studies, and art. Later in the day there is story time, "a second circle, and outdoor play until [children's] parents come to pick them up again" (Wilson & Kamanā, 2001, pp. 151–152).

As the first Pūnana Leo students prepared to enter Hawai'i's English-dominant public schools, their parents pressed the state for Hawaiian immersion elementary and secondary programs. Parental boycotts and demonstrations led to the establishment of immersion streams or tracks within existing school facilities and to a full-immersion, pre-K–12 school, Anuenue (Warner, 2001). At this school, children are instructed entirely in Hawaiian until fifth grade, when English language arts is introduced, often in Hawaiian. The following description is from McCarty's 2004 observations of Anuenue School in Oahu:

> Arriving at Anuenue School on a sunny morning in early fall, we hear the voices of children singing the Hawaiian *oli* or chant in the yard outside the school. According to the Native Hawaiian colleagues who have arranged this visit, this is how every school day begins at Anuenue: Facing their teachers and principal, children sing [in Hawaiian], asking permission to enter the school. The adults respond, comparing students to blossoms and reminding them that they are the leaders of the future.[6] Throughout the day, children's songs can be heard in classrooms, breezeways, and the grassy areas adjoining the school; song is a primary element of the curriculum. In the classrooms, all instruction is in Hawaiian and children respond and

interact in Hawaiian, although our fifth-grade guides, who began learning Hawaiian in kindergarten, tell us they prefer to speak English during playtime. (field notes, September 16, 2004)

Anuenue's founding highlights the tension between safe and dangerous differences in Indigenous schooling. Although the immersion school's founders desired and requested a facility in close proximity to Native Hawaiian communities, the state department of education offered a facility perched on a remote hillside near Honolulu. "I think they thought we'd give up," one veteran Anuenue teacher reflected (field notes, September 16, 2004). Like the tribal–community schools described in Chapter 6, Anuenue—a public school—has had to grapple with inconsistent and insufficient funding. Founded as an immersion school in 1995, Anuenue did not receive state funding for transportation until the 2004–2005 school year. Lack of state funding for the immersion preschool caused it to shut down the very same year.

Anuenue has nonetheless persisted, as have Hawaiian immersion tracks within other public schools. In 2005, there were 11 full-day, 11-month immersion preschools, and the opportunity for an education in Hawaiian extended from preschool to graduate school (see Table 7.1). In addition, an alternative community outreach Hawaiian language and culture program had been implemented to encourage Hawaiian-language learning in the domains of sports and the home (Warner, 1999a). In 2005, the total pre-K–12 enrollment in Hawaiian public and charter school immersion programs was 1,750 (Shapiro, 2005), and approximately 2,000 children had learned to speak Hawaiian through immersion schooling (Warner, 1999b, 2001; Wilson, 1999). Wilson and Kamanā (2001) cite two other accomplishments of Hawaiian immersion schools: the development of a network of young parents who are learning Hawaiian and the creation of a more diffuse environment of language support. And, although Hawaiian immersion has emphasized language revitalization rather than academic achievement, immersion students have performed as well or better on standardized tests than Native Hawaiian children in English-medium schools, even in English language arts, in which instruction is often in Hawaiian (Kamanā & Wilson, 1996; Wilson & Kamanā, 2001). There is also evidence that Hawaiian immersion strengthens the development of critical literacy and cultural pride. "I understand who I am as a Hawaiian, and where Hawaiians stood, and where they want to go," a graduate of Anuenue School states (Infante, 1999, p. E3).

These outcomes did not materialize without contention or strife. According to Warner (2001, 2004), for years parents fought state laws and regulations that prevented Native speakers from obtaining state-required certification to teach in the preschools. Warner (2001) also expresses concern that immersion schooling often assumes there is a one-to-one correspondence between

Table 7.1. Pre-K–12 Hawaiian language immersion programs, 2005.

Level	Number	Program Type
Pre-K	11	Private, community-based 'Aha Pūnana Leo preschools
K–12		Hawaiian-medium public schools:
	9	Elementary sites
	3	Intermediate sites
	2	Intermediate/high school sites
	2	High school sites
	1	K–11 site
	1	Comprehensive pre-K–12 site
	5	Charter school sites
Summary: Pre-K–12	34	Private, public, and public charter schools

Source: Department of Education State of Hawai'i, Office of Curriculum, Instruction and Student Support/Instructional Services Branch, 2005.

curriculum designed for the English classroom and the Hawaiian classroom, with the result being the "default" promotion of an English worldview (see also Wong, 1999, 2004). Finally, as the vignette from Anuenue suggests, Hawaiian remains restricted largely to the domain of schooling, which, as Warner (2001) and others have observed, is not sufficient to reverse the shift toward English.

Nevertheless, immersion schooling has succeeded in strengthening Hawaiian mauli, heightening consciousness and self-determination within the Native Hawaiian community, and enhancing children's academic success. In the process, the program has served as a catalyst for other Indigenous-language revitalization efforts, including the programs that follow.

NAVAJO IMMERSION: "BUCKING THE TIDE"

Navajo belongs to the Athabaskan language family, one of the most widespread Indigenous language families in North America. The language is spoken primarily in the Four Corners region of the U.S. Southwest, where the 25,000-square-mile Navajo Nation stretches over parts of Arizona, New Mexico, and Utah. With a written language history dating to the 19th century,

Navajo claims the largest number of speakers—more than 175,000—of any Indigenous language group in the United States (Benally & Viri, 2005).

These facts notwithstanding, by the late 20th century, English had become the primary language for a growing number of school-age Navajo children. In a 1991 survey of 682 Navajo preschoolers, Navajo linquist Paul Platero (1992, 2001) found that over half were considered by their teachers to be English monolinguals. In 1993, Wayne Holm conducted a study of over 3,300 kindergarteners in 110 Navajo schools and found that only half spoke any Navajo; less than a third were considered reasonably fluent speakers of Navajo (Holm & Holm, 1995). In contrast, just a few decades prior to Holm's study, Spolsky had found that 95% of Navajo 6-year-olds spoke fluent Navajo on entering school (Spolsky, 1975, 2002; Spolsky & Holm, 1977).

Given these statistics, the Navajo Nation initiated a major language immersion effort in Head Start preschools. Several pre-K–12 schools also launched language immersion programs. One of the better-documented programs began at a public elementary school in Fort Defiance, Arizona, adjacent to the tribal headquarters in Window Rock and very near the reservation border. A hub of commercial activity with a growing professional class, Fort Defiance is cross-cut by two major highways. The town's children are served by the Window Rock Unified School District. According to program cofounders Marie Arviso and Wayne Holm, when the Fort Defiance immersion program began in 1986, less than a tenth of the school's 5-year-olds were considered "reasonably competent" Navajo speakers; a third were judged to have passive knowledge of Navajo (Arviso & Holm, 2001, p. 204; see also Holm & Holm, 1995). At the same time, a high proportion of students were identified as "limited English proficient," possessing conversational English abilities but less proficiency in more decontextualized uses of English (Arviso & Holm, 2001). Given this sociolinguistic profile, program founders believed that "something more like the Māori [and Hawaiian] immersion programs might be the only type of program with some chance of success" (Arviso & Holm, 2001, p. 205).

Initially the Fort Defiance program involved reading and writing in Navajo, then English, and math in both languages, with other subjects included as content for speaking or writing (Holm & Holm, 1995). A heavy emphasis was placed on language and critical thinking as well as on process writing and cooperative learning. In the lower grades, all communication occurred in Navajo. By the second and third grades, the curriculum included a half-day in Navajo and a half-day in English. Fourth graders received at least 1 hour each day of Navajo instruction. In addition, the program required that adult caretakers or relatives "spend some time talking with the child in Navajo each evening after school" (Arviso & Holm, 2001, p. 210). Parental involvement became one of the program's most impressive accomplishments: "We began to realize," Arviso and Holm (2001) write, "that we had reached a number of those parents who had been 'bucking the tide' in trying to give their child[ren] some appreciation of what it meant to be Navajo in the late 20th century" (p. 211).

Table 7.2 summarizes findings from the project's first 7 years. By the fourth grade, Navajo immersion students were performing as well on local tests of English as comparable nonimmersion students at the school. Immersion students performed better on local assessments of English writing and were "way ahead" on standardized tests of mathematics. On standardized tests of English reading, students were slightly behind but closing the gap. In short, like students in the bilingual programs described in Chapter 6, immersion students were acquiring Navajo as a heritage language without cost, performing as well as or better than their nonimmersion peers by the fifth grade (Arviso & Holm, 2001; Holm & Holm, 1995).

An additional finding from the Fort Defiance study is worthy of note. By the fourth grade, not only were Navajo immersion students outperforming comparable nonimmersion students on assessments of Navajo, nonimmersion students actually performed *worse* on these assessments than they had in kindergarten (see Table 7.2). There is much debate about what schools can and cannot do to reverse language shift (see, e.g., Fishman, 1991; Krauss, 1998; McCarty, 1998). The Fort Defiance data demonstrate the powerful *negative* effect of the absence of instruction in the heritage language and,

Table 7.2. Achievement trends after the first seven years of Navajo immersion programming at Fort Defiance Elementary School.

Assessment Type	Navajo Immersion (NI) Students	Mainstream English (ME) Students
Local English reading assessments	Same as ME students	Same as NI students
Local Navajo assessments	Better than ME students	Worse than NI students and worse than their own kindergarten performance
Local English writing assessments	Better than ME students	Worse than NI students
Standardized mathematics assessments	Substantially better than ME students	Worse than NI students
Standardized English reading tests	Slightly behind but catching up with ME students	Slightly ahead of NI students

Source: Holm & Holm (1995).

conversely, its positive effect on heritage-language maintenance as well as students' acquisition of English and mathematics content and skills.

In 2004, 245 immersion students were enrolled in 18 classrooms within a consolidated primary/intermediate school in the Window Rock School District. Immersion students continued to demonstrate significant improvements in their academic performance as measured by standardized tests, with nearly 70% of third-grade immersion students meeting or exceeding state standards in mathematics, compared to 15% of comparable students in nonimmersion classrooms. In English writing, 55% of Navajo immersion students met or exceeded state standards, compared to 35% of nonimmersion students. Student performance on English reading assessments was comparable for both groups, with 36% of immersion students and 37% of nonimmersion students meeting or exceeding standards (Johnson & Wilson, 2004). Although some might argue there is room for improvement for both groups, our point is that Navajo immersion students perform as well as or better than their peers in monolingual English programs, even on English standardized tests. Meanwhile, Navajo immersion students have the benefit of becoming bilingual and biliterate in their heritage language.

Like the Hawaiian experience, the Fort Defiance/Window Rock immersion program has become a model for school-based efforts to reclaim Indigenous languages and promote Indigenous- and minority-language rights. At the same time, these programs show convincingly that student achievement, as measured by local and national assessments, is enhanced by curricula that meaningfully incorporate Native languages and cultural knowledge. The findings from these programs also suggest that to be maximally effective, school-based language revitalization must be combined with community-based initiatives, an approach illustrated in the following section.

KERES IMMERSION: "THE COMMUNITY MUST DEFEND THEIR RIGHTS"

The Pueblos of the U.S. Southwest are among the most enduring Indigenous communities in North America. There are 20 Pueblo tribes, including the Hopis of northern Arizona, with the remaining 19 located in northern New Mexico. Four language families are represented among the New Mexico Pueblos. In this section, we focus on the Keres-speaking Pueblos of Acoma and Cochiti, both of which are actively involved in language reclamation.

Located 64 miles west of Albuquerque, Acoma Pueblo has a tribal enrollment of 5,000, approximately 3,000 of whom live on the quarter-million-acre Acoma reservation (Sims, 2001b). While retaining a traditional matrilineal clan system and a governing system of secular officials appointed annually by religious leaders, Acoma participates vigorously in the wider economy, including tourism, marketing its famed black-and-white pottery, and operating a large tribal casino. The 54,000-acre Pueblo of Cochiti is located farther north, about 30 miles southwest of Santa Fe at the base of the Jemez Mountains along the Rio Grande. There are approximately 1,200 tribal members, with a median age of 27 (Benjamin, Pecos, & Romero, 1996). Cochiti, too, retains a traditional religious calendar and a theocratic government, participation in which requires proficiency in the Native language (Pecos & Blum-Martínez, 2001). In both Pueblo communities, however, Native-language loss is a growing concern (Romero, 2001; Romero & McCarty, 2006; Sims, 2001b).

Cochiti and Acoma share with other New Mexico Pueblos a history of brutal Spanish colonization (see, e.g., Spicer, 1962). The U.S. government's acquisition of the New Mexico Territory in the 19th century and the forced incorporation of Pueblo communities into the expanding nation-state "introduced an even more rapid pace of new foreign influence, . . . especially in the socioeconomic and education domains" (Sims, 2001b, p. 65; see also Minge, 1976). Like other Native people, the Pueblos were subject to forced assimilation carried out in mission and federal boarding schools. Pueblo communities also were impacted by their proximity to a major east–west railroad and interstate highway, and by the more recent enrollment of their children in nearby public schools. At Cochiti, the construction of a large federal dam destroyed ceremonial sites and family farmlands, precipitating widespread familial and communal displacement and Native-language loss (Benjamin et al., 1996).

Beginning in the 1990s, both Cochiti and Acoma launched concerted community-based language-planning initiatives. According to Acoma tribal member and language educator Christine Sims (2001b), a year-long language-planning process revealed that "there were no children of preschool or elementary school-age speaking Acoma as a first language" (p. 67). Mary Eunice Romero (2001), former director of the Cochiti language immersion program, states that a similar survey at Cochiti showed that two-thirds of the population were not fluent Keres speakers. At the same time, both surveys showed a strong interest by adults and young people in revitalizing the language (Pecos & Blum-Martínez, 2001; Romero, 2001; Romero & McCarty, 2006; Sims, 2001b).

The two tribes began holding communitywide awareness meetings and language forums. "We had to convince the community, number one, that we were experiencing major language shift, and two, that there is something we can do about," Romero (2001, n.p.) reports. In 1996 Cochiti Pueblo launched an immersion program, and in 1997 Acoma held its first summer immersion camp. To model natural dialogue, both programs paired teams of fluent speakers with small groups of students. At Cochiti, pairing fluent with partially fluent speakers/teachers enabled young people and adult teacher-apprentices to learn Keres together.

Focus of community immersion programs for Pueblos

The focus in both programs has been strengthening oral skills rather than literacy. "There is widespread support for keeping [the Native language] in its oral form," Pecos and Blum-Martínez (2001) explain; "oral tradition . . . has been an important element in maintaining [community] values [and the] leaders know that writing the language could bring about unwanted changes in secular and religious traditions" (p. 76).

Recently, Cochiti extended its efforts to year-round instruction in the public elementary school, where students receive daily Keres immersion in grades 1 through 5. An important factor in these school-based efforts is tribal fiscal and operational control over the program. "We're accountable to the tribal council first since they fund the program," a Pueblo Native-language teacher relates (quoted in Suina, 2004, p. 291).

Success of programs

Preliminary program data show that on national assessments of English language arts, students who participated in immersion classes performed significantly better than those in English-only classes (Sims, 2001a). More important to community members are the facts that children have gained conversational ability in Keres and that there is growing evidence of Native-language use communitywide. Of Cochiti Pueblo, Pecos and Blum-Martínez (2001) report:

> Across the community and within individual families, one can see closer, more intimate relationships . . . as fluent speakers take the time to share their knowledge. In short, the children's success is the community's success, and many people are now aware of the need to speak Keres publicly and consistently. (p. 81)

The Cochiti and Acoma initiatives have been recognized as exemplars of community-based language planning (see discussions in Hinton & Hale, 2001; Hornberger, 1996; Romero & McCarty, 2006). "It is at the community level that people . . . must defend their rights to their own languages and cultures," Wong-Fillmore (1996) insists (p. 439). "Revitalizing the language is up to us," Romero (2001, n.p.) observes; "the true planners and implementers have to be local people."

NATIVE YOUTH LANGUAGE ATTITUDES AND IDEOLOGIES

The Hawaiian, Navajo, and Keres projects highlight the importance of understanding the sociohistorical circumstances that have shaped the current status of Indigenous languages. These projects also suggest the enormity of the challenges in turning the present situation around. Teachers must be trained (sometimes including, as in the Hawaiian case, learning or relearning the heritage language as part of teacher preparation), materials must be produced, and, most importantly, community members and school officials must be committed to the effort over the long haul. The long-term success of these projects remains to be seen: Will the graduates of these programs choose to socialize *their* children in the heritage language?

In this penultimate section, we consider the youngest stakeholders in the "new American revolution"—Native youth—those ultimately entrusted with tribal language futures. What are Native youths' attitudes and ideologies toward their tribal/heritage languages?[7] How do these attitudes and ideologies influence young people's language choices?

Surprisingly little has been published on this topic, but the available research is both intriguing and troubling. Adley-SantaMaria (1999) notes that the "(mis)education of Native American youth is one cause of the crisis of language shift" (p. 17). Bielenberg (2002) and Nicholas (2005) document the family-, community-, and school-based dynamics impacting Hopi youths' language choices. In both of these studies, although youth indicated a desire to learn the language, they often expressed fear of being ridiculed for linguistic errors: "People sometimes laugh at you," one youth reported, "and you don't want to speak it anymore" (quoted in Bielenberg, 2002, p. 250). Lee's (1999) study of 200 Navajo adolescents in five reservation secondary schools suggests that as they aged, Navajo youth became more aware of the endangered status of their language and that this may have led them to speak more Navajo with siblings and adult family members as young adults (see also Lee & McLaughlin, 2001). Romero's (2003) study of child socialization and language shift in Cochiti Pueblo also documents reverence for and interest in learning Keres among the young, although most young parents were not fluent in Keres and therefore were raising their children in English.

As part of a national study of Native-language loss and revitalization, McCarty and colleagues (2006a, 2006b, 2006c) examined the language ideologies and choices among a sample of 45 Navajo youth. The following responses were typical of the majority of these youth, who in general expressed positive feelings toward their heritage language:

"Knowing Navajo is important because I get the best of both worlds."
"Knowing Navajo helps me not to lose the identity of who I am."
"Knowing Navajo helps me in school because I can compare the two different languages [Navajo and English]."
"English is important. . . . But you have to know your own language to succeed."
[McCarty et al., 2006a]

(handwritten margin note: Old + Some shame speaking Navajo)

These positive statements were tempered by those of youth who described speaking Navajo as unimportant or "just the past" (McCarty et al., 2006a). Even youth who were proficient speakers of Navajo and who expressed positive attitudes toward the language described the prevalence of feelings of shame associated with speaking Navajo. A 17-year-old reported that his peers frequently hid their ability to speak Navajo from their teachers: "They [peers] probably think [Navajo] is important, but . . . they're judged by other people that speak English more clear than they do and they just kind of feel dirty about the whole thing" (McCarty et al., 2006a). Some youth who spoke Navajo felt stigmatized as "uneducated," "backward," or "not having experienced anything in the world"; Navajo-speaking students also were overrepresented in remedial education programs (McCarty et al., 2006b). Commenting on the historical roots of these attitudes and practices, one youth stated, "It's [a result of] being told Navajo is stupid, . . . to speak Indian is the way of the devil" (McCarty et al., 2006a).

This research suggests that while many young people hold positive attitudes toward their heritage language, those attitudes may be undermined by sociohistorical and systemic forces that constrain their language choices. It is a deeply troubling irony that languages once proscribed as dangerous by the federal government have come to be perceived, in effect, as "unsafe" among the young. "You forsake who you are," one Navajo youth reported; "You give up having to learn Navajo in order to accommodate the mainstream life" (McCarty et al., 2006a).

CREATING NEW INDIGENOUS-LANGUAGE SAFETY ZONES

Although recent federal support for Native-language education is a welcome reversal of past policy, centuries of federal bans on and abuse for speaking Native languages have left an indelible mark. Working with drastically reduced numbers of speakers, Native communities are faced with transforming conditioned attitudes toward their languages as "dirty" and "backward"—"the way of the devil." Communities are now in the position of having to create new Indigenous-language safety zones, not only within the context of schools but even more important, within the informal and intimate contexts of family and community (Fishman, 1991, 2001). These challenges are heightened by the recent passage of English-only policies in states with large numbers of Indian pupils (e.g., Arizona and California) and by the conjoined march of technology, globalization, and English as a world language.

These are the tasks of the "new American revolution," and they are fraught with both contradiction and hope. The contradictions lie in the history of linguistic repression and the residue of ideological ambiguity left in its wake. At the same time, recent research indicates that many Native youth continue to value the heritage language, view it as central to their identities, want adults to teach it to them, and employ it as a strategic tool to facilitate their learning in school. Much more research is needed in this area, but these are hopeful signs. The future of Indigenous linguistic self-determination rests on our ability to capitalize on the interests and resources present in this generation of youth and on the lessons learned from successful language revitalization efforts such as those currently under way in Hawai'i, the Navajo Nation, the Pueblos, and, indeed, around the world.

CHAPTER 8

Testing Tribal Sovereignty: Self-Determination and High-Stakes Tests

At the beginning of the 21st century, . . . we are witnessing an un-
bridled, vulgar, corporate influence on American education. Through
the insistence on high stakes . . . testing as a means of advancing our
national competitive edge in world markets, American education is
in danger of devolving into a punitive, hierarchical and unforgiving
tournament that winnows and sifts students as if they were the wheat
and the chaff. The end goal of which is to declare that those who
pass have demonstrated competence and that those who do not are
the children of a lesser God, or at least a failing grade.
                          —Beverly Gordon, Past Vice President of the American
                              Educational Research Association (2000, pp. 1–2)

In this final chapter, we come to the present moment. American education
has reached a new zenith in its emphasis on standards and testing. "No
other country in the world tests their children to the extent that we do,"
Beverly Gordon (2000) writes (p. 3). What distinguishes the current standards movement from previous practices is both the quantity of standardized tests and their high stakes: Under a new labeling system in P.L. 107-110,
the federal No Child Left Behind (NCLB) Act of 2001, standardized tests
are administered not only to gauge student knowledge but as a surveillance
and gatekeeping device, enabling or curtailing educational opportunity as
never before.

The need to hold schools accountable for achievement results is, in principle, a laudable goal. Few would argue that schools should "leave children
behind." Unfortunately, as Crawford (2004b) points out, NCLB's approach
to school accountability "is overly rigid, punitive, unscientific, and likely to
do more harm than good for students who are now being left behind" (p. 1;
see also Goodman, Shannon, Goodman, & Rapoport, 2004). Even those who
have praised this policy because it requires schools to disaggregate achievement data by "race"/ethnicity, social class, ability, and English proficiency—
thereby motivating school districts to focus greater attention on students so
classified—note that teachers often respond to the pressures of high-stakes

150

accountability by implementing such detrimental practices as increasing special education placements, "preemptively" retaining students in grade, and limiting time spent on "low-stakes" subjects such as science and social studies (compare, e.g., Jacob, 2004; Roderick, Jacob, & Bryk, 2002; Amrein & Berliner, 2002). Moreover, as we elaborate further in this chapter, the law fails to address the most significant barrier to achievement parity: resource inequities (see also Crawford, 2004b).

Exacerbating these punitive policies is a burgeoning corpus of state constitutional amendments that make instruction in a language other than English illegal, despite students' English-language proficiency. In the most extreme cases, such as Arizona's Proposition 203, these statutes criminalize teachers and school administrators, threatening to rescind their state certification for failure to instruct limited-English-proficient pupils (relabeled as English language learners under NCLB) in English only.

These policies flatly contradict the provisions of the Native American Languages Act (NALA), described in Chapter 7. Jurisdictional issues surrounding these laws for public schools on reservations remain contested. However, even if questions regarding the authority of states to impose English-only requirements were resolved in favor of tribes, public school students in off-reservation schools remain affected, and both on- and off-reservation schools remain accountable to NCLB. NCLB is, in effect, an English-only law.[1] These new state and federal policies place "minority" languages outside the safety zone (the telling exception is foreign-language teaching, an elite form of second-language instruction not of concern in these policies), severely limiting the educational choices available to language minority youth.

Utilizing our three-pronged approach (policy, practice, Native experiences), this chapter examines these recent developments as they are impacting Native American education, their interface with tribal sovereignty, and tribal–community responses to these new "tests" of self-determination. This is a chapter about tests, both literal and metaphorical. Whether literal or metaphorical, they are high-stakes tests, because they challenge—test—the cornerstones of tribal sovereignty and democracy. The standards movement raises issues of educational equity and opportunity in which all citizens have a high stake.

We begin with some brief historical background, placing the present standards movement in the context of what is arguably the most salient organizing category in U.S. society: race (Hill, 2001; Moses, 2004). We then show how racial ideologies intersect with notions of safe versus dangerous difference within the standards movement. We analyze more closely the instructional consequences of this movement in Indigenous schools. We conclude by considering contemporary tribal challenges to the movement, including Native American charter schools and the development of "counter-standards" for culturally responsive schooling.

RACE AND INTELLIGENCE TESTING
IN AMERICAN EDUCATION

As a socially constructed concept, race has a long, ugly, and lingering history in American education. That this concept remains vigorous in American intellectual, social, educational, and political life is evident from the popularity of such texts as Hernnstein and Murray's (1994) *The Bell Curve* or psychologist J. Phillippe Rushton's (1999) racial "profiles" that place Asians and Blacks at opposite ends of an evolutionary pole, with Asians said to have larger brains and higher IQs and Whites falling "somewhere in the middle" (pp. 19–20).

Race-based testing for Native Americans is part of this larger race complex. According to policy analysts Terrence Wiley and Wayne Wright (2004), the rise of the educational testing movement in the early 20th century coincided with a period of intense Americanization and "widespread xenophobia toward non-English speaking immigrants, . . . lynching of African Americans and discrimination against other racial minority groups" (p. 158). By the start of World War I, corporate-financed racial intelligence testing "became a national movement," with such prominent educational researchers as Edward Thorndike and Lewis Terman supporting sterilization of the "feebleminded" (Wiley & Wright, 2004, p. 158).

> The so-called scientific testing movement of the early 20th century was intertwined with racism and linguicism at a time when the push for expanded uses of restrictive English-literacy requirements coincided with the period of record immigration. (Wiley & Wright, 2004, p. 159)

These demographic forces and social-educational responses are not unlike those in the United States today, and we will return to them later in our analysis. For present purposes, we simply wish to place Native American experiences within this larger ideological complex.

"Blood" and IQ

Previous chapters have shown the ways in which racial (and racist) ideologies pervaded educational practice in American Indian schools. Recall, for example, Superintendent of Indian Schools Estelle Reel's characterization of "the Indian child [as] of lower physical organization" and of "stolid mind"

(Lomawaima, 1996, p. 14; see Chapters 2 and 3, this volume). Intelligence testing of children said to possess varying degrees of Indian "blood" both reflected and served these ideological interests. In 1922, for instance, researchers from the University of Kansas tested 715 students at the Haskell Indian Institute on English paper-and-pencil tests, comparing scores among individual Indian students said to have different degrees of Indian "blood," as well as those of Indian students as a group with students identified simply as "White." Noting that one "should not overlook the possibility . . . that the white blood present in the various hybrids [so-called mixed-bloods] is of a low grade," these researchers concluded that intelligence decreases "with increasing amount of Indian blood" and that Indians were inferior to Whites in mental processes (Hunter & Sommermier, 1922, p. 259).

In a similar study of Native students in Ontario, Canada, researchers from the University of Toronto asserted that the "more white blood the Indian pupils have the higher their intelligence" and that in terms of intelligence, Indians of Ontario "occupy a point just below the Hebrews and above the Chinese" (Jamieson & Sandiford, 1928, pp. 540, 543). Well into the 20th century, researchers made claims for similar "scientific" findings, sometimes noting, parenthetically, related personal qualities of "rugged honesty and thriftiness" (Navajos), "amiability" (Pueblos), or "courage and endurance" (Lakota and Arapaho) (Garth, Serafina, & Dutton, 1925, p. 383).

Race-Based School Evaluation: The Erickson Report and Beyond

Within the Navajo Nation, a government-sponsored evaluation of the Rough Rock Demonstration School was undertaken in the late 1960s by Donald Erickson, a professor at the University of Chicago, and his assistant Henrietta Schwartz. The purpose of the evaluation was to determine whether the Rough Rock School and its "demonstration" of Indian control over Indian schooling was producing positive results in terms of the school's stated aims. Erickson and Schwartz used a variety of methods for their study, including a two-month "anthropological live-in" by Schwartz, a content analysis of school board minutes, standardized test scores, questionnaires, and interviews with school staff, students, and parents. Among the measures used with students was an "anxiety scale" that asked students to respond to such questions as:

- Do you bite your nails or chew your pencil?
- Can you feel your heart pounding in your chest?
- Have you had a lot of trouble with your teeth?
- Are your feelings easily hurt?

- Do you worry about many things?
- Do you feel unhappy and depressed?
(quoted in McCarty, 2002a, p. 105)

In the same evaluation, Rough Rock students also were asked "aspirational" questions such as: "Do most Navajo pupils sometimes wish they were Anglos?" "Who is smarter [Navajos or Anglos]?" "What grade do you think you will go to before you stop going to school?" (Erickson & Schwartz, 1969, pp. 7.15, 7.16, 7.18). These and other measures, including English standardized tests, were used to characterize Rough Rock students as "inferior academically" and to dismiss the Rough Rock Demonstration School altogether as "unrealistic and unnecessary" (Erickson & Schwartz, 1969, p. 9.8).

The invalidity of and racist assumptions informing these measures may appear to be self-evident. Yet similar measures have been used to buttress more recent studies of brain hemisphere and learning style differences based on race and ethnicity, with some researchers going so far as to assert that the "traditional Native American mode of thinking is uniquely different from modern man" (Ross, 1989, p. 72). Countering these claims is an abundance of scholarship from around the world documenting the inappropriateness of standardized testing as a measure of minority students' ability, learning styles, or school achievement (see, e.g., Cummins, 1984, 1989; Deyhle, 1986; Edelsky, 1991; Gipps, 1999; Lessow-Hurley, 2000; McCarty et al., 1991; Stefanakis, 1998; Troike, 1984; Valdés & Figueroa, 1994). Nevertheless, English standardized tests continue to be the "gold standard" for evaluating all students' educational progress, regardless of their language proficiency or cultural background vis-à-vis the instrument.

THE PRESENT STANDARDS MOVEMENT

Sense and Non-Sense: Problematizing NCLB

What are the implications of the standards movement for Indigenous students in U.S. schools today? Before proceeding to this question, it is instructive to consider the rationale for this movement, most recently embodied in the No Child Left Behind Act of 2001. According to the U.S. Commission on Civil Rights (USCCR), NCLB "is premised on the idea that by measuring student achievement, students, teachers, parents, and school administrators will improve their performance to meet or exceed national standards" (USCCR, 2004, p. 14). (Note that the standards themselves go unquestioned, a point we will return to later in this chapter.) The congressional Statement of Purpose for the law describes its goal as meeting "the educational needs of low achieving children in our Nation's highest-poverty schools, limited English proficient children, migratory children, children with disabilities, Indian children, neglected or delinquent children, and young children in need of reading assistance" (USCCR, 2004, p. 3).

We can see from this statement that NCLB and its standards, pedagogies, and consequences target specific student populations, the majority of whom are students of color, including Native American students, in economically poor school districts. These districts are overwhelmingly underresourced, with per-pupil expenditures one-third to one-half that of schools serving primarily White students. More than 80% of the nation's schools serving African Americans, Latinos, Native Americans, and some Asian students are in high-poverty areas, compared with 5% of schools serving primarily White students. Phoenix, Arizona, is typical; there, the difference between the richest and poorest districts is $1,500 per student per year, $36,000 per classroom per year, and $600,000 per year for an elementary school of 400 students (Meléndez, 2004). When reservation schools are factored in to these statistics, the differences in per-pupil expenditures are doubled. Federal funding levels for American Indian education are notoriously low; between 1998 and 2003, funding was completely absent for many U.S. Department of Education Indian education programs (USCCR, 2003).

NCLB fails to take these economic and social differentials into account, a failure that, in combination with the legislation's high-stakes "accountability" measures, virtually guarantees that poor and working-class students, students of color, English-language learners, and special-needs students will continue to be "left behind" (USCCR, 2004). NCLB requires annual reading and mathematics testing of students in grades 3–8; by 2007–2008, schools must test students in science at least once during elementary, middle, and high school (USCCR, 2004). Further, the tests must be aligned with standards approved by states (not tribes), and both students and schools are expected to meet annual goals for achievement, called "adequate yearly progress" (AYP). If students fail to meet AYP goals, schools become subject to outside remediation, including changes in governance (e.g., takeover by for-profit school management groups) and withdrawal of federal funds. The consequences for students include failure to graduate or retention in grade—a practice that exhaustive research shows actually increases school dropout rates, particularly for ethnic minority students (National Center for Education Statistics, 2001–2002; USCCR, 2004).

NCLB: Widening the Achievement Gap?

Research is only beginning to document the consequences of this policy on the students, communities, and schools it most directly affects. However, a recent U.S. Civil Rights Commission report found that NCLB has done little to close the achievement gap. In fact, the Commission notes that the prescriptive nature of the policy, its high stakes for minority students and schools, and the total lack of attention to closing the gap in financial resources between the richest and poorest schools are widening the gap between children of color and their more affluent White peers (USCCR, 2004; see also Wiley & Wright, 2004; Wright, 2002). Further, the Commission expressed concern that "the emphasis on testing built into NCLB will result in 'teaching to the test' at the expense of developing reasoning and critical thinking skills" (USCCR, 2004, p. 17). The report continues:

> There is concern that students who are most suffering from the achievement gap (i.e., the lower scoring students, predominantly minority and special needs students) will be coached to pass the tests rather than to learn a rich curriculum, and that schools will feel pressure to eliminate or reduce the emphasis on subjects not covered by the tests . . . many U.S. schools are reporting a narrowing of the curriculum as a result of the new mandates [and] the impact of NCLB has been particularly great in schools with large minority populations that have . . . the lowest test scores and are under the most pressure to improve. (USCCR, 2004, pp. 17–18)[2]

In 2005, the National Indian Education Association (NIEA) conducted 11 regional hearings on NCLB throughout the United States. The purpose of the hearings, which included testimony by 120 witnesses, was to gather information on the impact of NCLB, make recommendations to strengthen the law for Native students, and gather "information about what is working within NCLB and how to support [successful] programs" (Beaulieu, Sparks, & Alonzo, 2005, p. 1). In its report on the outcomes of these hearings, NIEA's leadership pointed out that making schools accountable to Native students is a "welcome change" but that there is widespread concern that NCLB compromises tribal sovereignty and Indigenous community choice, negatively impacts culturally based instruction, leads to hyperattention to standardized tests at the expense of pedagogically sound instruction, and is inadequately funded to enable tribes to meet its mandates. Further, "these [legislative] changes . . . have not included the Native voice" (Beaulieu et al., 2005, p. 4).

CONSEQUENCES OF THE STANDARDS MOVEMENT FOR INDIGENOUS STUDENTS AND SCHOOLS

According to the working group that outlined the 2001 American Indian and Alaska Native national education research agenda, the purpose of setting standards and assessing student performance "is not to punish children" but "to ensure that educators are accountable for the product they are providing" (Research Agenda Working Group, 2001, p. 37). The evidence to date, however, indicates that the effects of the current standards movement have been punitive rather than uplifting. Of all ethnic minorities in U.S. schools, American Indian and Alaska Native students are the "least likely to perform well on [standardized] tests" and the most likely to drop out of school (Tirado, 2001, p. 12). Their low test performance leads American Indian and Alaska Native students to be heavily overrepresented in remedial programs. In 1999–2000, for example, although American Indian and Alaska Natives students accounted for only 1% of public school enrollment, they accounted for 1.3% of all students served under the Individuals with Disabilities Education Act—a representation in special education programs and services 30% higher than would be expected (Tippeconnic & Faircloth, 2002, p. 1). Among all students identified as limited English proficient during the same time period, 1.9%—55,000 students, or more than 10% of total Indian enrollment in U.S. schools—were American Indian/ Alaska Native. In Bureau of Indian Affairs schools, 20% of students received special education services in 1999–2000, and nearly 60% were identified as limited English proficient (Tippeconnic & Faircloth, 2002, p. 1).

Conversely, the number and proportion of Native American students in gifted-and-talented programs is extremely low. In a study of giftedness among New Mexico Pueblo students, Romero (1994) found that although a high proportion of Native students were enrolled in remedial programs, none were identified by the school as gifted. Yet Pueblo communities have a coherent and well-articulated system of attributes for giftedness that include endurance, self-discipline, empathy, generosity, Native-language proficiency, "a keen interest in learning," and creativity in traditional artforms such as drum making, weaving, drumming, and dancing (Romero, 1994, pp. 41–49). Many students at Santa Fe Indian School, where Romero served as a diagnostician and conducted her research, possessed these qualities but had been assigned to remedial tracks on the basis of mainstream views of ability as reflected in standardized tests. Meeting the educational needs of American Indian children and addressing their underrepresentation in gifted programs "first requires an acceptance of Native principles, values, and traditions . . . [that] play a vital role in [their] lives and educational performance," Romero (1994) states (p. 56).

THE LARGER CONTEXT:
STANDARDS AND DANGEROUS DIVERSITY

The present standards movement cannot be decoupled from larger social, economic, and demographic forces. "Whenever people start talking about [an educational] crisis," literacy scholar Carole Edelsky notes, "you have to ask . . . , why this now?" (quoted in Teale, 1992, p. 328; see also McQuillan,

1998). It is not coincidental that the present standards movement, like that of
the early 20th century discussed earlier in this chapter, comes at a time when
the United States is experiencing an unprecedented demographic shift. Much
of this stems from the "new immigration"—those who have immigrated to
the United States following Congress's abolition of national-origin quotas in
1965. Unlike earlier waves of immigration, which originated in Europe and
were primarily White, recent immigrants come largely from Latin America,
Southeast Asia, and the Caribbean (Qin-Hilliard, Feinauer, & Quiroz, 2001;
Suárez-Orozco, 2001). Difference in the United States is taking on not only
new languages, but new colors. People of color now make up 28% of the
nation's population, with the numbers expected to grow to 38% in 2024 and
47% in 2050 (Banks, 2001). A significant proportion are English-language
learners, who, in addition to Native Americans, speak more than 150 languages.

According to Suárez-Orozco, more than 3.5 million English-language
learners are presently enrolled in U.S. schools. In the 500 largest public school
districts in the United States—New York, Los Angeles, Chicago, Houston,
and Detroit, for example—52% of the student population are ethnic minority students. In the 100 largest school districts, 61% of student enrollments
are minority students from low-income families (Moll, 2004). In light of these
demographics, current state-prescribed instructional and testing programs
can be seen as regulatory strategies aimed at stifling "dangerous" diversity.
"Consider that the dominant response to these radical demographic changes
has been to develop educational policies that obviate diversity in favor of
practices that seek to control the student population," Moll observes (2004,
p. 126). The fact that affluent and middle-class White students elude these
pedagogies (indeed, these students are explicitly excluded from the language
and requirements of NCLB) heightens the disparities between the privileged
and those already marginalized within these policies.

The present moment in American Indian education must be viewed in
light of this larger sociopolitical context. Tribal- and community-controlled
schools are not immune to the pressures of the standards movement, as their
funding depends on compliance with federal mandates. What are the implications for tribal sovereignty? How are tribes and Native communities
responding to these tests of tribal sovereignty? Using illustrative examples
from Native communities in the Southwest and Alaska, we consider these
questions in the sections that follow.

REASSERTING LOCAL CONTROL:
A CHARTER SCHOOL EXAMPLE

As the pressures for standardization have mounted, with no evidence that
the focus on standards and high-stakes testing improves educational out-

comes or opportunities for Native youth, many Indigenous communities
have looked to alternative institutional arrangements as a means of retaining control over their schools and ensuring that the curriculum is infused with
local linguistic and cultural knowledge. Charter schools, linked through formal agreements to authorizing entities such as public school districts but
chartered by a distinctive mission, have become an increasingly popular—
if controversial—option.[3] The hallmarks of charter schools are (1) a certain degree of autonomy from state regulations (charter schools are still
accountable for increased student achievement, and most charter schools
participate in whatever statewide testing is in place); and (2) the opportunity to exercise an alternative to BIA or public schools. Forty states and
the District of Columbia have charter school legislation; in 2005, approximately 3,400 charter schools enrolled a million children across the country (Center for Education Reform, 2005; U.S. Charter Schools, 2004).
According to the U.S. Department of Education, in 1997–1998, nearly one-
tenth of all American Indian/Alaska Native student enrollment—5,310
students—were in charter schools (Tirado, 2001). "For Native Americans,"
Tirado (2001) writes, these schools "offer the opportunity to create and
offer curriculums geared toward local cultures" (p. 14).

In this section, we focus on one Native American charter school, which
we call Bahidaj High (a pseudonym).[4] Bahidaj High is located in an urban
metropolitan area of the southwestern U.S.; it serves Native American students in grades 9–12. Bahidaj High is a particularly relevant case for examination, as its mission is to serve as an academically rigorous, bicultural,
community-based high school for Native youth. "By infusing all aspects
of the educational experience with elements of [Native] language and Native
history," a school brochure reads, "the school will nurture individual students, helping them become strong and responsible contributors to their
communities."

Bahidaj High was founded in 1998 by a small group of Native and non-
Native educators and parents dissatisfied with the BIA and public schools available for Native youth in the area. "The schools on the reservation weren't even
requiring the courses students would need to be accepted into universities," the
school's founding director notes (quoted in Zehr, 2001). The pathway to founding an alternative school was far from easy, and up until the school's opening
day, the group was confounded with both political and financial obstacles.
Another school cofounder and Native-language teacher describes the prover-
bial "leap of faith" required to make Bahidaj High a reality:

> Roadblocks immediately appeared in our way. Our financial resources were
> almost nonexistent, and vested interests on the . . . reservation made acquiring
> a reservation site impossible. Several times our small group considered . . . giving
> up. . . . But each time a new problem or obstacle appeared, we found a solu-

tion, and it became obvious to us that [Bahidaj] was meant to be a reality. . . .
We applied for loans [and a] federal charter schools grant came our way, allowing us to assemble a core faculty. (Mendez et al., 2003, p. 74)

In 2004–2005, approximately 150 students attended Bahidaj High;
many were bused in daily from their home reservation some 70 miles away.
That this is a different kind of school is evident at first glance. Located in
a residential area near a large university campus, the school facility was
formerly a church. Repainted in vibrant colors, the school is surrounded
by working gardens and native desert trees planted by students and their
teachers. The gardens are part of Bahidaj High's ethnobotany and permaculture curriculum and are enhanced by straw-bale cold frames and a traditional Native outdoor kitchen that "serves as a meeting place for both the
neighborhood residents and parents of [Bahidaj High] students" (Woelfle-
Erskine, 2003, p. 72). Inside the school, the organization of space is equally
distinctive, with student projects and the Native language evident throughout the building.

Bahidaj High teachers, many of whom are Native American, describe
their goals as "helping kids really understand the things that they can do with
their talents" (Bahidaj teacher, personal communication, 2003). In addition
to required standardized tests, teachers maintain portfolios for every student
in every class, conducting their own teacher research on the portfolios over
time (Bahidaj teacher, personal communication, 2005). The curriculum com-
bines Native language and culture with conventional courses. English literature courses, for example, emphasize the work of poets and writers of color,
including Native American authors. The U.S. history text is Howard Zinn's
(1980/2003) *A People's History of the United States*, which begins with a
critique of the Christopher Columbus story: "Even allowing for the imper-
fection of myths, it is enough to make us question . . . the excuse of progress
in the annihilation of races, and the telling of history from the standpoint of
the conquerors and leaders of Western civilization" (p. 22). This critique is
evident in the writings of Bahidaj High School students: "My teacher doesn't
teach us out of a textbook," one student states, "because . . . they're often
too one-sided. Instead, she tells us both sides of history":

> It makes me think of [the Chiricahua Apache leader] Geronimo and what they
> did to him when he was captured. They dressed him up and made him dance
> like crazy, just to give the public the idea that Indians acted like that. After
> learning all that it makes me wonder about what else people lied about. (Juan,
> 2003, p. 27)

In addition to Spanish, students' tribal language is taught as a "foreign"
language (state statutes require foreign-language teaching, and many public

schools serving primarily Native students use this as an opportunity to teach Native languages); even teachers at Bahidaj who do not speak the Native language take classes in the language. "I choose to learn about my culture," a student states, "so I can know where I come from, and know who I am" (Juan, 2003, p. 29). Other curricular areas include traditional Native basket weaving, ethnobotany, and permaculture. Although teachers recognize that "most . . . students won't weave baskets after the class stops," some do; one graduate has become a prize-winning basket weaver. The primary purpose of these and other Native culture classes, according to one teacher, is to develop a respect for the craft from experiencing it firsthand. Of the ethnobotany curriculum, which features the cultivation of traditional Native crops, a teacher says: "The presence of a garden in a struggling neighborhood can be a wellspring for building pride and self-esteem" (quoted in Woelfle-Erskine, 2003, p. 72).

This type of firsthand, experiential, and community-based learning is central to the Bahidaj School philosophy and curriculum. Senior capstone projects, for example, investigate important issues in students' communities, using human as well as textual resources and including an action component (interview with Bahidaj teacher, 2003). During the 2003–2004 school year, one student was researching sweatshops. Another was investigating diabetes in the local Native community and organizing a health fair for younger Native students. Other student projects have included a volunteer mission to Chiapas, Mexico, to help build a school, a cultural exchange program with students in Germany, and regular field investigations in the surrounding desert region to learn about the use and terminology of local flora in the Native language and English (Tirado, 2001). The school houses a technology lab that students use to create newsletters. A cofounding teacher provides this description of learning activities at the school:

> Visitors to [Bahidaj] will observe students writing essays on problems facing the [local Native American] Nation; others in the [Native] class may be fashioning and decorating traditional gourd rattles for use in the [Native] singing and culture class. In the computer lab, students might be searching the Internet for information about colleges and universities they want to attend or sources of financial aid. Seniors in the college prep class will be busy writing résumés or completing admissions forms. In the school garden, ethnobotany students are busy planting traditional [Native] plants, while science students pile into the school vans for a trip to the main . . . reservation, where they will study nature or work in a community garden. (Mendez et al., 2003, pp. 74–75)

In 2003–2004, Bahidaj was rated by the state education agency as "meeting adequate yearly progress" according to NCLB. Every senior had applied to at least one college or university, and some had won scholarships. The following school year, Bahidaj students not only improved their performance on state-required tests over previous years, they also gained significantly more than the state and county averages in many subject areas and grade levels. A Bahidaj student was one of two to win a local newspaper's annual award for academic achievement, leadership, and school and community involvement. Perhaps most impressive are the students' statements about the quality of their education. "I can always look toward the future," a student writes, "while still looking back at the past to find out who I am. As long as I know my background, I can have some sense of pride, and can know that I won't get lost" (Juan, 2003, p. 29).

We do not endorse charter schools as a panacea and in general are wary that the larger charter school movement may undermine the financial justice efforts of struggling noncharter public schools. For Indigenous communities that have experienced centuries of discrimination and educational malpractice, however, Native-operated charter schools represent one option for mediating the pressures of the standards movement and exerting local control. Charter schools are not the only option; BIA and public schools must become more responsive and accountable to the Native communities they serve. In this regard, Alaska Native communities have taken a strong stand in developing "counterstandards" and guidelines for culturally responsive schooling—a story we turn to next.

ACCOUNTABLE TO WHOM? ALASKA NATIVE STANDARDS FOR CULTURALLY RESPONSIVE AND RESPONSIBLE SCHOOLING

The standards movement is replete with the language of accountability. We agree that holding schools accountable for providing a healthy, uplifting, quality education is important. Yet we must ask: Accountable to what or to whom? In the U.S. Department of Education's introduction to NCLB, the legislation's primary purpose is stated as providing "stronger accountability for results" (USCCR, 2004, p. 1). Six U.S. Department of Education web pages, each with multiple links, are devoted to "stronger accountability"— for meeting adequate yearly progress, "getting results," closing the achievement gap, and meeting state standards (U.S. Department of Education, 2004; see also http://www.ed.gov/nclb/overview/intro/index.html; http://www.ed.gov/nclb/accountability/achieve/edpicks.jhtml?arc=ln). In response to the question, "Accountable to what or to whom?", current federal education policy appears to answer with a single word: "tests."

In contrast to test-driven accountability, some Native nations and states are adopting formal approaches to assessment that hold schools and educators accountable to the children, Native nations, and communities they serve. Cochiti educator Joseph Suina (2004) notes that Native language teachers in some New Mexico BIA and public schools feel "accountable to the tribal council first" (p. 291). "I let my elders advisory group know how the kids are doing," one Native teacher reports; "they are the ones most interested and concerned" (quoted in Suina, 2004, p. 292).

In Alaska, a statewide initiative has created a parallel set of cultural standards and guidelines intended to complement (not replace) standards adopted by the state. These cultural standards "are predicated on the belief that a firm grounding in the heritage language and culture indigenous to a particular place is a fundamental prerequisite for the development of culturally-healthy students and communities associated with that place, and thus an essential ingredient for identifying the appropriate qualities and practices associated with culturally-responsive educators, curriculum, and schools" (Assembly of Alaska Native Educators [AANE], 1998, p. 2). The standards grew out of a collaboration between the University of Alaska–Fairbanks and the Alaska Federation of Natives, who created the Alaska Native Rural Systemic Initiative (AKRSI), a statewide network of 20 partner school districts representing 176 rural schools and 20,000 primarily Alaska Native students (Barnhardt & Kawagley, 2005). According to Ray Barnhardt and A. Oscar Kawagley (2005), university-based educators who were instrumental in forming the partnership:

> The activities associated with the AKRSI have been aimed at fostering connectivity and complementarity between the Indigenous knowledge systems . . . and the formal education systems imported to serve the educational needs of rural Native communities. The underlying purpose of these efforts has been to implement research-based initiatives to systematically document the Indigenous knowledge systems of Alaska Native people and to develop pedagogical practices and school curricula that appropriately incorporate Indigenous knowledge and ways of knowing into the formal education system. (p. 15)

The Alaska Standards for Culturally Responsive Schools are specifications for students, educators, curriculum, and communities intended to ensure that students achieve state standards "in such a way that they become responsible, capable and whole human beings in the process" (AANE, 1998, p. 3). The emphasis is on fostering strong connections between students' in-school and out-of-school lives, recognizing multiple ways of knowing and worldviews. "The cultural standards are not intended to produce standardization," the AANE (1998) asserts, "but rather to encourage schools to nurture and build upon the rich and varied cultural traditions that continue to be practiced in communities throughout Alaska" (pp. 3–4).

Alaskan Cultural Standards

Within this framework, culturally knowledgeable students are expected to assume responsibilities for the well-being of their communities; recount their family histories; understand the role of the heritage language in their identities; and determine the place of their Native community within wider state, regional, national, and international economic systems (AANE, 1998). Culturally responsive educators recognize the validity and integrity of traditional knowledge systems, incorporate the expertise of elders in their teaching, and "continually involve themselves in learning about the local culture" (AANE, 1998, p. 9). A culturally responsive curriculum reinforces the cultural knowledge students bring to school, drawing on substantive elements of that knowledge base while tapping local languages and oral traditions to plumb deeper meanings. Schools and communities are expected to demonstrate respect for Native elders by providing multiple pathways for them to interact with students and "a place of honor in community functions" (AANE, 1998, pp. 17, 21).

Accompanying the standards are guidelines for preparing culturally responsive teachers, strengthening Indigenous languages, nurturing culturally healthy youth, respecting cultural knowledge, and developing cross-cultural orientation programs. Teacher preparation guidelines, for example, use the Alaska teacher standards as a framework, offering parallel guidelines in each of eight areas. We provide illustrations of those guidelines here:[5]

- *Philosophy*: Teachers should "develop a philosophy of education that is able to accommodate multiple world views." (AANE, 1999, p. 4)
- *Learning theory and practice*: Teachers should build on students' prior knowledge "and reinforce the positive parenting . . . practices from the community." (AANE, 1999, p. 6)
- *Diversity*: Teachers should "learn about the local language[s] and culture[s] of the community in which they are situated." (AANE, 1999, p. 8)
- *Content*: Teachers should understand and be able to apply local knowledge systems.
- *Instruction and assessment*: Teachers should use multiple instructional strategies grounded in local ways of teaching and learning as well as a broad assortment of assessment tools "that maximize the opportunities for students to demonstrate their competence." (AANE, 1999, pp. 12–13)
- *Learning environment*: Teachers should build classroom contexts modeled after natural learning environments in the community.
- *Family and community*: Teachers should work as partners with parents, elders, families, community members, and local school board members.

- *Professional growth*: Teachers should "engage in critical self-assess-ment," participating in and learning from local community events in culturally appropriate ways. (AANE, 1999, p. 16)

"All teachers should be provided with a cross-cultural orientation," the guidelines advise—a practice now in place through the AKRSI (AANE, 1999, p. 17).

In 2005, the AKRSI entered its 10th year. According to Barnhardt and Kawagley (2005), AKRSI initiatives have strengthened the quality of educa-tion and improved the academic performance of students in participating schools. In all of these efforts, elders have been recognized as key repositories of cultural and linguistic knowledge and expertise. "In the course of imple-menting AKRSI initiatives," Barnhardt and Kawagley (2005) state, "we have come to recognize that there is much more to be gained from further mining the fertile ground that exists within Indigenous knowledge systems" (p. 15).

CONCLUDING THOUGHTS: BEYOND THE SAFE VERSUS DANGEROUS DIVIDE

> If education could do all or if it could do nothing, there would be no reason to speak about its limits. We speak about them, precisely because, in not being able to do everything, education can do something. As educators . . . it behooves us to see what we can do so that we can competently realize our goals. (Freire, 1993, p. 25)

Critical pedagogue Paulo Freire recorded these thoughts in an interview dur-ing his first year as Minister of Education in São Paulo, Brazil. To rephrase Freire's words, recognizing education's systemic limits, it nonetheless "behooves us to see what we can do" to transform the standardizing practices that deny quality education for Indigenous and other minoritized children. In this chap-ter, we have shown the deeply historical and racialized roots of these prac-tices. We also have provided illustrations of two significant countermovements: Native American charter schools and Native standards for culturally respon-sive schools. Although we have focused on only two examples of these counterinitiatives, they are not the only illustrations of Indigenous challenges to standardization we might cite. In the Lower Kuskokwim School District in Juneau, Alaska, for example, children are taught almost exclusively in Yup'ik until fourth grade. The Alaska education commissioner has requested a waiver of NCLB to defer English-language testing until sixth grade, when students will have had 3 years of English instruction—the minimum, research shows, for developing academic proficiency in a second language (Cummins, 1989; Krashen, 1996). In Window Rock, Arizona—the only district in the state with a full (Navajo) immersion program for students in grades K–6 (see Chap-ter 6, this volume)—the district has effectively contested Arizona's English-only law that would eliminate the district's immersion program. Interestingly, in support of its case, the district has cited NCLB's goal of preparing students for meaningful citizenship. In Navajo society, school officials point out, "If students do not speak Navajo, they cannot be a meaningful participant in Navajo society" (Johnson & Wilson, 2004).

We can learn much from certain state initiatives as well. Exercising its sovereignty as a state, Nebraska has refused to bow to the pressure of "50-minute tests that will determine whether . . . teachers and their schools are considered successful" (Dell'Angela, 2004, n.p.). Instead, all of Nebraska's 517 school districts design their own portfolio assessments—compendia of students' written and creative work that demonstrate students' progress to-ward particular learning goals over time. "We decided . . . to take NCLB and integrate it into our plan, not the other way around," the state educa-tion commissioner reports. "If it's bad for kids, we're not going to do it" (quoted in Dell'Angela, 2004, n.p.).

Some Native educators have argued that standards-based reform can be a "lever for improving education for Native children" (Research Agenda Working Group, 2001, p. 37). For instance, such reforms might lead to clearer learning expectations within and across the various school systems—public, private, BIA, tribal, mission—that Native students attend, enhancing oppor-tunities to involve parents and communities in infusing the curriculum with locally appropriate content and assessment (Fox, 2001). The full realization of these opportunities has yet to be seen; as the Research Agenda Working Group (2001) points out, "It is not clear to what extent representatives of American Indian and Alaska Native communities or tribal governments [have been] involved in deciding upon the standards to be used in their states or why some BIA-funded schools have opted to go with their state's system rather than the national one" (p. 37).

The history of American Indian education has been one of relentless attempts by both secular and religious agencies to standardize, assimilate, and recast Native people. As we have shown here, those standardizing prac-tices have not gone uncontested by Native communities. These practices have nonetheless been enormously wasteful of human talent and lives. Native American charter schools and culturally responsive standards are two dem-onstrations of hopeful, self-determinant counterinitiatives to the standard-izing regimes that continue to characterize federal education policy. These initiatives point the way beyond the policies that reproduce "safe" versus "dangerous" divides, illuminating, in Freire's words, "what we can do" to ensure a critically conscious and uplifting education for all learners.

Coda:
Consummating the
Democratic Ideal

We in this country are slowly learning to appreciate the significance
of the problem of Indian rights for the cause of democracy here in
the United States and throughout the Western Hemisphere.
> —Nathan R. Margold, Solicitor, Interior Department,
> Franklin D. Roosevelt administration (1986, p. xxi)

We must ask, which is more destabilizing to democratizing societies:
the efforts of an ethnic group to emphasize its distinctiveness, or the
strategy of a state to forcibly create a unitary, homogeneous "nation"
from a diverse, multiethnic, multilingual population? For students of
democracy, the key question . . . is, which policies are more likely to
reinforce democracy: those that protect the interests of distinct sub-
cultures, or those that strive to unify national interests?
> —Donna Lee Van Cott (1994, pp. 2–3)

In the preceding chapters, we have traced the footprints of Indigenous
struggles for educational, linguistic, and cultural self-determination from
the early 20th century to the present day. These footprints record not only physical presence but also enduring emotional, moral, and spiritual commitments—
the day-to-day, generation-to-generation accretion of human knowledge and
experience, accommodation and resistance, that have shaped conditions in
Native America today. Our three-pronged approach has connected official,
"authorizing" federal and state policies with everyday social and educational
practices, linking policy and practice to the lived experiences of Native people
inside and outside of schools.

The voices and perspectives of Native people occupy center stage: accounts of their own, carefully designed education systems; experiences in
boarding schools; self-reflections on language, culture, and identity; and the
windows of opportunity they have pried open to exercise choice in the content and process of their education. Choice, we argue—the right to "remain

167

an Indian" on local, Indigenous terms—is the defining expression of tribal sovereignty and self-determination.

Linking past and present, we see a discernible pattern of federal support for innocuous or safe expressions of tribal sovereignty and of manifold constraints on the exercise of genuine sovereignty. The exercise of federal powers is most evident in the overweening surveillance within the federal boarding schools; as essential elements of the civilizing project, boarding schools were laboratories of domestication, the primary means by which Native languages, cultures, and identities were to be pounded out and re-shaped. And yet, as will be recalled from Thisba Huston Morgan's description of the miniature Lakota camp set up at Ogalalla Boarding School, from the example of Indian arts and crafts instruction established under Superintendent of Indian Schools Estelle Reel, and from early federal support for the development of bilingual literacy materials, we also see seemingly contradictory policies in support of Indigenous languages and cultural practices. We have argued that these policies are not contradictory at all but are highly consistent with federal goals to define and delimit a safety zone—physical, social, intellectual, and affective domains in which certain differences are deemed allowable or safe, while others are marked off as threatening to the interests of the nation-state and therefore proscribed.

More subtle and complex manifestations of the safe/dangerous paradigm are evident in federal language policies. Whereas the use of Native languages was strictly prohibited in federal boarding schools throughout most of the 20th century, by the end of the century—a time when Native languages had reached a nearly irredeemable decline—the federal government had passed the Native American Languages Act, vowing to protect and promote Indigenous languages and authorizing funding for teaching Native languages in school. Given the precarious state of Indigenous languages, this policy reversal is entirely consistent with the safe/dangerous paradigm. Even more complex and insidious, however, are federal policies for self-determination, which, as we have seen, both enable and constrain Indigenous control over local schools.

Within this sociopolitical context, the struggle for Indigenous self-determination may be conceptualized as two very different yet coexistent realities. One is the reality of a revolution in Indigenous education, of opportunity seized by Native people in the name of self-determination. From this perspective, the passage of the Native American Languages Act was, in fact, a crucial assertion of Indigenous language rights. Indigenous-controlled bilingual/bicultural schooling, heritage-language immersion, Native charter schools, and Native standards for culturally responsive schooling are further examples of these self-determinant initiatives.

A second reality is of an entrenched federal bureaucracy that, despite its public rhetoric, has protected its own powers and stifled Native self-determination at every turn. When Indigenous initiatives have crossed the line between allowable, safe difference and radical, threatening difference, federal control has been reasserted in explicit, diffuse, and unmistakably constricting ways. At the present moment of unprecedented demographic shift, we see these controlling forces at work in state and federal policies that strip bilingual children of their most powerful learning resource—their mother tongue—and that segregate students of color and English-language learners, targeting them for remedial, reductionist literacy pedagogies. Divested of the resources and opportunities for high-level intellectual engagement, these students and their teachers are then held accountable to high-stakes, English-only standardized tests. The entrapment could not be more complete.

These dual realities raise the question of the legitimacy of Indigenous education control. Is genuine self-determination, the right to choice in the content and process of schooling, possible? Or is it, as Senese (1986) and Senese and Page (1995) argue, an illusion that serves to perpetuate rather than dismantle federal paternalism? We believe the policy of self-determination can be a lever for Indigenous empowerment, but only if the ideologies that have motivated federal repression of tribal sovereignty and cultural/linguistic difference are exposed and transformed.

This book is an attempt to unveil and confront the tangled forces that simultaneously constrain and enable Indigenous control over Indigenous education. Throughout the 20th century and into the 21st, Native Americans and federal authorities have drawn and redrawn the boundaries of the safety zone. An enormous investment of time and energy has been poured into attempts to eradicate American Indian cultural and linguistic distinctiveness. Despite this sustained effort, Native Americans have survived as distinctive and productive peoples.

Can Native American cultural distinctiveness be maintained without the concomitant economic, political, and social marginalization of Indigenous communities? Can places of difference be maintained without denying educational, economic, political, and social rights and opportunities to their inhabitants?

These questions lie at the core of a larger debate. Can social justice and democracy coexist? The current political resurgence of tribes clearly threatens many U.S. citizens, who are struggling to understand or fighting vigorously to deny tribal sovereign rights to hunt, fish, tax businesses, or operate casinos. No wonder, then, that focusing on American Indian education—the enterprise charged with remaking and standardizing Indigenous people as "Americans"—forces us all to confront the fault lines in the topography of the American democracy.

We began by stating that we intend to reveal the falseness of the fears embedded in the safe/dangerous paradigm. Danger lies not in diversity, but in attempts to standardize and homogenize the linguistically and culturally diverse peoples who comprise the nation's citizenry. Disguised as an equalizing force, standardization in fact stratifies, segregates, and undercuts human potential, denying equality of opportunity for all. We have only to consider the history of Native American education to see the standardizing juggernaut in its true form.

We conclude by arguing for more hopeful, empowering education policies and practices that capitalize on human diversity and embrace its systematic cultivation as a national resource. The choices Native people and other minoritized communities make need not be either–or ones, nor must there be an immutable dividing line between Indigenous and nontribal citizens.

A healthy sense of tribal sovereignty can most profitably be viewed as an invigorating challenge to democracy. Vital and persisting Native American communities can inspire the nation's citizens to rise to the challenge of securing a democracy in which equality is more than rhetoric and social justice prevails. Schools, especially, can be constructed as places of difference in which children are free to learn, question, and grow from a position that affirms who they are. This vision of critical democracy, long held within Indigenous communities, has the power to create a more just and equitable educational system for all.

A VISION OF THE FUTURE

"Indian schools" reveal the cancer at the heart of the American educational system, the powerful forces that conspire to standardize, homogenize, and "dumb down" some groups of citizens. In contrast, Native visions for an Indigenously rooted and inspired education hold a promise for schools and a promise for a nation that can look cultural difference in the face, not as an enemy but as an ally. American Indian schools today, run by Indian parents and communities in accord with their deeply rooted, persistent, but not unchanging cultural values provide a model for meaningful, challenging, locally controlled education for all Americans.

Luther Standing Bear (Lakota) began his life on the Dakota plains not far from where Ogalalla Boarding School would one day stand. He attended Carlisle Indian School in Pennsylvania, made his living as an entertainer in Wild West shows and the movies of 1930s Hollywood, and published four books. More than 70 years ago, he issued a challenge to his fellow citizens:

> Why not a school of Indian thought, built on the Indian pattern and conducted by Indian instructors? Why not a school of tribal art? Why should not America be cognizant of itself; aware of its identity? In short, why should not America

be preserved? . . . In denying the Indian his ancestral rights and heritages the white race is but robbing itself. But America can be revived, rejuvenated, by recognizing a native school of thought. The Indian can save America. (Standing Bear, 1933/1978, pp. 254–255)

We have come a long way since Standing Bear first published these words in 1933. Why not a school of Indian thought? Today, many Native communities operate their own schools (see, for example, Figures C.1 and C.2), from preschool through the more than 35 tribal colleges united under the American Indian Higher Education Consortium. Why not a school of tribal art? The Institute of American Indian Arts in Santa Fe, New Mexico, is a "multitribal center of higher education dedicated to the preservation, study, creative application, and contemporary expression of American Indian and Alaska Native arts and cultures" (Warrior, 2003).

On the other hand, some things have not changed so much. Our nation still struggles with cultural difference, still denies or devalues its identity as

Figure C.1. Navajo schoolchildren at Rough Rock Community School (photograph by Fred Bia, courtesy of Rough Rock Community School).

Figure C.2. Navajo schoolchildren at Rough Rock Community School (photograph by Teresa L. McCarty, courtesy of Rough Rock Community School).

a multilingual, multiethnic, multicultural polity. We believe that the story of Native American education can lead to a better understanding of our individual and collective identities; Native America's experiences provide lessons from which all citizens can learn. We take to heart Standing Bear's vision that "America can be revived, rejuvenated, by recognizing a native school of thought. The Indian can save America."

Notes

Chapter 1

1.   Readers will note highly gendered language in many of the historical quotes, such as *free men*, and consistent references to *he* and *him*. We have not altered the language quoted here, as we find the repeated insertion of [*sic*] distracting and assume the reader can understand the language in the context of its times.

2.   Throughout the book, we use the notion of a "safety zone" and safety zone theory in an apposite way to the construct of a "zone of safety" developed by Begay et al. (1995), Lipka and McCarty (1994), McCarty (2002a), and McCarty and Dick (2003). In the latter works, the "zone of safety" describes a co-constructed social and intellectual space in which Native teachers, often working with elders, are free to interrogate their own education histories and conventional teaching methods; this critical inquiry process becomes the basis for new pedagogies that Indigenize the curriculum and open possibilities for radical school change. Lipka and his associates (1998) also refer to this as a "'zone of possibility' where [cultural] insiders and outsiders ferret out the meanings, conflicts, and confusions surrounding the practical question of how to negotiate [Native] cultural knowledge within a school context" (p. 26).

Chapter 2

1.   Some 19th-century mission education in the Southeast and tribally controlled educational systems set up by southeastern tribes after removal to Indian territory merged community and school to various degrees, including the use of Native languages in the classroom (Noley, 1979). We do not mean to slight the importance of these examples to their communities, but few of these local efforts survived into the 20th century. Also, although tribally controlled, these systems did not necessarily incorporate Indigenous knowledge into their curricula (Mihesuah, 1993).

2.   Many Native communities have a litany of names attached to them over time. In this case, the set of names attached to groups of related Algonquian-language speakers in the Great Lakes area is notable for its diversity, each with a diverse range of spellings: Chippewa, Chippeway; Ojibwe, Ojibwa, Ojibway; Anishinaubae (s.) and Anishinaubaek (pl.) (Johnston, 1995), Anishinaabeg (pl.) (Vizenor, 1984). See Vizenor

(1984) for a discussion of etymologies and definitions. We use Anishinabe (s.) and Anishinabeg (pl.).

3. We have reproduced here Deborah Neff's poetic transcription style, designed to capture Frances Manuel's narrative rhythms. Capitalized words are spoken louder; line breaks indicate slight pauses (approximately ½ second); periods indicate full stops.

Chapter 5

1. The federal agency charged with responsibility for Indian affairs was known in the early part of the 20th century as the Office of Indian Affairs, or OIA, or the Indian Service. In the 1930s the Office became the Bureau of Indian Affairs, or BIA. We refer to the office during this transition period interchangeably as the OIA, the Indian Office, the Bureau, or the BIA.

2. The current standard orthography for Hopi, as used in the *Hopi Dictionary* (Hopi Dictionary Project, 1998) was developed by Emory Sekaquaptewa, Third Mesa dialect speaker, working with a team of linguists, scholars, and Hopi-language consultants. Hartman Lomawaima is not trained in this orthography; the spellings we use here for village names approximate his Second Mesa dialect and the spellings with which he is familiar. The dictionary spelling of *Misongnovi* is *Musangnuvi*; *Sipaulovi* is *Supawlavi*.

Chapter 6

1. The title of this subsection comes from Holm and Holm's retrospective account of the Rock Point bilingual education program, "Rock Point, a Navajo Way to Go to School: A Valediction" (Holm & Holm, 1990).

2. This characterization reflects the many "Long Marches" and "Long Walks" into exile and incarceration endured by Native groups who were forcibly removed from their homelands and relocated by the U.S. government.

3. Portions of this section are adapted from McCarty (2002a, 2003) and from McCarty and Dick (2003).

4. Portions of this section are adapted from McCarty, Watahomigie, Yamamoto, and Zepeda (2001b).

5. Between 1994 and 2002, AILDI recruited and graduated 28 Native and 6 non-Native participants in language-related master's degree programs and 4 Native students in education specialist programs (McCarty, 2002b).

Chapter 7

1. Language researcher and activist Tove Skutnabb-Kangas refers to this process as linguicide. Speaking of languages that have been exterminated, she notes that they "have died . . . *not* because this has been a 'natural' development, but because they have been 'helped' on their way. They have not 'died' because of old age or lack of adaptability—they have been murdered" (Skutnabb-Kangas, 2000, p. 222;

see also Phillipson, 2000; Skutnabb-Kangas & Phillipson, 1994). Others have referred to these processes as *language dispossession* (see, e.g., Nicholls's [2005] discussion of Aboriginal language repression in Australia's Northwest Territory).

2.   NALA funding is competitive and is administered by the Administration for Native Americans (ANA) in Washington, D.C. Thus, individual grant amounts differ, and not all tribes apply for or receive ANA awards.

3.   These were Senate Bill (S.) 2688 and 575, the Native American Languages Act Amendments Act of 2000 and 2003, respectively. At the time of this writing, none of these amendments had been passed, and another bill had been introduced: H.R. 4766, the Native American Languages Preservation Act of 2006. This bill would amend NALA and authorize grants through the U.S. Department of Education to establish Native American language programs for young children and their families, as well as Native American language survival schools.

4.   Parts of the discussion of Native American immersion programs is adapted from McCarty (2003).

5.   In 1993, Congress acknowledged U.S. culpability in overthrowing the Indigenous Hawaiian government in the Hawaii Apology Act: "the United States Minister assigned to the sovereign and independent Kingdom of Hawaii conspired with a small group of non-Hawaiian residents . . . to overthrow the indigenous and lawful Government of Hawaii. . . . On the occasion of the 100th anniversary of the illegal overthrow of the Kingdom of Hawaii, [the Congress] acknowledges the historical significance of this event which resulted in the suppression of the inherent sovereignty of the Native Hawaiian people" (Preamble, Sect. I[1]). This is a noteworthy symbolic act, but does not right the wrongs perpetrated by the U.S. government on Native Hawaiians.

6.   According to Kawakami and Dudoit (2000), the *oli* "is a significant part of the Hawaiian oral tradition and is used to convey information from person to person, generation to generation, and to uphold structures of protocol" (p. 384). The teachers' response "is filled with references to these people, places, and things that make [the local area] a special place" (Kawakami & Dudoit, 2000, p. 384).

7.   Language ideologies refer not to language per se but to "the very notion of the person and social group" (Woolard, 1998, p. 3). Thus, language ideology connotes ideas and attitudes about language that are integrally connected to sociohistorically constituted relations of power.

Chapter 8

1.   Title III of NCLB, "Language Instruction for Limited English Proficient and Immigrant Students," contains a section allowing "programs of instruction, teacher training, curriculum development, evaluation, and assessment designed for Native American children learning and studying Native American languages and [Puerto Rican] children of limited Spanish proficiency," providing the program outcome is "increased English proficiency" (Part B, Subpart 1, Sec. 3216). It is clear, however, that this subpart is not intended to maintain Indigenous languages (or Spanish for Puerto Rican children), or to develop these languages as mother tongues.

NCLB's de facto English-only orientation is reflected in the fact that schools and students are accountable to English standardized tests and in the change in the title of the former Bilingual Education Act, to the English Language Acquisition, Language Enhancement, and Academic Achievement Act (at the time of this writing, Title III Part A). For the text of NCLB, see http://www.ed.gov/nclb.

2. See also Amrein and Berliner's (2002) analysis of high-stakes testing, which indicates "that high school graduation exams increase dropout rates, decrease high school graduation rates, and increase the rates by which students enroll in GED [General Education Diploma] programs" (p. 47). Using the best external measures available, these researchers found that "high-stakes tests do create the negative, unintended consequences about which critics worry. . . . The adverse consequences of high-stakes tests appear to outweigh what few benefits such tests may have" (Amrein & Berliner, 2002, p. 48). In a subsequent meta-study using National Assessment of Education Progress tests, Nichols, Glass, and Berliner (2006) found, moreover, that "accountability pressure" in the form of high-stakes testing produced no gains in mathematics achievement at the 4th- and 8th-grade levels or in reading achievement at any grade level for any ethnic student subgroup.

3. Charter school legislation varies from state to state, but typically one of four entities authorizes these schools: a local school board, a state university, community colleges, or the state board of education (U.S. Charter Schools, 2004).

4. Bahidaj High is a pseudonym for a research site that is part of the Native Language Shift and Retention Project discussed in Chapter 7. In accordance with Human Subjects protocols, we use a pseudonym for the school and do not name the tribal nation involved. However, some sources cited in this section are from public documents. We therefore name the authors but have substituted the pseudonym where the actual name exists in our reference list. We realize this accommodation is less than ideal but have sought to balance our obligations to protect research participants while acknowledging their published contributions to this discussion and to the field.

5. These guidelines parallel the "12 Essential Principles for Teaching and Learning in a Multicultural Society" developed by a consensus panel of interdisciplinary scholars "to determine what we know from research and experience about education and diversity" (Banks et al., 2001, p. 3).

References

ARCHIVAL RECORDS

Clark Papers: Ann Nolan Clark Papers in the Special Collections of the University of Arizona Main Library, Tucson, Arizona.

Oklahoma Historical Society, Records of the Chilocco Indian School, Oklahoma City, Oklahoma.

Reel Papers: Estelle Reel Papers in the collections of the Northwest Museum of Arts and Cultures/Eastern Washington State Historical Society, Spokane, Washington.

NATIONAL ARCHIVES

NARA: National Archives & Records Administration, Washington, D.C.

NARA/LN: National Archives & Records Administration, Regional Branch, Laguna Niguel, California.

NARA/FW: National Archives & Records Administration, Regional Branch, Fort Worth, Texas.

(All Office of Indian Affairs/Bureau of Indian Affairs records are found under Record Group 75, which is categorized by entry numbers (see list below of consulted records) or titles, such as "Superintendent's Subject Files [SSF]."

Entry 121 [Central Classified Files] is also used to organize records in the regional branches such as Laguna Niguel [NARA/LN] and Fort Worth [NARA/FW]).

LIST OF ENTRIES USED FOR NARA RECORDS IN THE WASHINGTON, D.C. REPOSITORY

Entry 91: Letters received by the Education Division, 1881–1907.

Entry 121: Central Classified Files (CCF) are filed alphabetically by agency name, such as reservation (e.g., Pima), school (e.g., Chilocco), or consolidated agency name (e.g., Western Navajo, which in some years includes Hopi records).

Entry 177: Records of the office of the Commissioner of Indian Affairs, personal and semiofficial files, 1921–1932, [1933].

NARA, Washington, D.C. Repository, Records of the Education Division

Entry 135: Orders, circulars, and circular letters issued by the General Superintendent and replies, 1926–1928.
Entry 718: Circulars issued by the Education Division, 1897–1909.
Entry 719: Circulars issued by the Superintendent of Indian Schools, 1899–1908.
Entry 722: Office files of Hervey B. Peairs, Chief Supervisor of Education and General Superintendent, 1910–1927.
Entry 723: Office files of Will Carson Ryan Jr., Director of Education, 1931–1935.
Entry 724: Office file, Mary Stewart, Assistant Director of Education, 1929–1936.
Entry 756: Reference file, Carrie A. Lyford, ca. 1921–1932.
Entry 758: Reports of School Social Workers, 1932–1936.
Entry 761: Records Of Industries Section, Records Concerning Former Students, 1910–1925.

NARA, Washington, D.C. Repository, Records of the Division of Extension and Industry

Entry 785: Annual reports of the Director, 1932–1939 [1931].

WORKS CITED

Adams, D. W. (1977). Education in hues: Red and Black at Hampton Institute, 1878–1893. *The South Atlantic Quarterly, 76,* 159–176.
Adams, D. W. (1988). Fundamental considerations: The deep meaning of Native American schooling, 1880–1900. *Harvard Educational Review, 58*(1), 1–28.
Adams, D. W. (1995). *Education for extinction: American Indians and the boarding school experience, 1875–1928.* Lawrence: University Press of Kansas.
Adley-SantaMaria, B. (1999). Interrupting White Mountain Apache language shift: An insider's view. *Practicing Anthropology, 20*(2), 16–19.
American Indian Policy Review Commission (AIPRC). (1976). *Report on Indian education.* Washington, DC: U.S. Government Printing Office.
Amrein, A., & Berliner, D. C. (2002). *An analysis of some unintended and negative consequences of high-stakes testing.* Tempe: Education Policy Research Unit, College of Education, Arizona State University.
Annual reports of the Commissioner of Indian Affairs (ARCIA). 1899–1939.
Appleton, N. (1983). *Cultural pluralism in education.* New York: Longman.
Archuleta, M. L., Child, B. J., & Lomawaima, K. T. (2000). *Away from home: American Indian boarding school experiences, 1879–2000.* Phoenix, AZ: Heard Museum.
Aronowitz, S., & Giroux, H. A. (1985). *Education under siege.* South Hadley, MA: Bergin & Garvey.

Arviso, M., & Holm, W. (2001). Tséhootsooídi Ólta'gi Diné bizaadbíhoo'aah: A Navajo immersion program at Fort Defiance, Arizona. In L. Hinton & K. Hale (Eds.), *The green book of language revitalization in practice* (pp. 203–215). San Diego, CA: Academic Press.

Assembly of Alaska Native Educators (AANE). (1998). *Alaska standards for culturally-responsive schools*. Anchorage: Alaska Native Knowledge Network.

Assembly of Alaska Native Educators (AANE). (1999). *Guidelines for preparing culturally responsive teachers for Alaska's schools*. Anchorage: Alaska Native Knowledge Network.

Au, K., & Jordan, C. (1981). Teaching reading to Hawaiian children. In H. Trueba, G. Guthrie, & K. Au (Eds.), *Culture and the bilingual classroom* (pp. 139–152). Rowley, MA: Newbury House.

Balenquah, K. L. (1981). *Mö'wi*. Hotevilla, AZ: Hotevilla-Bacavi Community School.

Banks, J. A. (2001). Series foreword. In G. Valdés, *Learning and not learning English: Latinos in American schools* (pp. ix–xii). New York: Teachers College Press.

Banks, J. A., Cookson, P., Gay, G., Hawley, W. D., Irvine, J. J., Nieto, S., Schofield, J. W., & Stephan, W. G. (2001). *Diversity within unity: Essential principles for teaching and learning in a multicultural society*. Seattle: Center for Multicultural Education, University of Washington.

Barnhardt, R., & Kawagley, A. O. (2005). Indigenous knowledge systems and Native Alaska ways of knowing. *Anthropology and Education Quarterly, 36*(1), 8–23.

Barth, P. J. (1945). *Franciscan education and the social order in Spanish North America, 1502–1821*. Unpublished doctoral dissertation, University of Chicago, Chicago.

Basso, K. (1989). *Western Apache language and culture: Essays in linguistic anthropology*. Tucson: University of Arizona Press.

Bauer, E. (1970). Bilingual education in BIA schools. *TESOL Quarterly, 4*(3), 223–229.

Beatty, W. W. (1943). Bilingual readers. In A. N. Clark, *The hen of Wahpeton* (pp. 90–91). Lawrence, KS: Haskell Institute, for Education Division, U.S. Office of Indian Affairs.

Beatty, W. W. (1950). *Indians yesterday and today*. Chilocco, OK: Bureau of Indian Affairs.

Beatty, W. W. (1953). *Education for cultural change: Selected articles from Indian education, 1944–1951*. Chilocco, OK: U.S. Department of the Interior, Bureau of Indian Affairs.

Beaulieu, D., Sparks, L., & Alonzo, M. (2005). *Preliminary report on No Child Left Behind in Indian Country*. Washington, DC: National Indian Education Association.

Begay, S., Dick, G. S., Estell, D. W., Estell, J., McCarty, T. L., & Sells, A. (1995). Change from the inside out: A story of transformation in a Navajo community school. *Bilingual Research Journal, 19*, 121–139.

Begay, S. M., Clinton-Tullie, V., & Yellowhair, M. (1983). *Kinaaldá: A Navajo puberty ceremony.* Rough Rock, AZ: Navajo Curriculum Center, Rough Rock Demonstration School.

Begishe, K. (n.d.). *Nitsáhákees bee haho'dilyaa. One's development through thoughts.* Unpublished manuscript.

Benally, A., & Viri, D. (2005). Diné bizaad (Navajo language) at a crossroads: Extinction or renewal? *Bilingual Research Journal, 29*(1), 85–108.

Benes, R. C. (2004). *Native American picture books of change: The art of historic children's editions.* Santa Fe, NM: Museum of New Mexico Press.

Benjamin, R., Pecos, R., & Romero, M. E. (1996). Language revitalization efforts in the Pueblo de Cochiti: Becoming "literate" in an oral society. In N. H. Hornberger (Ed.), *Indigenous literacies in the Americas: Language planning from the bottom up* (pp. 115–136). Berlin: Mouton de Gruyter.

Benton, N. A., & Kinsland, J. E. (1953). *Please fill the tank.* Ogden, UT: Defense Printing Service, U.S. Department of the Interior, Bureau of Indian Affairs.

Bialystok, E. (Ed.). (1991). *Language processing in bilingual children.* Cambridge, UK: Cambridge University Press.

Bibby, B. (1996). *The fine art of California Indian basketry.* Sacramento, CA: Crocker Art Museum.

Bielenberg, B. T. (2002). *"Who will sing the songs?" Language renewal among Puebloan adolescents.* Unpublished doctoral dissertation, Graduate School of Education, University of California, Berkeley.

Bishop, R. (2003). Changing power relations in education: Kaupapa Māori messages for "mainstream" education in Aotearoa/New Zealand. *Comparative Education, 39*(2), 221–238.

Blackburn, T. C., & Anderson, K. (1993). *Before the wilderness: Environmental management by Native Californians.* Menlo Park, CA: Ballena Press.

Blackman, M. B. (1982). *During my time: Florence Edenshaw Davidson, a Haida woman.* Seattle: University of Washington Press.

Borden, J. (producer). (1988). *Seasons of a Navajo.* Washington, DC: PBS Video.

Brewer, A. (1977). On Indian education. *Integrateducation, 15,* 21–23.

Bronson, R. M. (1944). *Indians are people, too.* New York: Friendship Press.

Brown, A. D. (1980). Cherokee culture and school achievement. *American Indian Culture and Research Journal, 4*(3), 55–74.

Brumble, H. D., III. (1981). *An annotated bibliography of American Indian and Eskimo autobiographies.* Lincoln: University of Nebraska Press.

Bryde, J. (1970). *The Indian student: A study of scholastic failure and personality conflict* (2nd ed.). Vermillion, SD: Dakota Press.

Buckley, T. (1997, November). *Love, rage, grief and salvage ethnography as a cultural system.* Paper presented at the annual meeting of the American Society for Ethnohistory, Mexico City.

Cajete, G. (1994). *Look to the mountain: An ecology of indigenous education.* Skyland, NC: Kivakí Press.

Cantoni, G. (Ed.). (1996). *Stabilizing indigenous languages.* Flagstaff: Northern Arizona University Center for Excellence in Education.

Carlo, P. (1978). *Nulato: An Indian life on the Yukon.* Caldwell, ID: Caxton Printers.

Castile, G. P. (1998). *To show heart: Native American self-determination and federal Indian policy, 1960–1975.* Tucson: University of Arizona Press.

Castile, G. P., & Bee, R. L. (Eds.) (1992). *State and reservation: New perspectives on federal Indian policy.* Tucson: University of Arizona Press.

Cazden, C., & Leggett, E. L. (1981). Culturally responsive education: Recommendations for achieving Lau remedies II. In H. Trueba, G. Guthrie, & K. Au (Eds.), *Culture and the bilingual classroom* (pp. 69–86). Rowley, MA: Newbury House.

Center for Education Reform. (2005). Charter schools. Retrieved September 15, 2005, from http://www.edreform.com/index.cfm?fuseAction=stateStats&pSectionID=15&cSectionID=44

Child, B. J. (1998). *Boarding school seasons: American Indian families, 1900–1940.* Lincoln: University of Nebraska Press.

Chrisjohn, R. D., & Peters, M. (1989, August). The right-brained Indian: Fact or fiction? [Special issue]. *Journal of American Indian Education,* 77–83.

Clark, A. N. (1940a). *Little boy with three names: Stories of Taos Pueblo.* Illustrated by Tonita Lujan. Chilocco, OK: U.S. Department of the Interior, Bureau of Indian Affairs.

Clark, A. N. (1940b). *Little herder stories. 1. In autumn. Na'niłkaadí yázhí baa hani'. 1.'Aak'eedgo.* Illustrated by Hoke Denetsosie. Phoenix, AZ: Phoenix Indian School, for U.S. Department of the Interior, Office of Indian Affairs.

Clark, A. N. (1940c). *Little herder stories. 3. In spring.* Illustrated by Hoke Denetsosie. Phoenix, AZ: Phoenix Indian School, for U.S. Department of the Interior, Office of Indian Affairs.

Clark, A. N. (1941a). *In my mother's house.* New York: Viking.

Clark, A. N. (1941b). *The Pine Ridge porcupine.* Illustrated by Andrew Standing Soldier. Lawrence, KS: Haskell Institute, for Office of Indian Affairs, Education Division.

Clark, A. N. (1942a). *About the Slim Butte raccoon: Paha zizipela wic'iteglega kin.* Illustrated by Andrew Standing Soldier. Lawrence, KS: Haskell Institute, for Office of Indian Affairs, Education Division.

Clark, A. N. (1942b). *Little herder stories. 2. In winter. Na'niłkaadí yázhí baa hani'. 2. Haigo.* Illustrated by Hoke Denetsosie. Phoenix, AZ: Phoenix Indian School, for U.S. Department of the Interior, Office of Indian Affairs.

Clark, A. N. (1942c). *Little herder stories. 4. In summer. Na'niłkaadí yázhí baa hani'. 2. Shį́į́go.* Illustrated by Hoke Denetsosie. Phoenix, AZ: Phoenix Indian School, for U.S. Department of the Interior, Office of Indian Affairs.

Clark, A. N. (1943a). *About the Grass Mountain mouse: Hep'eji it' unkala kin.* Illustrated by Andrew Standing Soldier. Lawrence, KS: Haskell Institute, for Bureau of Indian Affairs, Branch of Education.

Clark, A. N. (1943b). *About the hen of Wahpeton: Unjincala Wahpet'un etanhin kin he.* Illustrated by Andrew Standing Soldier. Lawrence, KS: Haskell Institute, for U.S. Office of Indian Affairs, Education Division.

Clark, A. N. (1969). *Journey to the people: Recollections of an inspired educator and writer's experiences teaching Indian children.* New York: Viking.

Clark, A. N. (1988). *Sun journey: A story of Zuni pueblo*. Illustrated by Percy Tsisete Sandy. Santa Fe, NM: Ancient City Press. (Original work published 1945)

Cohen, F. S. (1953). The erosion of Indian rights, 1950–1953: A case study in bureaucracy. *Yale Law Review 62*, 349–390.

Crawford, J. (1992). *Language loyalties: A source book on the Official English controversy*. Chicago: University of Chicago Press.

Crawford, J. (1997). *Best evidence: Research foundations of the Bilingual Education Act*. Washington, DC: National Clearinghouse for Bilingual Education.

Crawford, J. (2004a). *Educating English learners: Language diversity in the classroom* (5th ed.). Los Angeles: Bilingual Educational Services.

Crawford, J. (2004b). *No Child Left Behind: Misguided approach to school accountability for English language learners*. Washington, DC: National Association for Bilingual Education.

Crow, L., Murray, W., & Smythe, H. (1966). *Educating the culturally disadvantaged child*. New York: David McKay.

Cruikshank, J. (1998). *The social life of stories: Narrative and knowledge in the Yukon Territory*. Lincoln: University of Nebraska Press.

Cummins, J. (1984). *Bilingualism and special education: Issues in assessment and pedagogy*. San Diego, CA: College-Hill Press.

Cummins, J. (1989). *Empowering minority students*. Sacramento, CA: California Association for Bilingual Education.

Cummins, J. (2000). *Language, power, and pedagogy: Bilingual children in the crossfire*. Clevedon, UK: Multilingual Matters.

Cummins, J., & Corson, D. (1997). *Encyclopedia of language and education: Vol. 5. Bilingual education*. Dordrecht, The Netherlands: Kluwer.

Dalton, S. S., & Youpa, D. G. (1998). Standards-based teaching reform in Zuni Pueblo middle and high schools. *Equity and Excellence in Education, 31*(1), 55–68.

Danielson, C. (1989). *Teaching for mastery* (2nd ed.). Princeton, NJ: Outcomes Associates.

Darder, A. (1991). *Culture and power in the classroom: A critical foundation for bicultural education*. New York: Bergin & Garvey.

Dell'Angela, T. (2004, April 12). Nebraska schools skip mandatory tests. *Seattle Times*. Retrieved September 15, 2005, from http://seattletimes.nwsource.com/html/education/2001901192_nebraska12.html

Deloria, V., Jr., & Lytle, C. M. (1983). *American Indians, American justice*. Austin: University of Texas Press.

Deloria, V., Jr., & Lytle, C. M. (1984). *The nations within: The past and future of American Indian sovereignty*. New York: Pantheon Books.

Deloria, V., Jr., & Wilkins, D. E. (1999). *Tribes, treaties and constitutional tribulations*. Austin: University of Texas Press.

deMarrais, K., Nelson, P., & Baker, J. (1992). Meaning in mud: Yup'ik Eskimo girls at play. *Anthropology and Education Quarterly, 23*(2), 120–144.

Deyhle, D. (1986). Success and failure: A micro-ethnographic comparison of Navajo and Anglo students' perceptions of testing. *Curriculum Inquiry, 16*(4), 365–389.

Dick, G. S. (1998). I maintained a strong belief in my language and culture: A Navajo language autobiography. *International Journal of the Sociology of Language, 132,* 23–25.

Dick, G. S., Estell, D., & McCarty, T. L. (1994). Saad naakih bee'enootíílji na'alkaa: Restructuring the teaching of language and literacy in a Navajo community school. *Journal of American Indian Education, 33*(3), 31–46.

Dick, G. S., & McCarty, T. L. (1996). Reclaiming Navajo: Language renewal in an American Indian community school. In N. H. Hornberger (Ed.), *Indigenous literacies in the Americas: Language planning from the bottom up* (pp. 69–94). Berlin: Mouton de Gruyter.

Dinges, N. G., & Hollenbeck, A. R. (1978). Field dependence-independence in Navajo children. *International Journal of Psychology, 13*(3), 215–220.

Dongoske, K., Jenkins, L., & Ferguson, T. J. (1993). Understanding the past through Hopi oral tradition. *Native Peoples, 6*(2), 24–35.

Dorsey, G. (1904). *Traditions of the Arikara.* Washington, DC: Carnegie Institution of Washington.

Dumont, R. V., Jr. (1972). Learning English and how to be silent: Studies in Sioux and Cherokee classrooms. In C. Cazden, V. John, & D. Hymes (Eds.), *Functions of language in the classroom* (pp. 344–369). New York: Teachers College Press.

Dumont, R. V., Jr., & Wax, M. L. (1969). Cherokee school society and the intercultural classroom. *Human Organization, 28*(3), 217–226.

Dupuis, V. L., & Walker, M. (1989). The circle of learning at Kickapoo. *Journal of American Indian Education, 28*(1), 27–33.

Eastman, C. A. (1971). *Indian boyhood.* New York: Dover Publications. (Original work published 1902)

Eastman, E. G. (1900, October). The education of the Indian. *The Arena, 24*(4), 412–414.

Edelsky, C. (1991). *With literacy and justice for all: Rethinking the social in language and education.* London: Falmer.

Ellis, C. (1996). *To change them forever: Indian education at the Rainy Mountain Boarding School, 1893–1920.* Norman: University of Oklahoma Press.

Emerson, G. (2004). Foreword. In R. Benes, *Native American picture books of change: The art of historic children's editions* (pp. ix–xiv). Sante Fe: Museum of New Mexico Press.

Engle, B. (1935, October 27). Students at Chilocco getting "New Deal" in education. *Wichita Eagle,* p. 32.

Epley, L., Benton, N., & Bitsie, W. (1953). *Do you need a plumber?* Brigham City, UT: Materials Preparation Department, Intermountain School.

Erickson, D., & Schwartz, N. (1969). *Community school at Rough Rock.* Washington, DC: U.S. Office of Economic Opportunity.

Ferrero, P. ((producer). (1983). *Hopi songs of the fourth world,* San Francisco, CA: Ferrero Films.

Fishman, J. A. (1991). *Reversing language shift: Theoretical and empirical foundations of assistance to threatened languages.* Clevedon, UK: Multilingual Matters.

Fishman, J. A. (Ed.). (2001). *Can threatened languages be saved? Reversing language shift, revisited: A 21st century perspective.* Clevedon, UK: Multilingual Matters.

Fishman, J. A. (2002). Commentary: What a difference 40 years make! *Journal of Linguistic Anthropology, 12*(2), 144–149.

Fixico, D. (2002). Federal and state policies and American Indians. In P. Deloria & N. Salisbury (Eds.), *A companion to American Indian history* (pp. 379–396). Malden, MA: Blackwell.

Foucault, M. (1994). *The order of things: An archaeology of the human sciences.* New York: Vintage. (Original work published 1970)

Fox, S. (2001). American Indian/Alaska Native education and standards-based reform. *ERIC Digest* EDO RC-01-2 (December). Charleston, WV: ERIC Clearinghouse on Rural Education and Small Schools.

Freire, P. (1970). *Pedagogy of the oppressed.* New York: Seabury.

Freire, P. (1978). *Education for critical consciousness.* New York: Seabury.

Freire, P. (1993). *Pedagogy of the city.* New York: Continuum.

Freire, P. (1998). *Pedagogy and freedom: Ethics, democracy, and civic courage.* Trans. Patrick Clarke. Lanham, MD: Rowman & Littlefield.

Frisbie, C. J. (1964). *Kinaaldá: A study of the Navaho girl's puberty ceremony.* Middletown, CT: Wesleyan University Press.

Frisbie, C. J., & McAllester, D. P. (Eds.). (1978). *Navajo Blessingway ceremony: The autobiography of Frank Mitchell, 1881–1967.* Tucson: University of Arizona Press.

Fuchs, E., & Havighurst, R. (1972). *To live on this earth: American Indian education.* Garden City, NY: Doubleday.

Garcia, E. E. (2003). Bilingualism and schooling in the United States. *International Journal of the Sociology of Language, 155/156,* 1–92.

Garcia, E. E. (2005). *Teaching and learning in two languages: Bilingualism and schooling in the United States.* New York: Teachers College Press.

Garth, R. R., with Serafina, T. J., & Dutton, D. (1925). The intelligence of full blood Indians. *Journal of Applied Psychology, 9,* 382–389.

Gill, S., & Sullivan, I. (1992). *Dictionary of Native American mythology.* Oxford, UK: Oxford University Press.

Gipps, C. (1999). Socio-cultural aspects of assessment. In A. Iran-Nejad & P. D. Pearson (Eds.), *Review of Research in Education Volume 24* (pp. 355–392). Washington, DC: American Educational Research Association.

Giroux, H. A. (2001). English Only and the crisis of memory, culture, and democracy. In R. D. González & I. Melis (Eds.), *Language ideologies: Critical perspectives on the Official English movement* (pp. ix–xviii). Urbana, IL, and Mahwah, NJ: National Council of Teachers of English and Erlbaum.

Goddard, I. (1996). The description of the Native languages of North America before Boas. In W. C. Sturtevant (Gen. Ed.) & I. Goddard (Vol. Ed.), *Handbook of North American Indians: Vol. 17. Languages* (pp. 17–42). Washington, DC: Smithsonian Institution.

Goodman, K., Shannon, P., Goodman, Y., & Rapoport, R. (2004). *Saving our schools: The case for public education, Saying no to "No Child Left Behind"*. Berkeley, CA: RDR Books.

Gordon, B. M. (2000, Autumn). On high-stakes testing. *Division Generator*, pp. 1–4.

Greenbaum, P. E., & Greenbaum, S. D. (1983). Cultural differences, nonverbal regulation, and classroom interaction: Sociolinguistic interference in American Indian education. *Peabody Journal of Education*, 61(1),16–33.

Guilmet, G. M. (1978). Navajo and Caucasian children's verbal and nonverbal visual behavior in the urban classroom. *Anthropology and Education Quarterly*, 9(3), 196–215.

Guilmet, G. M. (1981). Oral-linguistic and nonoral-visual styles of attending: Navajo and Caucasian children compared in an urban classroom and on an urban playground. *Human Organization*, 40(2), 145–150.

Hawaii Apology Act (P. L. 103-150, S.J. res. 19). (1993). 100th Anniversary of the Overthrow of the Hawaiian Kingdom. Washington, DC: 103rd Congress of the United States of America. Retrieved March 9, 2006, from http://mauimapp .com/moolelo/apology.htm

Herrnstein, R. J., & Murray, C. (1994). *The bell curve: Intelligence and class structure in American life*. New York: Free Press.

Hill, J. (2001). The racializing function of language panics. In R. D. González & I. Melis (Eds.), *Language ideologies: Critical perspectives on the Official English movement* (Vol. 2, pp. 245–267). Urbana, IL, and Mahwah, NJ: National Council of Teachers of English and Erlbaum.

Hinton, L. (1991). The Native American Languages Act. *News from Native California*, 5(2), 22–23.

Hinton, L. (2001). Language revitalization: An overview. In L. Hinton & K. Hale (Eds.), *The green book of language revitalization in practice* (pp. 3–18). San Diego, CA: Academic Press.

Hinton, L., & Hale, K. (Eds.). (2001). *The green book of language revitalization in practice*. San Diego: Academic Press.

Holm, A., & Holm, W. (1990). Rock Point, a Navajo way to go to school: A valediction. *Annals, AAPSS, 508*, 170–184.

Holm, A., & Holm, W. (1995). Navajo language education: Retrospect and prospects. *Bilingual Research Journal*, 19(1), 141–167.

Hopi Dictionary Project. (1998). *Hopi dictionary/Hopìikwa lavàytutuveni: A Hopi-English dictionary of the Third Mesa dialect*. Tucson: University of Arizona Press.

Hornberger, N. H. (Ed.). (1996). *Indigenous literacies in the Americas: Language planning from the bottom up*. Berlin: Mouton de Gruyter.

Horne, E. B., & McBeth, S. (1998). *Essie's story: The life and legacy of a Shoshone teacher*. Lincoln: University of Nebraska Press.

Hoxie, F. E. (1989). *A final promise: The campaign to assimilate the Indians, 1880–1920*. Cambridge: University of Cambridge Press. (Original work published 1984)

Hunter, W. S., & Sommermier, E. (1922). The relation of degree of Indian blood to score on the Otis Intelligence Test. *Comparative Psychology, 2*, 257–277.

Hyer, S. (1990). *One house, one voice, one heart: Native American education at Santa Fe Indian School.* Santa Fe: Museum of New Mexico.

Infante, E. J. (1999, May 30). Living the language: Growing up in immersion school taught its own lessons. *Honolulu Advertiser*, pp. E1, E3.

Jacob, B. A. (2004). Accountability, incentives and behavior: The impact of high-stakes testing in the Chicago Public Schools. NBER Working Paper No. 8968. Retrieved August 23, 2005, from http://www.nber.org/papers/w8968.pdf

Jamieson, E., & Sandiford, P. (1928). The mental capacity of southern Ontario Indians. *Journal of Educational Psychology, 19,* 536–551.

John, V. (1972). Styles of learning–styles of teaching: Reflections on the education of Navajo children. In C. Cazden, D. Hymes, & V. John (Eds.), *Functions of language in the classroom* (pp. 331–343). New York: Teachers College Press.

Johnson, B. H. (1968). *Navaho education at Rough Rock.* Rough Rock, AZ: Rough Rock Demonstration School.

Johnson, F. T., & Wilson, J. (2004, June 23). Embracing change for student learning. Diné language immersion school. Paper presented at the 25th annual American Indian Language Development Institute, Tucson, AZ.

Johnston, B. H. (1976). *Ojibway heritage.* New York: Columbia University Press.

Johnston, B. H. (1989). *Indian school days.* Norman: University of Oklahoma Press.

Johnston, B. H. (1995). *The Manitous.* New York: HarperCollins.

Juan, M. J. B. (2003, September). Modern nomad. *110°,* pp. 26–30.

Kamanā, K., & Wilson, W. H. (1996). Hawaiian language programs. In G. Cantoni (Ed.), *Stabilizing indigenous languages* (pp. 153–156). Flagstaff: Northern Arizona University Center for Excellence in Education.

Kawagley, A. O. (1995). *A Yupiaq worldview: A pathway to an ecology and spirit.* Prospect Heights, IL: Waveland Press.

Kawagley, A. O. (1999). Alaska Native education: History and adaptation in the new millennium. *Journal of American Indian Education, 39*(1), 31–51.

Kawakami, A. J., & Dudoit, W. (2000). *Ua ao Hawai'i/*Hawai'i is enlightened: Ownership in a Hawaiian immersion classroom. *Language Arts, 77*(5), 384–390.

Kennard, E. A. (1944). *Field mouse goes to war: Tusan homichi tuwvöta.* (Hopi text by Albert Yava.) Pueblo Series 1. Education Division, U.S. Indian Service. Phoenix, AZ: Phoenix Indian School.

Kennard, E. A. (1948). *Little Hopi Hopihoya.* Pueblo Series 5. Lawrence, KS: Haskell Institute.

King, C. S. (1951). *Away to School: 'Ólta'góó.* (Navajo text by M. Nez.) Phoenix, AZ: Phoenix Indian School for the U.S. Indian Service.

King, C. S. (1956). *The flag of my country: Shikéyah bidah Na'at'a'í.* (Navajo text by Marian Nez.) Phoenix, AZ: Phoenix Indian School for the U.S. Indian Service.

Kleinfeld, J., & Nelson, P. (1991). Adapting instruction to Native Americans' "learning styles": An iconoclastic view. *Journal of Cross-Cultural Psychology, 22*(2), 273–283.

Krashen, S. (1996). *Under attack: The case against bilingual education.* Culver City, CA: Language Education Associates.

Krauss, M. (1998). The condition of Native North American languages: The need for realistic assessment and action. *International Journal of the Sociology of Language, 132*, 9–21.

LaFlesche, F. (1978). *The middle five: Indian schoolboys of the Omaha tribe*. Lincoln: University of Nebraska, Bison Book edition. (Original work published 1900)

Lang, J. (1989). It's hard to be an Indian. *News From Native California, 3*(1), 3.

Lee, T. (1999). *Sources of influence over Navajo adolescent language attitudes and behavior*. Unpublished doctoral dissertation, Graduate School of Education, Stanford University.

Lee, T., & McLaughlin, D. (2001). Reversing Navajo language shift, revisited. In J. A. Fishman (Ed.), *Can threatened languages be saved? Reversing language shift, revisited: A 21st century perspective* (pp. 23–43). Clevedon, UK: Multilingual Matters.

Left-Handed Mexican Clansman, Gorman, H., & Young, R. (1952). *The trouble at Round Rock*. Navajo Historical Series, 2. U.S. Indian Service. Phoenix, AZ: Phoenix Indian School.

Lessow-Hurley, J. (2000). *The foundations of dual language instruction* (3rd ed.). New York: Longman.

Levinson, B. A. U., & Sutton, M. (2001). Introduction: Policy as/in practice—A sociocultural approach to the study of educational policy. In M. Sutton & B. A. U. Levinson (Eds.), *Policy as practice: Toward a comparative sociocultural analysis of educational policy* (pp. 1–22). Westport, CT: Ablex.

Lindsey, D. F. (1995). *Indians at Hampton Institute, 1877–1923*. Urbana: University of Illinois Press.

Lipka, J. (1991). Toward a culturally based pedagogy: A case study of one Yup'ik Eskimo teacher. *Anthropology and Education Quarterly, 22*(3), 203–223.

Lipka, J. (2002). Schooling for self-determination: Research on the effects of including Native language and culture in the schools. *ERIC Digest*. ERIC Document Reproduction Service No. EDO-RC-01-12. Charleston, WV: ERIC Clearinghouse on Rural Education and Small Schools.

Lipka, J., & Ilustik, E. (1997) Ciulistet and the curriculum of the possible. In N. H. Hornberger (Ed.), *Indigenous literacies in the Americas: Language planning from the bottom up* (pp. 45–67). Berlin: Mouton de Gruyter.

Lipka, J., & McCarty, T. L. (1994). Changing the culture of schooling: Navajo and Yup'ik cases. *Anthropology and Education Quarterly, 25*(3), 266–284.

Lipka, J., with Mohatt, G. V., & the Ciulistet Group. (1998). *Transforming the culture of schools: Yup'ik Eskimo examples*. Mahwah, NJ: Erlbaum.

Littlebear, R. E. (1996). Preface. In G. Cantoni (Ed.), *Stabilizing indigenous languages* (pp. xiii–xv). Flagstaff: Northern Arizona University Center for Excellence in Education.

Littlebear, R. (2004). One man, two languages: Confessions of a freedom-loving bilingual. *Tribal College Journal, 15*(3), 11–12.

Littlefield, A. (1989). The B.I.A. boarding school: Theories of resistance and social reproduction. *Humanity and Society, 13*(4), 428–441.

Littlefield, A. (1993). Learning to labor: Native American education in the United States, 1880–1930. In J. Moore (Ed.), *The political economy of North American Indians* (pp. 43–59). Norman: University of Oklahoma Press.

Locust, C. (1988). Wounding the spirit: Discrimination and traditional American Indian belief systems. *Harvard Educational Review, 58*(3), 315–330.

Lomawaima, H. H. (1989). Hopification, a strategy for cultural preservation. In D. H. Thomas (Ed.), *Columbian consequences: Vol. 1. Archaeological and historical perspectives on the Spanish borderlands west* (pp. 93–99). Washington, DC: Smithsonian Institution Press.

Lomawaima, K. T. (1993). Domesticity in the federal Indian schools: The power of authority over mind and body. *American Ethnologist, 20*(2), 1–14.

Lomawaima, K. T. (1994). *They called it Prairie Light: The story of Chilocco Indian School.* Lincoln: University of Nebraska Press.

Lomawaima, K. T. (1995). Educating Native Americans. In J. Banks & C. M. Banks (Eds.), *Handbook of research on multicultural education* (pp. 331–347). New York: Macmillan.

Lomawaima, K. T. (1996). Estelle Reel, Superintendent of Indian Schools, 1898–1910: Politics, curriculum, and land. *Journal of American Indian Education, 35*(3), 5–31.

Lomawaima, K. T. (1999). The un-natural history of American Indian education. In K. G. Swisher & J. Tippeconnic III (Eds.), *Next steps: Research and practice to advance Indian education* (pp. 3–31). Charleston, WV: ERIC Clearinghouse on Rural Education and Small Schools.

Lomawaima, K. T. (2002). American Indian education: *By* Indians vs. *for* Indians. In P. J. Deloria & N. Salisbury (Eds.), *A companion to American Indian history* (pp. 422–440). Malden, MA: Blackwell.

Lomawaima, K. T. (2003). Educating Native Americans. In J. Banks & C. A. McGee Banks (Eds.), *Handbook of research on multicultural education* (2nd, rev. ed.) (pp. 441–461). New York: Jossey-Bass.

Lomawaima, K. T., & McCarty, T. L. (2002a). Reliability, validity, and authenticity in American Indian and Alaska Native research. *ERIC Digest.* Charleston, WV: ERIC Clearinghouse on Rural Education and Small Schools.

Lomawaima, K. T., & McCarty, T. L. (2002b). When tribal sovereignty challenges democracy: American Indian education and the democratic ideal. *American Educational Research Journal, 39*(2), 279–305.

Longstreet, W. S. (1978). *Aspects of ethnicity.* New York: Teachers College Press.

Lowry, L. (1970). Differences in visual perception and auditory discrimination between American Indian and White kindergarten children. *Journal of Learning Disabilities, 3,* 359–363.

Lyford, C. A. (1931). *The use of Indian designs in the government schools.* Indian Handcrafts Series, W. W. Beatty (Ed.). Department of Interior, Bureau of Indian Affairs, Branch of Education.

Lyford, C. A. (n.d.). *Quill and beadwork of the Western Sioux.* Indian Handcrafts Series 1. W. W. Beatty (Ed.). Department of Interior, Bureau of Indian Affairs, Branch of Education.

Manuel, F., & Neff, D. (2001). *Desert Indian woman: Stories and dreams.* Tucson: University of Arizona Press.

Margold, N. R. (1986). Introduction. In R. Bennett & F. Hart (Eds.), *Felix Cohen's handbook of federal Indian law* (pp. xxi–xxix). Five Rings Corporation (no location listed).

May, S. (2001). *Language and minority rights: Ethnicity, nationalism and the politics of language*. Harlow, UK: Longman/Pearson Education.

McCarty, T. L. (1984). *Bilingual-bicultural education in a Navajo community*. Unpublished doctoral dissertation, Department of Anthropology, Arizona State University.

McCarty, T. L. (1993). Language, literacy, and the image of the child in American Indian classrooms. *Language Arts, 70*(3), 182–192.

McCarty, T. L. (1998). Schooling, resistance, and American Indian languages. *International Journal of the Sociology of Language, 132*, 27–41.

McCarty, T. L. (2002a). *A place to be Navajo: Rough Rock and the struggle for self-determination in indigenous schooling*. Mahwah, NJ: Erlbaum.

McCarty, T. L. (2002b). Memorandum regarding the American Indian Language Development Institute. Unpublished document.

McCarty, T. L. (2002c). Between possibility and constraint: Indigenous language education, planning, and policy in the United States. In J. W. Tollefson (Ed.), *Language policies in education: Critical issues* (pp. 285–307). Mahwah, NJ: Erlbaum.

McCarty, T. L. (2003). Revitalising Indigenous languages in homogenising times. *Comparative Education, 39*(2), 147–163.

McCarty, T. L. (2004). Dangerous difference: A critical-historical analysis of language education policies in the United States. In J. W. Tollefson & A. B. M. Tsui (Eds.), *Medium of instruction policies: Which agenda? Whose agenda?* (pp. 71–93). Mahwah, NJ: Erlbaum.

McCarty, T. L., & Dick, G. S. (2003). Telling The People's stories: Literacy practices and processes in a Navajo community school. In A. I. Willis, G. E. García, R. B. Barrera, & V. J. Harris (Eds.), *Multicultural issues in literacy research and practice* (pp. 101–122). Mahwah, NJ: Erlbaum.

McCarty, T. L., & Romero, M. E. (2005, Fall). What does it mean to lose a language? Investigating heritage language loss and revitalization among American Indian students. *Show and Tell*, 14–17. Tempe: Arizona State University College of Education.

McCarty, T. L, Romero, M. E., & Zepeda, O. (2006a). Reclaiming the gift: Indigenous youth counter-narratives on Native language loss and revitalization. *American Indian Quarterly, 30*(1/2), 28–48.

McCarty, T. L., Romero, M. E., & Zepeda, O. (2006b). Reclaiming multilingual America: Lessons from Native American youth. In O. García, T. Skutnabb-Kangas, & M. Torres-Guzmán (Eds.), *Imagining multilingual schools: Languages in education* (pp. 91–110). Clevedon, UK: Multilingual Matters Ltd.

McCarty, T. L., Romero, M. E., & Zepeda, O. (2006c, forthcoming). Native American youth discourses on language shift and retention: Ideological cross-currents and their implications for language planning. *International Journal of Bilingual Education and Bilingualism*.

McCarty, T. L., Wallace, S., Lynch, R., & Benally, A. (1991). Classroom inquiry and Navajo learning styles: A call for reassessment. *Anthropology and Education Quarterly, 22*(1), 42–59.

McCarty, T. L., Watahomigie, L. J., & Yamamoto, A. Y. (1999). Introduction: Reversing language shift in Indigenous America—Collaborations and views from the field. *Practicing Anthropology, 20*(2), 2–4.

McCarty, T. L., Watahomigie, L. J., & Yamamoto, A. Y. (Eds.). (2001a). Reversing language shift in Indigenous America: Collaborations and views from the field. [Special issue]. *Practicing Anthropology, 21*.

McCarty, T. L., Watahomigie, L. J., Yamamoto, A. Y., & Zepeda, O. (2001b). Indigenous educators as change agents: Case studies of two language institutes. In K. Hale & L. Hinton (Eds.), *The green book of language revitalization in practice* (pp. 371–383). San Diego, CA: Academic Press.

McLaughlin, D. (1995). Strategies for enabling bilingual program development in American Indian schools. *Bilingual Research Journal, 19*(1), 169–178.

McQuillan, J. (1998). *The literacy crisis: False claims, real solutions*. Portsmouth, NH: Heinemann.

McShane, D. A., & Plas, J. M. (1984). The cognitive functioning of American Indian children: Moving from the WISC to the WISC-R. *School Psychology Review, 13*(1), 61–73.

Melendez, M. (with R. Konig). (2004, May 16). [No headline.] *The Arizona Republic*, p. A1.

Mendez, A., Reeves, A., Braun, D., Bird, N., Macias, M., & Redhorn, C. (2003). Warriors of tomorrow. *Learning communities, 7*(1), 72–80.

Meriam, L., Brown, R. A., Roe Cloud, H., Dale, E. E., Duke, E., Edwards, H. R., McKenzie, F. A., Mark, M. L., Ryan, W. C., & Spillman, W. J. (1928). *The problem of Indian administration*. Baltimore, MD: Johns Hopkins Press for the Institute for Government Research.

Mihesuah, D. A. (1993). *Cultivating the rosebuds: The education of women at the Cherokee Female Seminary, 1851–1909*. Urbana: University of Illinois Press.

Miller, A. G., & Thomas, R. (1972). Cooperation and competition among Blackfoot Indian and urban Canadian children. *Child Development, 43*, 1104–1110.

Minge, W. A. (1976). *Ácoma: Pueblo in the sky*. Albuquerque: University of New Mexico Press.

Moll, L. C. (2004). Rethinking resistance. *Anthropology and Education Quarterly, 35*(1), 126–131.

More, A. J. (1989, August). Native Indian learning styles: A review for researchers and teachers. *Journal of American Indian Education* [Special issue], 15–28.

Morgan, T. H. (1958). Reminiscences of my days in the land of the Ogalalla Sioux. *Report and historical collections 29*, 21–62. Pierre: South Dakota State Historical Society.

Morris, W. (Ed.). (1975). *The American Heritage dictionary of the English language*. Boston: American Heritage Publishing and Houghton Mifflin.

Moses, Y. (2004). The continuing power of the concept of "race." *Anthropology and Education Quarterly, 35*(1), 146–148.

Nabokov, P. (Ed.). (1991). *Native American testimony: A chronicle of Indian-White relations from prophecy to the present, 1492–1992*. New York: Viking Penguin.

National Center for Education Statistics. (1995). *Digest of education statistics*. Washington, DC: U.S. Government Printing Office.

National Center for Education Statistics. (2001–2002). *Characteristics of American Indian and Alaska Native education*. Washington, DC: U.S. Department of Education, Office of Educational Research and Improvement.

Native American Languages Act of 1990 (P.L. 101-477). (1990). Washington, DC: United States Congress. Retrieved March 9, 2006, from http://nabe.org/docu-ments/policy_legislation/NALanguagesAct.pdf

Nettle, D., & Romaine, S. (2000). *Vanishing voices: The extinction of the world's languages*. New York: Oxford University Press.

Newcomb, F. (1964). *Hosteen Klah, Navaho medicine man and sand painter*. Norman: University of Oklahoma Press.

Nicholas, S. (2005). Negotiating for the Hopi way of life through literacy and school-ing. In T. L. McCarty (Ed.), *Language, literacy, and power in schooling* (pp. 29–46). Mahwah, NJ: Erlbaum.

Nichols, S. L., Glass, G. V., & Berliner, D. C. (2006). High-stakes testing and stu-dent achievement: Does accountability pressure increase student learning? *Education Policy Analysis Archives, 14*(1), 1–172. Retrieved February 1, 2006, from htpp://epaa.asu.edu

Nicholls, C. (2005). Death by a thousand cuts: Indigenous language bilingual education programmes in the Northern Territory of Australia, 1872–1998. *International Journal of Bilingual Education and Bilingualism, 8*(2 & 3), 160–177.

Noley, G. (1979). Choctaw bilingual and bicultural education in the nineteenth century. In *Multicultural education and the American Indian* (pp. 25–39). Los Angeles: American Indian Studies Center, University of California.

Okakok, L. (1989). Serving the purpose of education. *Harvard Educational Review, 59*(4), 405–422.

Olson, J. S., & Wilson, R. (1984). *Native Americans in the twentieth century*. Ur-bana: University of Illinois Press.

Ovando, C. J., Collier, V. P., & Combs, M. C. (2003). *Bilingual and ESL class-rooms: Teaching in multicultural contexts* (3rd ed.). Boston: McGraw Hill.

Payne, N. A., Wallace, L., & Shorten, K. S. (1953). *Be a good waitress*. Brigham City, UT: Materials Preparation Department, Intermountain School.

Pecos, R., & Blum-Martínez, R. (2001). The key to cultural survival: Language planning and revitalization in the Pueblo de Cochiti. In L. Hinton & K. Hale (Eds.), *The green book of language revitalization in practice* (pp. 75–82). San Diego, CA: Academic Press.

Philips, S. U. (1972). Participant structures and communicative competence: Warm Springs children in community and classroom. In C. Cazden, V. John, & D. Hymes (Eds.), *Functions of language in the classroom* (pp. 370–394). Pros-pect Heights, IL: Waveland.

Philips, S. U. (1983). *The invisible culture: Communication in classroom and com-munity on the Warm Springs Indian reservation*. New York: Longman.

Phillipson, R. (Ed.). (2000). *Rights to language: Equity, power, and education*. Mahwah, NJ: Erlbaum.

Philp, K. R. (1977). *John Collier's crusade for Indian reform, 1920–1954*. Tucson: University of Arizona Press.

Philp, K. R. (1986). *Indian self-rule: First-hand accounts of Indian-White relations from Roosevelt to Reagan*. Salt Lake City, UT: Howe Brothers.

Platero, D. (1970). Let's do it ourselves! *School Review, 79*(1), 57–58.

Platero, P. (1992). *Navajo Head Start language study.* Unpublished manuscript, Navajo (Diné) Division of Education, Navajo Nation, Window Rock, AZ.

Platero, P. (2001). Navajo Head Start language study. In L. Hinton & K. Hale (Eds.), *The green book of language revitalization in practice* (pp. 67–97). San Diego, CA: Academic Press.

Pommersheim, F. (1995). *Braid of feathers: American Indian law and contemporary tribal life.* Berkeley: University of California Press.

Pratt, R. H. (1964). *Battlefield and classroom: Four decades with the American Indian, 1867–1904* (R. Utley, Ed.). New Haven, CT: Yale University Press.

Prucha, F. P. (1984). *The Great Father: The United States government and the American Indians* (Vols. I and II). Lincoln: University of Nebraska Press.

Qin-Hilliard, D. B., Feinauer, E., & Quiroz, B. G. (2001). Introduction. *Harvard Educational Review, 71*(3), v–ix.

Qoyawayma, P. (Elizabeth Q. White), as told to Carlson, V. (1964). *No turning back: A Hopi Indian woman's struggle to live in two worlds.* Albuquerque: University of New Mexico Press.

Ramírez, J. D. (1992). Executive summary. *Bilingual Research Journal, 16*(1 & 2), 1–62.

Ramstad, V., & Potter, R. (1974). Differences in vocabulary and syntax usage between Nez Percé Indian and White kindergarten children. *Journal of Learning Disabilities, 7*(8), 491–497.

Reel, E. (1901). *The uniform course of study.* National Archives, Record Group 75.

Research Agenda Working Group, with Strang, W., & von Glatz, A. (2001). *American Indian and Alaska Native education research agenda.* Washington, DC: U.S. Department of Education and U.S. Department of the Interior.

Reyhner, J., & Eder, J. (2004). *American Indian education: A history.* Norman: University of Oklahoma Press.

Rhodes, J. (1953). *Shoe repairing dictionary.* Brigham City, UT: Materials Preparation Department, Intermountain Indian School.

Rhodes, R. W. (1988). Native American learning styles: Implications for teaching and testing. In Arizona Department of Education (Ed.), *Proceedings of the eighth annual Native American Language Issues Institute* (pp. 11–21). Choctaw, OK: Native American Language Issues Institute.

Rhodes, R. W. (1990). Measurements of Navajo and Hopi brain dominance and learning styles. *Journal of American Indian Education, 29*(3), 29–40.

Riney, S. (1999). *The Rapid City Indian School, 1898–1933.* Norman: University of Oklahoma Press.

Rivera, K. (1999). Popular research and social transformation: A community-based approach to critical pedagogy. *TESOL Quarterly, 33*(3), 485–500.

Roderick, M., Jacob, B. A., & Bryk, A. S. (2002). The impact of high-stakes testing in Chicago on student achievement in promotional gate grades. *Educational Evaluation and Policy Analysis, 24*(4), 333–357.

Roessel, R. A., Jr. (1966). *The first monthly report of Rough Rock Demonstration School month of August 1966.* Rough Rock, AZ: Rough Rock Demonstration School.

Roessel, R. A., Jr. (1977). *Navajo education in action: The Rough Rock Demonstration School.* Chinle, AZ: Navajo Curriculum Center Press.

Romero, M. E. (1994). Identifying giftedness among Keresan Pueblo Indians: The Keres study. *Journal of American Indian Education, 34*(1), 35–58.

Romero, M. E. (2001, June 9). Indigenous language immersion: The Cochiti experience. Paper presented at the 22nd Annual American Indian Language Development Institute, Tucson, AZ.

Romero, M. E. (2003). *Perpetuating the Cochiti way of life: A study of child socialization and language shift in a Pueblo community.* Unpublished doctoral dissertation, Graduate School of Education, University of California, Berkeley.

Romero, M. E., & McCarty, T. L. (2006). *Language planning challenges and prospects in Native American communities and schools.* Tempe: Arizona State University Education Policy Studies Laboratory. Retrieved February 27, 2006, from http://www.asu.edu/educ/epsl/EPRU/documents/EPSL-0602-105-LPRU.pdf

Rosier, P., & Farella, M. (1976). Bilingual education at Rock Point—Some early results. *TESOL Quarterly, 10*(4), 379–388.

Ross, A. C. (1989, August). Brain hemispheric functions and the Native American. *Journal of American Indian Education* [Special issue], 72–76.

Rough Rock English-Navajo Language Arts Program (RRENLAP) grant proposal. (1989). Unpublished document. Rough Rock, AZ: Rough Rock Community School.

Rushton, J. P. (1999). *Race, evolution and behavior* (abridged ed.). New Brunswick, NJ: Transaction.

Rydell, R. W. (Ed.). (1999). *The reason why the colored American is not in the World's Columbian Exposition.* Urbana: University of Illinois Press.

Salisbury, L. H. (1974). Teaching English to Alaska Natives. In R. Deever, W. Abraham, G. Gill, H. Sundwall, & P. Gianopulos (Eds.), *American Indian education* (pp. 193–203). Tempe: Arizona State University.

Schiffman, H. F. (1995). *Linguistic culture and language policy.* London: Routledge.

Schlesinger, A., Jr. (1986). *The cycles in American history.* Boston: Houghton Mifflin.

Schwarz, M. T. (1995). The explanatory and predictive power of history: Coping with the "mystery illness," 1993. *Ethnohistory 42*(3), 375–401.

Schwarz, M. T. (1997). *Molded in the image of changing woman: Navajo views on the human body and personhood.* Tucson: University of Arizona Press.

Scollon, R., & Scollon, S. (1981). *Narrative, literacy, and face in interethnic communication.* Norwood, NJ: Ablex.

Senese, G. (1986). Self-determination and American Indian education: An illusion of control. *Educational Theory, 36*(2), 153–164.

Senese, G. B., & Page, R. (1995). *Simulation, spectacle, and the ironies of education reform.* Westport, CT: Bergin and Garvey.

Shapiro, T. (2005, November 7). Renaissance waiting to bloom. *Honolulu Advertiser.* Retrieved February 27, 2006, from http://honoluluadvertiser.com/apps/pbcs/pbcs.dll/article?AID=20051107/NEWS07/511070321/1001

Shaw, A. M. (1974). *A Pima past.* Tucson: University of Arizona Press.

Sims, C. P. (2001a, June 9). Indigenous language immersion. Paper presented at the 22nd Annual American Indian Language Development Institute, Tucson, AZ.

Sims, C. P. (2001b). Native language planning: A pilot process in the Acoma Pueblo community. In L. Hinton & K. Hale (Eds.), *The green book of language revitalization in practice* (pp. 63–73). San Diego, CA: Academic Press.

Skutnabb-Kangas, T. (2000). *Linguistic genocide in education—Or worldwide diversity and human rights?* Mahwah, NJ: Erlbaum.

Skutnabb-Kangas, T., & Cummins, J. (1988). *Minority education: From shame to struggle.* Clevedon, UK: Multilingual Matters.

Skutnabb-Kangas, T., & Phillipson, R., with Rannut, M. (1994). *Linguistic human rights: Overcoming linguistic discrimination.* Berlin: Mouton de Gruyter.

Snell, A. H. (2000). *Grandmother's grandchild: My Crow Indian life* (B. Matthews, Ed.). Lincoln: University of Nebraska Press.

Snipp, C. M. (1989). *American Indians: The first of this land.* New York: Russell Sage Foundation.

Spack, R. (2002). *America's second tongue: American Indian education and the ownership of English, 1860–1900.* Lincoln: University of Nebraska Press.

Spicer, E. H. (1962). *Cycles of conquest: The impact of Spain, Mexico, and the United States on the Indians of the Southwest, 1533–1960.* Tucson: University of Arizona Press.

Spolsky, B. (1974). *American Indian bilingual education.* Navajo Reading Study Progress Report No. 17. Albuquerque: University of New Mexico.

Spolsky, B. (1975). Linguistics in practice: The Navajo Reading Study. *Theory into Practice, 14*(5), 347–352.

Spolsky, B. (2002). Prospects for the survival of the Navajo language: A reconsideration. *Anthropology and Education Quarterly, 32*(2), 139–162.

Spolsky, B., & Holm, W. (1977). Bilingualism in the six-year-old child. In W. F. Mackey & T. Andersson (Eds.), *Bilingualism in early childhood* (pp. 167–173). Rowley, MA: Newbury House.

Spring, J. (1996). *The cultural transformation of a Native American family and its tribe 1763–1995, A basket of apples.* Mahwah, NJ: Erlbaum.

Standing Bear, L. (1975). *My people the Sioux.* Lincoln: University of Nebraska Press. (Original work published 1928)

Standing Bear, L. (1978). *Land of the spotted eagle.* Lincoln: University of Nebraska Press. (Original work published 1933)

Standing Bear, L. (1988). *My Indian boyhood.* Lincoln: University of Nebraska Press. (Original work published 1931)

Stefanakis, E. H. (1998). *Whose judgment counts? Assessing bilingual children, K–3.* Portsmouth, NH: Heinemann.

Stewart, M. (1934). Summary of a survey of vocational training facilities and occupational opportunities. NARA, Entry 724.

Suárez-Orozco, M. (2001). Globalization, immigration, and education: The research agenda. *Harvard Educational Review, 71*(3), 345–365.

Suina, J. H. (2004). Native language teachers in a struggle for language and cultural survival. *Anthropology and Education Quarterly, 35*(3), 281–302.

Svensson, F. (1981). Language as ideology: The American Indian case. *Bilingual Resources, 4*(2–3), 34–40.

Swisher, K. G., & Deyhle, D. (1987). Styles of learning and learning of styles: Educational conflicts for American Indian/Alaskan Native youth. *Journal of Multilingual and Multicultural Development*, 8(4), 345–360.

Swisher, K. G., & Deyhle, D. (1989, August). The styles of learning are different, but the teaching is just the same: Suggestions for teachers of American Indian youth. *Journal of American Indian Education* [Special issue], 1–14.

Szasz, M. C. (1974). *Education and the American Indian: The road to self-determination*. Albuquerque: University of New Mexico Press.

Szasz, M. C. (1977). *Education and the American Indian: The road to self-determination since 1928* (2nd ed.). Albuquerque: University of New Mexico Press.

Teale, W. (1992). A talk with Carole Edelsky about politics and literacy. *Language Arts*, 69(5), 324–329.

Thomas, W. P., & Collier, V. (1997). *School effectiveness for language minority students*. Washington, DC: National Clearinghouse for Bilingual Education.

Tippeconnic, J. W. III, & Faircloth, S. C. (2002). Using culturally and linguistically appropriate assessments to ensure that American Indian and Alaska Native students receive the special education programs and services they need. *ERIC Digest*, EDO-RC-02-9. Charleston, WV: ERIC Clearinghouse on Rural Education and Small Schools.

Tirado, M. (2001, September). Left behind: Are public schools failing Indian kids? *American Indian Report*, pp. 12–15.

Tonigan, R. F., Emerson, G., & Platero, P. (1975). *Annual review and evaluation of the Rough Rock contract school—Second interim report*. Unpublished manuscript on file at Rough Rock Community School, Rough Rock, AZ.

Trennert, R. A., Jr. (1988). *The Phoenix Indian School: Forced assimilation in Arizona, 1891–1935*. Norman: University of Oklahoma Press.

Troike, R. (1984). SCALP: Social and cultural aspects of language proficiency. In C. Rivera (Ed.), *Language proficiency and academic achievement* (pp. 44–54). Clevedon, UK: Multilingual Matters.

Tyack, D. B. (Ed.). (1967). *Turning points in American educational history*. Waltham, MA: Blaisdell.

Udall, L. (as told to). (1969). *Me and mine: The life story of Helen Sekaquaptewa*. Tucson: University of Arizona Press.

U.S. Charter Schools (2004). U.S. charter schools. Overview. Retrieved February 28, 2006, from http://www.uscharterschools.org/pub/uscs_docs/o/faq.html#3

U.S. Commission on Civil Rights (USCCR). (2003). *A quiet crisis: Federal funding and unmet needs in Indian country*. Washington, DC: Author.

U.S. Commission on Civil Rights (USCCR). (2004). *Closing the achievement gap: The impact of standards-based education reform on student performance*. Draft report for Commissioners' Review, July 2. Washington, DC: Author, Office of the General Counsel.

U.S. Congress, Senate Committee on Labor and Public Welfare, Special Subcommittee on Indian Education. (1969). *The study of the education of Indian children, Part 3*. Washington, DC: U.S. Government Printing Office.

U.S. Department of Education. (2004). No Child Left Behind. Overview. Retrieved February 28, 2006, from http://www.ed.gov/nclb/accountability/index.html

U.S. Department of the Interior, Office of Indian Affairs (1927). *Education of the Indians*. Bulletin 9. Chilocco, OK: Chilocco Indian Agricultural School.

Valdés, G., & Figueroa, G. (1994). *Bilingualism and testing: A special case of bias.* Norwood, NJ: Ablex.

Van Cott, D. L. (1994). *Indigenous peoples and democracy in Latin America.* New York: St. Martin's Press and the Inter-American Dialogue.

Van Hamme, L. (1996). American Indian cultures and the classroom. *Journal of American Indian Education, 35*(2), 21–36.

Van Ness, H. (1981). Social control and social organization in an Alaskan Athabaskan classroom: A microethnography of "getting ready" for reading. In H. Trueba, G. Guthrie, & K. Au (Eds.), *Culture and the bilingual classroom* (pp. 120–138). Rowley, MA: Newbury House.

Vizenor, G. (1984). *The people named the Chippewa.* Minneapolis: University of Minnesota Press.

Vogt, L. A., & Au, K. H. P. (1995). The role of teachers' guided reflection in effecting positive program change. *Bilingual Research Journal, 19*(1), 101–120.

Vogt, L. A., Jordan, C., & Tharp, R. G. (1993). Explaining school failure, producing school success: Two cases. In E. Jacob & C. Jordan (Eds.), *Minority education: Anthropological perspectives* (pp. 53–65). Norwood, NJ: Ablex.

Warner, S. N. (1999a). Hawaiian language regenesis: Planning for intergenerational use of Hawaiian beyond the school. In T. Huebner & K. A. Davis (Eds.), *Sociopolitical perspectives on language policy and planning in the USA* (pp. 313–332). Amsterdam: John Benjamins.

Warner, S. L. N. (1999b). *Kuleana:* The right, responsibility, and authority of indigenous peoples to speak and make decisions for themselves in language and culture revitalization. *Anthropology and Education Quarterly, 30*(1), 68–93.

Warner, S. L. N. (2001). The movement to revitalize Hawaiian language and culture. In L. Hinton & K. Hale (Eds.), *The green book of language revitalization in practice* (pp. 133–144). San Diego, CA: Academic Press.

Warner, S. L. N. (2004, September). *Aia i kula ika''ala'alapuloa* (We're off on a wild goose chase). Paper presented at the Cultural Diversity and Language Education Conference, University of Hawai'i Manoa, Honolulu.

Warrior, D. (2003). President's message and mission statement, Institute of American Indian Arts. Retrieved February 28, 2006, from http://www.iaiancad.org/president.php

Washburn, W. E. (Vol. Ed.). (1988). *History of Indian-White relations: Vol. 4. The Handbook of North American Indians.* W. C. Sturtevant (Gen. Ed.). Washington DC: Smithsonian Institution.

Watahomigie, L. J. (1988). *Hualapai Bilingual Academic Excellence Program: Blending Tradition and Technology model replication training manual.* Peach Springs, AZ: Hualapai Bilingual Academic Excellence Program, Peach Springs School District No. 8.

Watahomigie, L. J. (1995). The power of American Indian parents and communities. *Bilingual Research Journal, 19*(1), 189–194.

Watahomigie, L. J. (1998). The Native language is a gift: A Hualapai language autobiography. *International Journal of the Sociology of Language, 132,* 5–7.

Watahomigie, L. J., & McCarty, T. L. (1994). Bilingual/bicultural education at Peach Springs: A Hualapai way of schooling. *Peabody Journal of Education*, 69(3 & 4), 26–42.

Watahomigie, L. J., & McCarty, T. L. (1996). Literacy for what? Hualapai literacy and language maintenance. In N. H. Hornberger (Ed.), *Indigenous literacies in the Americas: Language planning from the bottom up* (pp. 95–113). Berlin: Mouton de Gruyter.

Watahomigie, L. J., & Yamamoto, A. Y. (1987). Linguistics in action: The Hualapai bilingual/bicultural education program. In D. D. Stull & J. J. Schensul (Eds.), *Collaborative research and social change: Applied anthropology in action* (pp. 78–98). Boulder, CO: Westview.

Wauters, J. K., Bruce, J. M., Black, D. R., & Hocker, P. N. (1989, August). Learning preferences of capable American Indians of two tribes. *Journal of American Indian Education* [Special issue], 53–62.

Webb, G. (1959). *A Pima remembers*. Tucson: University of Arizona Press.

Webster, S. (Ed.). (1966). *Understanding the educational problems of the disadvantaged learner*. San Francisco, CA: Chandler.

Whaley, R., & Bresette, W. (1994). *Walleye warriors: An effective alliance against racism and for the earth*. Philadelphia, PA: New Society Publishers.

White House Conference on Indian Education. (1992). *The final report of the White House Conference on Indian Education* (Vols. 1 and 2). Washington, DC: Author.

Whiteley, P. (1992). *Hopitutungwni*: "Hopi names" as literature. In B. Swann (Ed.), *On the translation of Native American literatures* (pp. 208–227). Washington, DC: Smithsonian Institution.

Wiley, T. G., & Wright, W. E. (2004). Against the undertow: Language-minority education policy and politics in the "age of accountability." *Educational Policy*, 18(1), 142–168.

Wilkins, D. E. (1997). *American Indian sovereignty and the U.S. Supreme Court: The masking of justice*. Austin: University of Texas Press.

Wilkins, D. E, & Lomawaima, K. T. (2001). *Uneven ground: American Indian sovereignty and federal law*. Norman: University of Oklahoma Press.

Wilkinson, C. F. (1987). *American Indians, time, and the law: Native societies in a modern constitutional democracy*. New Haven, CT: Yale University Press.

Williams, R. A., Jr. (1990). *The American Indian in Western legal thought: The discourses of conquest*. New York: Oxford University Press.

Williamson, V. (1954). *I am a good citizen*. Ogden, UT: Defense Printing Service, Department of the Interior, Bureau of Indian Affairs.

Wilson, G. L. (1981). *Waheenee: An Indian girl's story*. Lincoln: University of Nebraska Press. (Original work published 1927)

Wilson, W. H. (1998). *I ka 'oleloHawai'i ke ola*, "Life is found in the Hawaiian language." *International Journal of the Sociology of Language*, 132, 123–137.

Wilson, W. H. (1999). The sociopolitical context of establishing Hawaiian-medium education. In S. May (Ed.), *Indigenous community-based education* (pp. 95–108). Clevedon, UK: Multilingual Matters.

Wilson, W. H., & Kamanā, K. (2001). "*Mai loko mai o ka 'i'ni*: Proceeding from a dream." The 'Aha Pūnana Leo connection in Hawaiian language revitalization. In L. Hinton & K. Hale (Eds.), *The green book of language revitalization in practice* (pp. 147–176). San Diego, CA: Academic Press.

Woelfle-Erskine, C. (2003). Feed a village: An interview with Farmer Dave and [Bahidaj] students. In C. Woelfle-Erskine (Ed.), *Urban wilds: Gardeners' stories of the struggle for land and justice* (pp. 69–74). Oakland, CA: Urban Wilds and AK Press.

Wolcott, H. (1967). *A Kwakiutl village and school.* New York: Holt, Rinehart and Winston.

Wong, L. (1999). Authenticity and the revitalization of Hawaiian. *Anthropology and Education Quarterly, 30*(1), 94–115.

Wong, L. (2004, September). What, brah! *A'oilehiki ke' olelo Hawai'i?* Paper presented at the Cultural Diversity and Language Education Conference, University of Hawai'i Manoa, Honolulu.

Wong-Fillmore, L. (1996). What happens when languages are lost? An essay on language assimilation and cultural identity. In D. I. Slobin, J. Gerhardt, A. Kyratzis, & J. Guo (Eds.), *Social interaction, social context, and language: Essays in honor of Susan Ervin-Tripp* (pp. 435–445). Mahwah, NJ: Erlbaum.

Woolard, K. A. (1998). Introduction. Language ideology as a field of inquiry. In B. B. Schieffelin, K. A. Woolard, & P. V. Kroskrity (Eds.), *Language ideologies: Practice and theory* (pp. 3–47). New York: Oxford University Press.

Wright, W. E. (2002). The effects of high-stakes testing on an inner-city elementary school: The curriculum, the teachers, and the English language learners. *Current issues in Education, 5*(5). Retrieved February 28, 2006, from http://cie .asu.edu/volume5/number5

Young, R. W., & Morgan, W. (1954). *Navajo historical selections.* Navajo Historical Series, 3. Bureau of Indian Affairs. Phoenix, AZ: Phoenix Indian School.

Zehr, M. A. (2001). Ethnic-based schools popular. *Education Week.* Retrieved September 12, 2001, from http://www.edweek.org

Zinn, H. (2003). *A people's history of the United States: 1492–present.* New York: HarperCollins. (Original work published 1980)

Index